A Guide to

Paddle Adventure

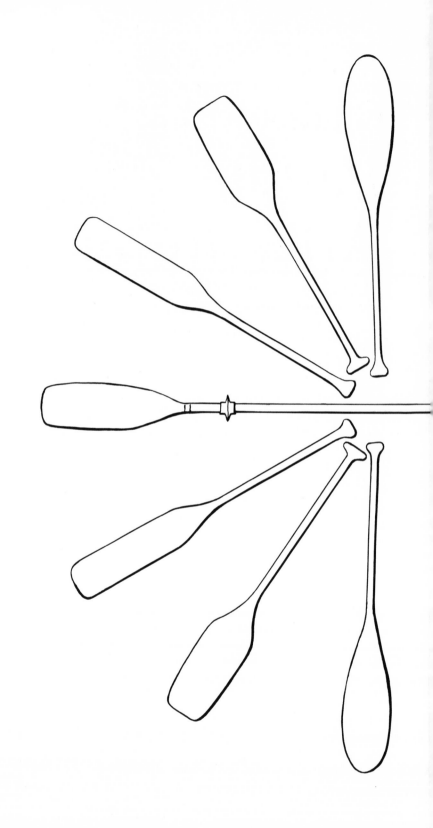

# A Guide to Paddle Adventure

How to Buy Canoes, Kayaks, and
Inflatables, Where to Travel,
and What to Pack Along

by
## RICK KEMMER

VANGUARD PRESS, INC.

NEW YORK

1975

ACKNOWLEDGMENTS

The information for this guide was supplied by
many enthusiastic canoeists and kayakists as well as
numerous manufacturers, outfitters, government agencies and dealers.
I am grateful to them for their help.
Special thanks to my typist,
Ann Selof, who never missed a deadline.

To my wife,
Mary Ann,
who made a home
while I cloistered myself
to write a book,
and
To my sons
Ross, Scott, and Brett
for their companionship on
the rivers of Wisconsin and Illinois
I dedicate this book.

# CONTENTS

## PART FIVE: PADDLE TRAILS IN THE UNITED STATES AND CANADA

# PREFACE

## Boating without Energy

In the affluent decades since World War II, Americans came to prefer their water recreation in high-powered motorboats that roared across little landlocked lakes, beating the water white and dousing the foam with oil slicks. More than any other recreational vehicles, powerboats drank excessively from the gasoline trough.

Now the demand for howling engines and planing hulls is diminishing. Not because Sunday boaters have lost their taste for speed and power. Rather because their fuel resources have been tapped to the limit. Gas prices have risen so unconscionably that many motorboats are lying idle in their slips, their owners no longer able to run them.

Fortunately, people who like water recreation have an alternative to powerboating. It is an ancient one that has endured over the years with little fanfare. While speedboaters have taken over the lakes, uncelebrated canoeists and kayakists have paddled the streams, exploring, daydreaming, sometimes even challenging the forces of nature. Now the time has come for paddlers to speak out, to make boaters everywhere aware of the healthful and exciting sport in which they participate. In this time of critical fuel shortages, exorbitant gas prices, and overriding concern for tidying up the environment, it is absolutely crucial for paddlers to present a strong case for their sport. Not only are canoeing and kayaking easy on gasoline and ecologically respectable, they are great fun for men and women, young and old, married or single.

The craft used by paddlers vary in construction and materials but include canoes, kayaks, and inflatable boats. Despite the pre-eminence of motorboating, sales of these craft have grown slowly. It is estimated that every year more than 90,000 new canoes are sold in the United States, and with conservation of energy and preservation of the environment paramount, a monumental increase in the number of canoeists and kayakists is anticipated for the immediate future.

This book is offered as a guide for the newcomer entering the world of paddle adventure. Although it touches on whitewater excitement and some strenuous trips for paddlers, it is meant primarily to help the person or family that purchases a canoe, kayak, or inflatable for enjoyment and that is interested in trips not too far from home—trips that can be taken on weekends and vacations.

Here is an overview of the latest paddlecraft * to help in purchasing the one that is exactly right for you as well as a discussion of related camping equipment. Tips are included for trip planning: using maps, planning menus, what to pack and how to pack it, establishing a pace, scouting for information at the point of embarkation, practicing ecology, and preventing injury. Finally, there is a lengthy list of paddle trails across the United States and Canada, and directions on where to obtain additional information on them.

Note: The prices that are included for canoes, kayaks, and inflatables, as well as for some other equipment, were obtained from manufacturers at the time of writing. In most cases they will have risen by the time this book is published, and they will continue to rise after that. They have been retained in the text because they provide a basis for comparison. The assumption is that inflation will affect all in approximately the same degree.

# INTRODUCTION

## The Pleasures and Problems of Paddling

In recent years, canoeing and kayaking have received twin stimulants from television coverage of the Olympic kayak competition and the movie *Deliverance*. The Olympics brought to the eyes of millions of viewers, for the first time, the heroic spectacle of superbly muscled athletes in kayaks, pitting their stamina against current and clock. There can be no doubt: piloting a lightweight craft through buffeting rapids, exulting in the spray on one's face and the feeling of total exhaustion after the course has been conquered all combine to provide a thrill matched in few other sports.

*Deliverance* aroused a massive audience to the excitement that can accompany the more violent aspects of canoeing in the wilderness. It depicted the trials of a party of four canoeists who took a float trip down the Cahulawassee River. (In reality, the river was the Chattooga, which flows through North Carolina and forms part of the border between Georgia and South Carolina.) Before the trip was finished one member had been killed, one canoe had been smashed to pieces as it went over a rapid that not even the most experienced whitewater expert should have attempted, the members of the expedition had been sexually molested by hillbillies, a member of the expedition had suffered a broken leg, and countless other mishaps had occurred. Despite the horrors of *Deliverance,* libraries and other information sources across America were deluged by calls from moviegoers asking the location of the river and in the summer of 1973, as a result of this impetuousness, the Chattooga received more than its share of paddle traffic and inflicted an extraordinary number of injuries on inexperienced and naive paddlers.

In retrospect, the thrills of the Olympics and the suspense of *Deliverance* were self-defeating publicity for the sport of paddling. The image of canoeing and kayaking as dangerous, requiring maximum stamina and physical skill, deters many newcomers from taking up the hobby. Often, the potential canoeist is afraid to make his first trip for fear of tumbling over a dam or down a rapid.

What one must remember is that Olympic kayaking is a sophisticated and esoteric aspect of paddling. It is highly specialized, and while a few experts participate, the vast majority of paddlers are content to try gentler water. And keep in mind that *Deliverance* was fiction. There is no reason why one should ever encounter a river like the Chattooga; instead there are countless pleasant canoe paths that do not even require portaging, much less challenging rapids, falls, or whitewater. Paddling a kayak or canoe need not be strenuous; it can be lazy, relaxing, ambling, lackadaisical, or any other pace one cares to set. And in most places the fictitious hillbillies of the movie are in reality friendly campers and paddlers, always ready to help and exchange information.

In addition to a misconception about the kind of water usually traveled by canoes and kayaks, many people harbor the pernicious idea that these craft are inherently unsafe. How many people have you heard exclaim "I wouldn't set foot in that tippy thing," when they spot a paddlecraft?

Such fears are exaggerated. Often they result from strict Boy Scout or Girl Scout training that so stresses safety that it frightens the young canoeist. This cautionary training is fine in itself, aimed as it is at instructing the novice in the limitations of his craft so that he will always use it as intended. But once he learns to handle it in this manner, his craft should be very safe, even under rather untenable conditions—and he should recognize this fact.

In fact, done properly, paddling is so safe that it is ideal recreation for any family that delights in the free-breathing outdoor world. Therefore, the entire family should be included in one's paddling plans right from the start. Before making the necessary expenditures to get started in canoeing or kayaking, sound out the family on their opinions of your soon-to-be-developed hobby. Does your spouse approve? Are the children enthusiastic? Whatever you do, don't force paddling on other members of the family. The arrangement worked out with them is a highly personal affair and should be satisfactory to everyone concerned.

An intransigent mate can turn dollars spent on a canoe or kayak to total waste. Does your wife or husband refuse to abandon a deep-seated aversion to canoes, considering them too tippy? Is he or she terrified by rain or wind? If you intend to camp during your travels, does he or she have an unscratchable phobia for mosquitoes? shiver upon hearing animal calls in the night? become sleepless at hearing flapping canvas or nylon in the night breeze? Does he or she feel it an unendur-

*Paddling is recreation for the entire family. Short trips on nearby streams offer excellent opportunities for waterside picnics.*

able sacrifice to forsake linen bedsheets and posh mattress in exchange for a sleeping bag? These questions should be answered candidly before buying equipment.

Too often, a loving partner who actually abhors outdoor living will try to accommodate his or her mate, explaining that an effort will be made to take up and enjoy the hobby. The enthusiast then sallies forth to the sporting-goods store and buys the most expensive equipment available, only to discover on the first family trip downriver that his companion cannot tolerate "roughing it." If you harbor doubts about your spouse's enthusiasm, contact an outfitter who rents canoeing and camping equipment. (You should be able to rent a canoe and tent plus all the necessary gear for a short trip for about

$15.) Using rented equipment, take an overnight downstream, testing the reactions of all concerned and reaching a decision about whether you want to spend more time on the water and under canvas. If paddling proves not to be the sport for you, the expenditure will have been mighty small compared to what you would have lost had you completely outfitted yourself.

If, after your trip, your spouse dislikes canoeing and kayaking but you still want to have a go at it, all is not necessarily lost. You may be able to buy a paddlecraft to carry along on the yearly vacation. If your companion is an extra good sport, he may even be willing to transport you to your departure point for paddle trips, then drive on and wait for you at the end of the course.

In addition to your spouse, children may have to be considered. I have learned through countless errors and multiple trials with my own boys—seven, five, and three—that if children are taken along on a paddle trip, their behavior is much better than ever it is at home. True, I seldom take more than one at a time on overnights; but this is not due to misbehavior. The fact is that cooking for and bedding down more than one child is crushing work. Nevertheless, children are a joy to have along on day trips if certain accommodations are made for them.

First, youngsters must be kept occupied. A tip for how to do this seeming impossibility appeared in a national canoeing magazine a short time ago: give the kids a paddle like Mom's and Dad's, a small paddle suited to the diminutive size of its user. You'll find that changing junior into a working member of the expedition brings miraculous results and that youngsters often amuse themselves with this diversion for hours. The only problem here is that paddles are sometimes lost or broken. When they are lost too often, retrieving them can be a nuisance. It doesn't hurt to bring along a favorite toy or two. Rubber alligators and turtles are excellent toys that provide the needed diversion, although little cars, trucks, or dolls will do the job just as well.

It is also important to stop occasionally to let children stretch their legs. Paddling can be enjoyed by people from under one year old to more than eighty; but remember that the older we get, the more able we are to hold still for extended periods of time. Kids just cannot do it.

Finally, if you plan to camp with kids when both parents are canoeing together, a clear division of labor is necessary. Decide ahead of time on how you will split the workload. This is no spot for the unreconstructable male chauvinist; the husband

*Paddling is fun for the whole family. Children love it. (Photo Alumacraft)*

simply has to undertake domestic chores he may not normally do at home.

Families that don't like to travel long distances over the highways will find paddle adventure to their liking; almost everybody lives within at most a few hours of enjoyable, often exciting paddle trails. Despite the universal opportunities for canoeing and kayaking in virtually all parts of the nation, many people entertain the misconception that there is no place to "dip a blade" within a reasonable distance of their homes. This idea is reinforced by sports shows held yearly in major population centers. There, resplendent brochures extol the pure water (suitable for drinking right out of the lakes), tall pines and glittering white-trunked birches, heart-purifying solitude, fantastic fishing, and rustic hospitality of the wilderness. You are invited to fly deep into the voyageuring country of Canada, Minnesota, Maine or any number of locales, and begin your trip as the plane vanishes into the distance. You are urged to place yourself totally in the competent hands of outfitters and guides who have spent their lives canoeing.

The colorful literature advertising the rustic pleasures of American vacation lands notwithstanding, by no means are canoeing and kayaking confined to remote areas. Whatever state you live in, and whichever city, there are interesting and rewarding canoe trails near you. It is simply a matter of finding them and in part VI of this book you will be given pointers on where to go and how to get information on these areas.

What is it about canoeing and kayaking that makes them thoroughly enjoyable? Why were an ever-growing number of Americans already seeking out the country's backwaters and streams even before the oil shortage? Why do so many people favor primitive, muscle-powered locomotion to the speed of planing hulls? The benefits of paddling are of two kinds: physical and spiritual. First let's discuss the tangible physical benefits. Paddling improves health and gives the body tone.

Before undertaking extended trips, paddle your canoe or kayak for a few hours at a time in quiet backwaters where the fish are jumping and the willows are reflected on the surface of the water. At first even short jaunts will cause shoulder and neck muscles to tighten and remain sore for a few days. As you continue these short outings, the aches disappear, yielding to the satisfying feeling that accompanies good muscle toning. Once you pass the aches and pains of paddle-dipping boot camp, you can paddle for several days, for sixty or seventy miles or more, even to the edge of fatigue, without the soreness returning. When you come off the water, you will breathe deeper and more rhythmically; your stomach and abdominal muscless will be tighter; your chest and arm muscles will be taut and easily controllable; and your head will remain thrown back, chin out. Once you start paddling, you are likely to be astounded at what a really healthy activity it is. Of course, even the healthiest among us occasionally becomes ill. But if you take the normal precautions to protect your well-being, paddling should

*Don't save paddling for faraway places. Plenty of pleasant lakes and rivers flow in and around most major cities. (Photo Old Town)*

get your circulation going and help to keep you feeling top-notch.

Beyond the observable physical benefits of canoeing and kayaking, there are many other advantages pertaining to the spirit. One spiritual advantage is the chance paddling offers to identify with the American historical heritage. When you dip your paddle into the waters of a lake, stream, or river, you cannot avoid becoming caught up in a sense of kinsmanship with the rugged trappers, traders, and missionaries who first explored the heart of the North and the rivers of the American Midwest. Paddling lists among its practition-

*Many paddlers appreciate tradition. An ABS canoe from Whitewater Marine Products resurrects the ghost of voyageurs with "birchbark" design. (Photo Whitewater Marine Products)*

ers many great men whose ghosts haunt channels and backwaters—to know their presence one need only follow their trails. The names of Marquette and Joliet have been celebrated for three centuries—the first Europeans to discover the

Mississippi River. In the Midwest alone, street names, designations of counties, cities, and monuments bear witness to such famous pioneers as Hennepin, Beltrami, Duluth, Dubuque, LaSalle, Tonti, Lewis and Clark, and countless others. These men gave canoeing a history and a tradition, and their labors established the romance that still lingers when you paddle a canoe down a quiet backwater or through the whitecaps of a windy lake.

Paddling offers more than a romantic link to the men who discovered our country. It is a sport, and as such, holds its own type of competition. It offers challenge even when you are not competing directly against other canoe or kayak pilots. While many paddlers enjoy simply staying afloat to observe the surrounding countryside, others prefer to set goals that must be accomplished come what may. For them the joy of paddling lies in attaining those goals.

There is nothing difficult about planning the length of a trip so that you have to strain to reach the end. The challenge is in making time regardless of obstacles imposed by the current, portages, weather, or any other problems that may arise. Although overambition can lead to carelessness and subsequent disaster, surmounting a certain amount of challenge adds a worthwhile dimension of pride; for you have pitted your body and intellect against a problem and conquered it.

Another compelling spiritual advantage of paddling is that it provides a change of pace from your daily work. And that, after all, is what relaxation is all about. Remember vacations taken in the past? You probably worked harder during your free time than during the rest of the year. Similarly, canoeing and kayaking demand much more exertion than does your job. But ergs are not really important when considering vacations. What is meaningful is the change of pace. You may exert a thousand times more energy when you dip the blade than you do in your profession, but you are doing something entirely different from your normal activity. Your performance at work can be astonishingly gusty after a couple of days paddling and camping have shaken the cobwebs from your mind.

Another spiritual benefit of paddling is the communion it offers with nature. Out on the lakes and streams you develop a deep, mature love and respect for the world about you, and want to do more for ecology. Many canoeists make it a point of religion to pack out more garbage than they take into the wilderness. Even though their individual efforts are small, ever so slowly progress is being made to eliminate the beer cans, whiskey bottles, bedsprings, and other miscellany that pollute America's waterways and woods. It is not long before you reach an affinity with nature once you meet her on her own turf.

Perhaps the greatest spiritual benefit of paddling is the chance it gives you to test and know yourself. Contributing to this is the chance paddling affords for solitude: a paradoxical solitude that can be experienced even when paddling with a group. Although paddlers love to share experiences and often travel together, most greatly value being alone. Even when traveling in groups, canoes are usually spread out over a wide span of water with little communication between them. In this way each paddler is alone with his dreams, unmolested by interruptions and demands of others. Group canoeing combines the best of two contradictory but innately human desires —the need to cooperate and the desire to be alone.

Camping beside a kayak or canoe just a few times puts you at one with yourself. As other paddlers have done before, you also can come to know yourself while camped under the pines and stars in some remote, unspoiled setting. Here you cease to direct your body as a tool to execute the incessant creative demands of the brain. Soul and body work in harmony without one driving the other.

*Solitude. (Photo Old Town)*

# PART ONE

# DETERMINING YOUR NEEDS
# AND MATCHING
# A BOAT TO THEM

## Keeping Your Needs in Mind

$O$nce you decide to try paddle adventure, the first step toward getting started is the selection of a boat. A boat is your transport to adventure, so you should purchase one that is dependable and adequate for your needs.

Paddlecraft are proliferate, with hundreds of models, ranging from about four to over twenty feet long. Some are mottled for camouflage; there is the famous "Budweiser" canoe from Whitewater Marine Products, Incorporated, resplendently gaudy from bow to stern with red and white beer labels. Reds, aquas, sunshine yellows, oranges, and iridescent hues are popular, any of which would have dazzled old-time voyageurs who saw pragmatic beauty in bark.

Shape varies, as manufacturers vie with each other to catch the buyer's eye with the sleekest boats on the showroom floor. Take canoes, for instance. There are models with high bows and sterns and models with almost no upsweep at the ends. Some models have straight keels and others curve from end to end (have more rocker). Models are available with flaring sides, while others have steep tumblehome (*i.e.*, curve in at the gunwales). Some are narrow for speed; others have wide beams for stability.

These and many other factors should influence and determine your choice of a paddlecraft. You owe it to yourself to gather some knowledge of basics before investing in a boat that will bear you and your impedimenta, possibly for the rest of your life. Romantic dreams of high adventure should not cause you to buy equipment far more sophisticated than your

1

locality or time permit you to use. On the other hand, you cannot afford to "under buy." Essentially the wise choice of paddlecraft must be based on the same kind of analysis as that used for other buying decisions: first determine your needs, then match the right product to them within the strictures of your budget.

With whom will you paddle most of the time? Do you plan to take children along or will you and your spouse paddle together with no passengers? Do you plan to join a canoe club and travel with a group or will you go solo, to be alone for extended periods? The answers to these questions bear heavily on the type of craft you should choose. For example, when traveling alone, you probably require little space for cargo. When traveling with your family, adequate room is necessary to provide a suitable measure of comfort. Similarly, if you plan to travel as the only adult, either with youngsters or alone, you need a craft light enough for one man to hoist on top of the car or lift from the water. But if you plan to travel with a group of canoeists, then it is probably best to have a craft equal to others in the group, one that lets you do your share of toting gear. Of course there is no such thing as a canoe for all seasons, but by answering these questions it is possible to narrow the selection of a craft to one that best suits your requirements most of the time.

Other questions that should be asked before buying a paddlecraft concern where the boat will be used. Do you plan to paddle local lakes? Will you be buffeted in the washes of powerboats? Is whitewater in your future? Will most paddling be done on placid rivers or small streams? Is there a likelihood of encountering numerous snags? Is the area that you will usually paddle windy? Again, the answers will influence your decision as to the type of craft you buy. For example, if you will be canoeing or kayaking mostly on open lakes with high winds, you should look for a craft with a fairly deep keel, low ends, and a comparatively high freeboard (midship stance out of the water). On the other hand, if whitewater will be run, a light, maneuverable craft with as shallow a keel as possible—better yet, no keel at all—should be used.

Will your paddling be combined with camping or consist solely of day trips on weekends? And at what time of year will your boat be used the most? Should there be cool colors inside and out to stave off the summer sun, or heat-conducting colors to toast you in autumn while you hunt ducks or pick the last bass from his lair before the ice sets in? Where will you store the boat? How will it be transported? If by public transportation, perhaps a folding boat or an inflatable is better for you.

Since the boat is often the most expensive single piece of equipment purchased and must be dependable, it is worth spending time and effort to analyze craft that are available. The following discussion of types of paddlecraft will help you assess the models in dealers' showrooms according to your answers to the foregoing questions.

# 2

## Boat Characteristics and Capabilities

There are three basic types of paddlecraft: canoes, kayaks, and inflatables. Although all three are paddled, they are very different from one another. Usually one look at a paddle-powered boat can identify it as being in one category or another. But there are overlaps. For instance, many people would mistake the Old Town covered whitewater canoe for a kayak, taking note of its decks. On the other hand, inflatable kayaks, such as the Pyrawa, attempt to do away with the "mumps-in-the-bilges" appearance of most inflatables and adopt the kayak's sleek hull design. And the world-famous Klepper Aerius kayak sports inflatable sponsons (air tubes along the sides), but its predominantly rigid design precludes it from being classed as an inflatable. Although we will discuss the fundamental types of boats in more detail later, it is possible to provide here certain meaningful definitions to help distinguish them.

A canoe is a rigid boat in which the paddlers kneel. Although they may sit on seats when water conditions permit or on the floor when conditions demand, the fundamental position for safe, strong paddling is on the knees, with the butt or lower back against a seat or thwart.

A kayak, on the other hand, is paddled from a sitting position. The paddler sits in the bottom with legs extending in front, possibly bracing his feet or knees against the framework.

Inflatables may be of almost any configuration and may be propelled from either position suitable to a canoe or kayak. Their major distinguishing characteristic, obviously, is that they achieve their buoyancy by being "blown up" with air.

### INFLATABLES?

Why would anyone buy an inflatable for paddling? To the traditionalist who dotes on the graceful lines of a canoe, the inflatable is little more than a raft with a toothache—a bulbous affair that offers no aesthetic experience. Many people believe inflatables are all too apt to spring leaks, deflate, and sink. "What if I caught a fishhook in the side of it?" is a common question. "What if it hits a stump?"

Skepticism notwithstanding, every year more and more inflatables are sold, and many are happy with their performance. What, then, is the story on inflatables?

To begin with, they offer some advantages that rigid paddlecraft do not. They are generally lighter in proportion to their size, which makes them ideal for fishermen who trek into the woods to find little-known streams; they take up little space, since they can be transported flat; or, if left inflated, they are easily hoisted onto the top of a car. Because of their light weight, portages are no problem.

In addition to being lighter than rigid craft, inflatables are more easily stored. Whereas a canoe or kayak requires garage space in the winter or yard space in the summer, inflatables can be collapsed and stored in a basement or a closet. This is particularly advantageous if you happen to live in an apartment or trailer, or if you are located in the city and don't have a garage or large yard.

In some cases, inflatables are actually safer than their rigid counterparts. Although it is still possible to buy models that have only one air compartment, most now have several compartments that are pumped up separately and individually sealed. Thus if one air chamber punctures or springs a leak, the rest stay inflated, maintaining enough flotation to support the craft's pilot and passengers. The more compartments, the better—for example, the Pyrawa from Leisure Imports has three main compartments, making it virtually unsinkable.

Should the inflatables spring a leak, they can be patched with kits supplied by their manufacturers. The only exception to this occurs when a leak is sprung along a vulcanized seam. In this case, unless the manufacturer provides a remedy, the boat is finished. But such separations seldom occur, for the vulcanizing process, if done correctly, makes the seam stronger than the neoprene or fabric itself.

If inflatables have all these advantages, why do purists seem to prefer canoes and kayaks? Aside from poor aesthetics, there are also serious disadvantages to inflatables. For example, the light weight. This may well make portages or loading the boat onto the car easy, but it is also true that matter in motion tends to remain in motion, and that the heavier the matter, the more tendency for it to remain in motion. Thus, if speed is built up by paddling a heavy boat with a good hydrodynamic hull, and then paddling is stopped for a while, the boat continues to push forward through the water. On the other hand, if a light craft is taken to the same speed and paddling is stopped, the boat slows rapidly. While an inflatable is never as hard to paddle as a heavy craft, it demands continuous paddling, which becomes tedious.

Compounding the problem of constant paddling is the fact that on most inflatables hull design is not conducive to sliding gracefully and swiftly through the water with a minimum of effort. Here the "mumps-in-the-bilges" appearance becomes more than an artistic objection. These hulls simply are not fast; rather, they are bulky, cumbersome, and awkward. It is impossible to achieve firm control as one can in a canoe or kayak. Inflatable kayaks, which are narrower and somewhat longer for their width than other inflatables, improve on this situation. If the advantages of inflatables interest you and your travel happens to be on water where the ability of the boat to hold its course in a straight line is desirable, you should definitely examine the inflatable kayaks. They won't match the rigid craft in holding a course, but they exceed other inflatables in this regard.

The fact that inflatables are soft to sit in makes them popular for whitewater, where they can bounce from rock to rock while cushioning you from jolts on a pillow of air. (On a large scale, this is why rubber rafts are popular for the guided adventures offered on the Colorado, Snake, and other wild rivers.) But for normal paddling, the soft, cushiony effect becomes uncomfortable after a time. Also, when stroking the water, the paddle must impart motion to the boat. Ideally, the boat should gain forward force in equal measure to that which the paddle imparts in the opposite direction. But in an inflatable —soft of side, seat, and bottom—much of the force is absorbed by the boat itself, resulting in a lack of responsiveness to the paddle.

Most compartmentalized inflatables may be extremely safe, but they do puncture on occasion; and when they do, the change in hull shape makes them almost unmaneuverable. Moreover, although they can be patched easily, the puncture first has to be found—which may take some doing—and the craft entirely deflated in order to fix it. Deflation, patching, and repumping can mean needless delay on a paddle trip.

Other disadvantages include the fact that many inflatables small enough to be classed as paddlecraft require the paddler to sit on the "floor." If he brings any water into the boat or takes splash over the sides, he finds himself sitting in a puddle —no way to enjoy an extended trip. This problem is compounded because the lowest spot in the inflatable is where the paddler sits, so all the water rushes there. Water can cause additional problems if sleeping and camping gear are in the craft, since they must be kept dry. If you are in the market for an inflatable, by all means look for one that has raised seats, constructed as inflatable cushions.

If you plan to camp extensively, most inflatables will not be for you, since they normally have little space to store gear. This results from the fact that a good amount of their volume is usurped by the required "fatness" of the inflated tubes. Yet, despite all their disadvantages, inflatables are the best craft for some types of paddling, and too many people concentrate on their shortcomings while failing to consider their advantages.

CANOE OR KAYAK?

Most people who set out to purchase paddlecraft are guided by one of two prejudices: either they picture themselves in something traditional, or they want to achieve an individual identity by purchasing something unusual. According to the prejudice that motivates them more strongly, they wind up with either a canoe (traditional) or a kayak (unusual). The respective abilities of the boats themselves often are not considered. It is a pity that so few people look into what makes these boats different from each other, and that so many remain unaware of their respective strengths and weaknesses.

Canoes dominate sales statistics in the United States, while kayaks do better abroad. Here, canoes seem to be preferred for voyageuring, while kayaks are used mostly for competition. Nevertheless, there are fine whitewater canoes and there are large kayaks that are excellent for voyageuring and downriver camping trips.

It is interesting to listen to the comments of observers when paddling a kayak. They reveal a great deal about the attitudes of the buying public and show why canoes hold their big sales lead over kayaks.

"You wouldn't catch me dead in that thing," I heard a young woman tell a Klepper paddler on Illinois' Galena River. "It would tip over in the slightest wind."

"I like the speed of your boat," a neighbor told me when he was riding in my Folbot, "but if you hit anything, the bottom is going to tear out."

"This thing bends every time it hits a wave," said a member of the powerboat set riding in a homemade canvas-covered kayak on the Mississippi River south of LaCrosse, Wisconsin.

These statements represent typical attitudes that confine the popularity of kayaks. The image of kayaks as tippy boats comes from the publicity given to their ability to roll over and pop rightside up again—the famous Eskimo roll (esquimautage).

7

What is not generally known is that this roll can be done only in very narrow kayaks, usually competition craft built for speed. Most of the larger voyageuring kayaks are too heavy and far too wide for such acrobatics. Moreover, their cockpits are too large to hold out water effectively during a roll.

In order to understand exactly what kayaks and canoes can do, and what characteristics are inherent to each craft, it helps to know something about where they came from, who first made them, how they originally were constructed, and what they were first used for.

Both the kayak and canoe are indigenous to North America. Actually, their existence runs in geographical bands, with the kayak appearing in the far north, the canoe appearing farther south throughout what is now Canada, and dugouts becoming the most widely used craft below the birch line. Kayaks appeared all the way from Eastern Siberia to the icebound fastness of Greenland, canoes from the Atlantic seaboard to the western extremities of what is today known as the Midwest.

When Europeans first saw canoes and kayaks, both already represented the apex of long and arduous development. Hull designs as they existed in, say, the seventeenth century, were quite sophisticated, and many variations were employed to make them applicable to a wide range of use. Considering that canoes were made by a Stone Age people, their design and construction are astounding for their complexity and sagacious use of materials. The kayak is no less miraculous, especially considering the fact that it was designed and built by people who had little more to work with than driftwood, bone, and animal skins.

Neither the kayak nor canoe were designed in a vacuum; both are products determined, for the most part, by the needs of the men who built them and by the materials available. Basically, the canoe was employed for transportation. Although it was used in salt water and on open lakes, its primary use was for navigating shallow rivers. The Indian preferred a small pack canoe for hunting voyages because it transported him rapidly into the forests where the game hid. Indian families moving from one hunting ground to another used larger canoes to carry them and their belongings over considerable distances. The treacherous rocks and snags of the woodland streams necessitated craft that could be propelled while the pilot faced forward. For this reason paddling was a logical development as opposed to rowing, in which the pilot has his back facing the direction in which he is going and so cannot spot obstacles ahead. Shallow-water trails demanded a craft that drew very little water, hence the canoe was designed for minimal draft. And frequent portages meant a craft light enough to be carried easily. It also had to be repairable.

Given this set of requirements, neolithic Indians had to find in their environment materials that could be fashioned by their technology. The materials had to be as strong as possible, yet lightweight and flexible. The result of Indian attempts to fashion a suitable boat was little short of miraculous—the bark canoe. Birchbark was preferred for its durability and flexibility, but the barks of other trees, including elm, also were used on occasion.

The Eskimo, faced with a different environment, needed a different type of boat. And he was far more limited than the Indian in the materials available from which to fashion it. In the far northern region through which the Eskimo wandered, trees of any size were scarce. Birchbark was nonexistent, and the spruce roots with which the Indian sewed his craft often were absent. About all the Eskimo could build a boat with were hunks of bone and skin from the animals he slew and ate, and fragments of driftwood. How many people living in today's metropolises would ever fashion a boat from such unlikely materials, let alone achieve the fine hull design the Eskimos gave their kayaks? It is a tribute to the incredible resourcefulness of the Eskimo that modern man has been able to do little to improve his kayak's basic design.

The Eskimo seldom needed the shallow draft that the Indian did for his canoe because the kayak was used over bottomless waters. Nevertheless, the kayak has a shallow draft as does the canoe, because this feature is needed to achieve speed.

Lurking in the vast cold seas that surrounded his camps were such life-sustaining creatures as seals and walrus, from whom the Eskimo derived the staples of his life. And these animals had to be hunted in their own haunts. The kayak evolved as the Eskimo's hunting craft. It had to be extremely fast, for it was used to chase seals to the point where an Eskimo could hurl his lethal-barbed, bone-tipped harpoon. The kayak had to be completely maneuverable, and become an extension of the paddler's body. It had to be small, low, almost invisible in the sea, camouflaged by looking like the back of a seal darting through the water. It had to be absolutely watertight both above and below to prevent its being swamped in frigid, swollen seas. Thus, while the canoe was designed as a craft for transportation over the waterways that formed a roadwork for the North American wilderness, the kayak was the instrument of an ocean-going predator.

Canoes and kayaks also differed fundamentally in the method of construction used by their respective builders. When a novice contemplates building a boat, invariably he first considers a design in which the frame is constructed and then a covering applied. This concept is applied to most wooden runabouts and cabin cruisers. It is sturdy and logical, starting with a strong frame and using it to buttress a skin that holds out the water. The same method of construction is used on the kayak.

The kayak was built by first constructing a rigid frame of driftwood, saplings, and carved chunks of bone, all lashed together with sinews. Then the skin of a walrus, sea lion, seal, or caribou was sewn into an exact, tightly fitting outer cover. The cover was soaked before applying. When it dried, it shrank to fit perfectly over the frame. The holes in the seams, where pieces of skin were joined by stitches of sinew, were impregnated with animal fat, tallow, or resin to keep out the sea.

Canoes, on the other hand, were built from the outside in— that is, a skin was formed into a shape and then filled with ribs and sheathing to maintain that shape. Canoe-building was a difficult undertaking. It made use of such materials as birchbark, cedar sheathing, fir strips, and split balsam roots that were used to sew the bark cover and lash it to the gunwales. Before Europeans introduced the products of the Iron Age to their red brothers in America, even felling a tree to obtain bark was an exhaustive task. An ax made of a stone head tied to a stick with leather was no match for a healthy birch. In order to fell the tree, the Indian built a controlled fire at its base to char it. Then he used the stone ax to scrape away the charred wood, built another fire, and scraped again. The process was repeated over and over until the tree was weakened enough to be pushed over.

The rest of the job of building a canoe proceeded slowly too. Making a mortise-and-tenon joint required hours of scraping or drilling with stone implements. Splitting the balsam roots to make "thread" required cutting the roots with a stone knife, taking one side of the root into the teeth, and gripping its opposite side with one hand while holding the stone knife in the other, using it to slit the root down the middle lengthwise.

In building a bark canoe, the bark was obtained and stored until it was ready to use. The first step in construction was the fashioning of the gunwales from lengths of fir. These were carefully shaped and lashed at the ends with spruce roots. Then, making use of mortise-and-tenon joints, thwarts were inserted to hold the gunwales apart. The spread gunwales were

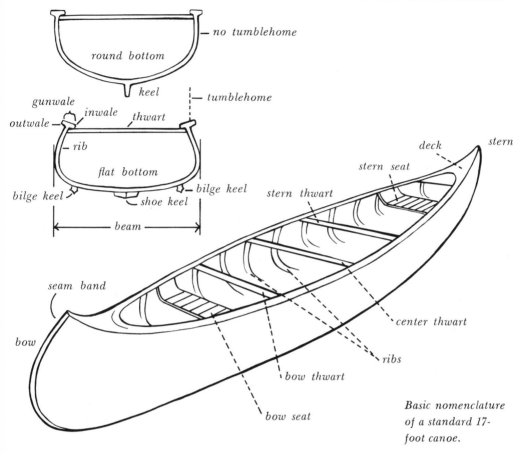

*Basic nomenclature of a standard 17-foot canoe.*

set upon the birchbark, which had been spread flat on the ground (bark had to be wet to make it pliable enough to work with) and the bark was lifted around them. The gunwales were then raised. Where imperfections appeared in the bark, or where it could not be stretched far enough to cover the craft, additional bark was sewn in. The covering was scored and sewn so that it took the proper shape. The problems involved can be appreciated if you take a flat piece of paper and try to fold it into the shape of a canoe. It bellies out too wide at the sides while maintaining almost no rocker. To alter this shape, sections of the paper must be cut away and the edges along the cuts butted together.

When the bark was finally shaped properly, it was lashed to the gunwales. Next, cedar sheathing was placed inside the covering to give strength to the floor. Then ribs, steamed and shaped exactly to fit the canoe crosswise at their respective points, were inserted an inch apart or closer. These provided strength and assured that the boat would retain its shape.

11

Canoe construction was an exacting, time-consuming, pains-taking, and complex job requiring true craftsmen. The finished craft were extremely sophisticated, exactly interrelating basic materials with design. Every detail was observed and intelli-gently considered. For example, numerous types of stitches were used on the hull. Toward the bow, the type of stitch used kept the roots close to the bark to eliminate protruding loops that would be snagged if the canoe brushed an obstacle. Be-cause the stern slanted away from obstacles, a different type of stitch was used. Stitching on underwater surfaces had to be waterproof, while that used above the waterline seldom needed to do more than join the segments of bark edge to edge.

All the characteristics of kayaks and canoes we have discussed were compromised from time to time and from locality to lo-cality to provide boats suited to precise individual and geo-graphic needs. There were canoes with both high and low bow and stern assemblies, humped gunwales, exaggerated rocker. Some were built wide to carry great amounts of cargo; others—the famed war canoes—were outsized to carry as many as twenty paddlers. Kayaks, too, were built in various sizes and shapes. They were available for one man, two men, and, on rare oc-casions, for three. Some had upswept bows and sterns, while others tapered gracefully into the water at each end. Some were fairly wide and stable, while others were scarcely wider than the paddler who rode inside—a paddler who could balance with consummate skill.

Although kayaks and canoes originally were fundamentally different craft, use of common materials such as aluminum and fiberglass has caused many of these differences to disappear in today's mass-produced models. Many canoes now are stamped from aluminum like washtubs, or molded from fiberglass. Many kayaks are molded from plastics. For this reason the structural differences have all but disappeared from the two types of craft. Yet, there are still excellent wood-and-canvas canoes available. (Canvas was introduced by Europeans to re-place bark and quickly appropriated by the red men.) And there still are fine kayaks available with skin-over-frame con-struction. Kayaks, however, have now been modified in design to accept tough synthetic skins.

Before deciding whether to buy a kayak or a canoe, reflect on where these boats came from and what they were originally used for. Many of the basic characteristics that made them de-sirable in their respective environments are still pertinent.

Eight factors should be checked for each canoe or kayak ex-amined in the showroom. They are: (1) durability of the boat's shell; (2) capacity; (3) patchability; (4) dryness; (5) flotation; (6) stability; (7) performance; and (8) maneuverability and handling. Let's first discuss these factors as they relate to kayaks and canoes generically.

## SHELL DURABILITY

The durability of canoe shells versus those of kayaks relates directly to the various materials of which these craft are made. The most popular materials for canoes are the traditional wood with wood covering, wood frame with canvas covering, aluminum, and fiberglass. Most whitewater kayaks, on the other hand, are built of polyurethane, fiberglass, or ABS laminate, a high-impact plastic which gives a rigid construction. But there are others covered with flexible skins—vinyl, Hypalon, and canvas.

How long do each of these materials last? The answer depends on how much the craft is used, the type of water challenged, and how the boat is cared for in the off-season.

The traditional canoe, built of wood over a wood frame or of canvas over a wood frame, is beautiful to behold. It is also difficult to maintain, since its highly finished thwarts, ribs, and gunwales must be revarnished periodically. Tears can develop in the canvas covering or scratches in the wood covering, both of which demand repair. Moreover, the skins of canvas-covered canoes tend to soak up water, a factor that makes the canoes heavy during the late season and that causes them to warp after extended use.

All in all, wood-frame canoes, whether covered by canvas or wood, tend to be the least durable if used where their hulls can be abraded. Don't buy such a canoe if you intend to push it

*A sectional view of a canoe made of wood and canvas. (Based on Old Town diagram)*

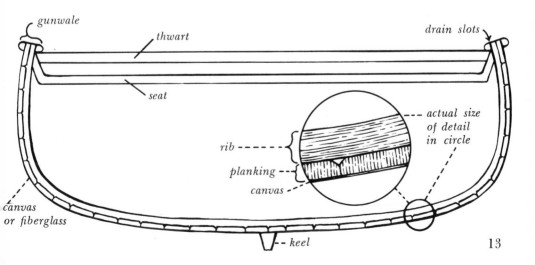

13

through whitewater or down stump-laden streams. On the other hand, when used on quiet waters or open lakes these canoes usually have fairly long lives.

Canoes built of aluminum are virtually indestructible and have justly won a legion of advocates for their performance in all types of use. They can be pounded over rocks, atop stumps, run up on gravel landings, and abused in countless ways, but they still last almost forever. It is possible to puncture or tear an aluminum canoe, but the likelihood of doing so is remote. It would have to ride the crest of a giant wave and be slammed down with terrific force on a sharp object to rend the hull. If an accident of this kind does occur, aluminum is more difficult to patch than fiberglass; but again, the probability of such an accident is small.

One reason aluminum is so durable is its ability to bend. It bends before it rips. When a canoe is dented, one simply pounds out the blemish. After this happens often enough, the canoe may be reduced in cosmetic value, but it still provides excellent transportation—and that, after all, is what it was purchased for.

*Sectional view of canoe constructed from fiberglass. (Based on Old Town diagram)*

Since many aluminum canoes are left in the original color, there is no problem with regard to painting them. Those that are painted do scratch and have to be painted from time to time.

Laminated fiberglass—especially treated with polyurethane resin—has become very popular for canoe and kayak construc-

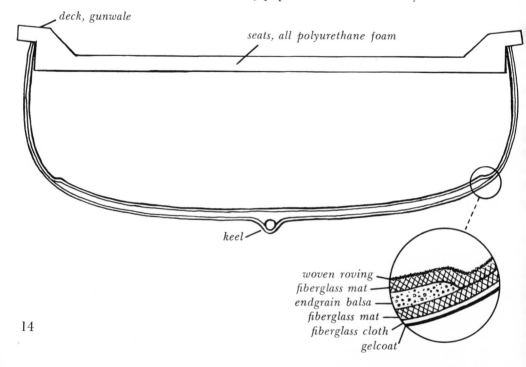

deck, gunwale

seats, all polyurethane foam

keel

woven roving
fiberglass mat
endgrain balsa
fiberglass mat
fiberglass cloth
gelcoat

tion. Even stronger is ABS laminate, now gaining in popularity. Using molds, these substances can be formed into complex shapes that eliminate the need for separately constructed gunwales and ribs. Carrying handles and cleats can be molded in; colors can be added to the hull material rather than painted on; two halves of the boat can be molded separately and joined together with flotation enclosed.

The durability of fiberglass is tremendous. If it does puncture, it can be repaired with a simple fiberglass-repair kit. Generally, fiberglass is exceptionally impact-resistant, and it has less tendency to tear than aluminum. Moreover, it lacks aluminum's propensity to dent, having what is known as a better memory—it "remembers" its original shape and returns to it. When all is said and done, you should be able to pound a fiberglass craft through rocks and down the most treacherous, snag-filled rivers over the course of a lifetime with only minimum maintenance.

ABS is a remarkable plastic that is applied to other products such as refrigerator liners and electrical-component encapsulations that must withstand abuse. It should produce a super canoe—virtually impregnable and invulnerable. I have, however, heard doubts expressed concerning its ability to withstand fatigue cracking in canoes. Also, it is reportedly difficult to repair when damage does occur. I cannot verify or discredit these observations from personal experience, but buyers would do well to check into the properties of this material and judge

*Sectional view of canoe constructed from ABS laminate. (Based on Old Town diagram)*

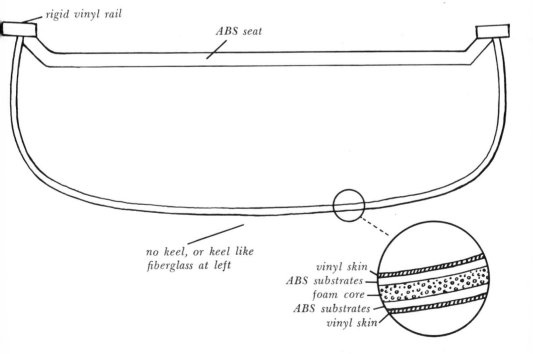

*rigid vinyl rail*

*ABS seat*

*no keel, or keel like fiberglass at left*

*vinyl skin*
*ABS substrates*
*foam core*
*ABS substrates*
*vinyl skin*

them in relation to their canoe's intended usage.

Thus, considering aluminum, fiberglass (and ABS), and wood durability, aluminum and fiberglass rate about equally (a slight edge goes to aluminum), with wood a distant third. But what about the flexible coverings of the popular voyageuring kayaks? Are they as flimsy as the casual observer often thinks?

Many kit-built kayaks and homemade craft utilize the same close-woven cotton fabric used on airplane wings. The material is doped to stretch it tight over the hulls, making a tough, and to some degree, flexible covering that withstands considerable abrasion. About the only thing that could endanger a covering of this type is a sharp stake. Such accidents do happen, especially where there are snags. But a hole in a kayak is less dangerous than might at first be imagined. Because the cloth used in the hull is strong, it does not tend to rip, but simply leaves a small opening where the stake entered. With quick thinking, the craft can be patched sufficiently to reach shore before it fills with water. A handkerchief, shirt, or other item of apparel stuffed into the opening provides a satisfactory stopgap. Once ashore, a simple roll of duct tape can be used to make the repair.

The world-famous Klepper folding kayaks have little need to prove their durability. They have given outstanding service in the hands of arctic explorers and men who have paddled deep into the tropics. The decks of the Klepper are of tough fabric, not likely to tear or puncture. The underside is constructed of Hypalon, a heavy, reinforced rubber compound that finds extensive use in electrical cable insulation, where it must stand up to the most abusive elements of the environment. On top of its inherent toughness, Hypalon stretches when it encounters a snag, which means that the kayak is apt to bounce away from even a sharp stake before the Hypalon gives way. True, the wooden frame of a Klepper is varnished and conceivably requires a little retouching during its life, but the frame in a kayak is not like the frame in a runabout: more of the wood is open to the air, and there is almost no chance for rot to set in. Rarely is it necessary to replace a frame member. With a minimum of maintenance a Klepper should last many years in moderate use, and it will not even require the finish rejuvenation of an aluminum or fiberglass boat.

A fact of nautical construction seldom considered by those buying a boat for the first time is that durability derives in part from flexibility. Actually, a boat that flexes with the waves and bends when it hits a stump has a better chance of living to fight another obstacle than a boat that is too rigid. This principle is elucidated on a grand scale in Thor Hyerdahl's remarkable book, *The Ra Expedition*. Mr. Hyerdahl expounds on the durability of his boat woven from papyrus reeds, and it was indeed the flexibility of the craft that accounted for its refusal to break apart even when the reeds had soaked up water and the boat had been twisted and tormented by winds and waves that would have snapped most modern (and more rigid) boats in two. The same principle applies in measure to a kayak's hull.

This principle was demonstrated to me the first time I paddled a Folbot. (The Folbot is constructed with a single layer of vinyl fiberplastic for its decks and two layers of cloth-backed vinyl fiberplastic for its underside.) My dad had purchased a kit from the Charleston, South Carolina, firm and assembled it in the garage. As soon as he finished the boat, I asked permission to try it. Dad helped me sling it on top of my '51 Chevy and sent me off with an admonition to be careful.

I drove out to Freiss Lake in the Kettle Morraine of Wisconsin, put the kayak in the water, and conducted a number of tests with it. After racing some counsellors from a nearby summer camp, I paddled down a channel that wound away from the lake and under Highway 67. At the highway was a low bridge. Not caring to lift the kayak from the water to carry it over the highway, I lay in the bottom and tried to sneak under the bridge. It was too low.

I lay in the boat, forcing it deep into the water by reaching up and pressing against the girders supporting the bridge. But the current was too strong and carried the boat forward faster than I wanted it to go. To my horror, I saw a sharp iron rod used as a concrete support sticking down from the bridge. The current carried the boat under it and jammed it into the deck. I was pinned on my back without enough room to stand or climb out of the boat, and I couldn't push away from the rod because of the heavy current. The deck began to stretch. And stretch. And stretch!

It was hard to believe. The vinyl gave more than eight inches before the rod finally penetrated. I managed to rock the boat far enough to one side so that I could roll out. Crouched in water about two feet deep, I worked the kayak free and pulled it from under the bridge.

An examination of the hole showed it was less than a quarter-inch in diameter, for the vinyl had a good memory and returned to its original shape. It had torn when stretched; but now, returned to its normal tension, it exhibited a hole smaller than the object that had punctured it.

17

I took the boat home when I was sure Dad would not be around, hauled out the patching kit, and masked my transgression by cutting the vinyl patch in the shape of a rather artistic fish and tried unsuccessfully to pass it off by saying it was an emblem for the new boat. Years have passed, and the fish still rides as an escutcheon on the Folbot's deck, a trophy of my maiden voyage.

The point here is hull durability. Any hull that stretches eight inches before giving way will bounce off just about anything without puncturing. The average paddler seldom encounters a strong current, immovable iron stake, and no alternative route for the kayak to take. And considering that the underside of the Folbot is twice as thick as the deck, the chances of having any difficulty with the hull are remote. In fact, aluminum or fiberglass sometimes are more likely to puncture, for they are less flexible.

One aspect of kayak construction that affects durability in any boat of this design should be mentioned. Any time you launch a kayak, you are almost sure to track sand into it. In a kayak, with its skin stretched tightly over its frame, sand can work its way in around the frame. Once there, it acts like sandpaper and has the same effect: since the kayak is flexible, the sand tends to work against the skin, eventually wearing it through. The Eskimo made an elaborate ritual of ridding himself of sand before entering his kayak, and it is recommended that you be extremely sand-conscious if you have a canvas- or cloth-covered kayak—it will ensure a longer life for the boat. In the case of vinyl or Hypalon kayaks, the skins are less affected by abrasion, but it is still a good idea to wash them thoroughly on the inside a couple of times a year, probing with a small stick of wood between the longitudinal members and the skin and letting the water run through to wash out any sand that might be trapped.

To summarize what has been said about durability, you should not purchase a wood-framed canoe with either wood or canvas skin unless your canoeing will be done on open water. All other types of construction will last indefinitely with proper care and if used for the purposes intended. If your boat must endure exceptionally rough use, the natural-finish aluminum canoe is probably best for durability. The average weekender who does some downriver paddling and challenges a little whitewater will probably be satisfied with the durability of fiberglass and will like the fact that dents do not appear in it as easily as they do in aluminum. Flexible-skin kayaks are satisfactorily durable: canvas is the most limiting type of cover, while Hypalon and fiberplastic prove virtually indestructible unless abused severely. If flexible-skin kayaks have an intrinsic disadvantage compared to aluminum and fiberglass canoes, it would have to be their wooden frames, which are more apt to snap than are the molded or stamped hulls of the latter. But even here, there is unbelievable strength in bent wood placed under tension; it would be an extreme situation that would cause frame breakage.

## DRYNESS

Even though water is an integral part of a paddle trip—indeed, the factor that creates most of the enjoyment—water must be conquered. It can ruin a trip if it gets into the boat or penetrates a camper's gear.

There are two ways water can enter: from below, or from rain above. The advantage of dryness falls squarely on the side of the kayak. Remember that the inventors of these craft designed them to transport men through the high seas of the arctic while keeping the paddlers dry. By the time the Eskimo covered the opening of his kayak with his clothing and rubbed himself with oil, he could even roll in the sea without moisture touching his body.

Because of its decks, the kayak is protected from spray and waves washing over it better than is a canoe. Waves that do break over decks that slant downward, away from the paddler, simply run off. When the craft is packed properly, the kayak's bow tends to float over, rather than plunge into, rising waves. In contrast, the paddlers in a canoe are positioned not centrally, but with one in the bow and one in the stern. The weight of the forward paddler can make the bow plunge into waves, causing water to find its way into the canoe. The problem is only partly alleviated by the fact that a canoe has a higher bow than does a kayak.

As far as keeping the rain from filling the bilges and wetting packed gear, again the kayak is superior because of its decks. Moreover, for most kayaks spray covers are available that feature elastic-rimmed holes in which paddlers can sit. When snapped to the edges of the cockpits, the spray covers can be drawn tight, protecting any underlying gear from both spray and rain. If a paddler wears a poncho when his spray cover is fixed over the cockpit, he can navigate in a downpour and still remain dry.

## CAPACITY

The capacity needed for carrying paddlers, passengers, and

19

gear is a definite determinant to whether you should choose a canoe or a kayak, and to which model of either type of boat is most suitable.

The next part of this guide examines a number of canoes and kayaks available on today's market and lists their important specifications. In general, you will be amazed at the amount of weight paddlecraft will bear. But our purpose here is to compare canoes and kayaks to help you choose a *type* of boat. And to make such a comparison, we must first analyze what capacity means.

Capacity can be looked at in two ways: it can be determined either by weight or by volume. This is an important distinction when judging the carrying ability of a canoe versus that of a kayak of equal length.

Let us first consider capacity as the weight the craft will bear. For comparison's sake, the 17-foot Grumman double-ended canoe is rated by its manufacturer for a carrying capacity of 805 pounds. Folbot rates its 17-foot Super for a somewhat lower carrying capacity of 750 pounds. The 55-pound difference in rated capacity between the two boats is substantial: approximately 12 percent; so if you plan to do especially heavy carrying, your choice would be the Grumman canoe. But for all practical purposes, it is unlikely you would ever pack either boat anywhere near its rated capacity. (The Grumman's rated capacity includes the mounting of a motor, as does Folbot's; but for the purposes of this discussion, canoes and kayaks are being considered as paddlecraft, and therefore judged without motors affixed.) The Grumman rating provides for four persons of 150 pounds each. For comfortable paddling with the 17-foot canoe and gear, you would normally accommodate only two paddlers and a possible passenger. Similarly, the seating configuration of the Folbot is conducive to use by only two paddlers. So in neither case are passengers likely to boast a combined weight much over 400 pounds. And no matter how heavy the camping equipment lugged along, it is unlikely to top 150 to 200 pounds. Usually it will be much less.

Capacity of kayaks versus that of canoes is another story entirely when capacity is considered as the volume the boats will hold. This is due mainly to the configuration of the respective hulls. Because the canoe is undecked, the sky is the limit for packing gear. Of course there are practical limitations, for piling gear too high is deleterious to stability. If equipment is to be piled high, heavy items should be placed on the bottom and lighter equipment piled on top. The entire bottom of the canoe between paddlers can be loaded with gear if it is packed low enough. If heavy items are kept in the boat's bottom, they actually increase stability.

In the kayak, on the other hand, gear must be packed forward and aft under the decks and under the side decks. Height, therefore, is limited. Since the paddler sits in the kayak with his legs extended in front, floor space is taken up that could otherwise be used for gear. Some kayaks even surrender much of the space under their side decks where storage space is replaced by sponsons * that provide flotation and keep the skin tight about the boat's frame. Thus, even though a kayak accommodates a large amount of weight, it may have to be packed with small, possibly heavy objects. Big items, even if light, may be too bulky.

That's the story: the canoe usually carries a greater *volume* of gear than a kayak of equal length. But what does this mean to the boat buyer?

How volume capacity affects your choice of boat depends in large measure on how many people and the type and quantity of gear you plan to take along. If you plan to paddle alone, a two-passenger kayak is more than sufficient for you and any gear you are likely to pack; certainly a canoe of equal size is just as satisfactory. If you will paddle with one other person, either boat should handle your needs. If you must carry a third adult or children in addition to your spouse, the canoe should definitely be your choice, since the sitting or kneeling position requires less floor space per paddler than the legs-extended-forward position used in the kayak.

If your boat will usually be manned by more than one paddler, you must consider the type of gear you have to carry. If you want to use camping equipment that has been stowed in the garage for some years—heavy tents, a two-burner stove, a large gas lantern, bulky sleeping bags, a canvas tarpaulin, etc.—a canoe can generally better handle the bulk and is a more practical choice than a kayak. On the other hand, if you already have, or are able to purchase, lightweight equipment that is readily adaptable to paddle camping, and plan to take only two paddlers, a kayak will fill the bill as well.

Do not sell the volume capacity of a kayak short. It may not match that of a canoe of comparable length, but it is still sur-

---

* Sponsons are air-filled tubes incorporated in the sides of a boat for floatation. Klepper is the only manufacturer discussed in this guide to use them. However, several other manufacturers offer "sponson type" designs, either with strips of foamed plastic outside the hull under the gunwales, or with bulges stamped into the hull at the waterline for extra width and, hence, stability. Throughout, the term "sponson" is used in its broadest sense to describe all these configurations.

21

prisingly large. When traveling with a companion, I have carried beneath the decks of a Super Folbot a lightweight tent, two fairly good-sized sleeping bags, four gallons of water in jugs, a packsack full of cooking gear, two duffel bags, a portable radio, two rolled-up foam mattresses, a large cook kit, a white-gas lantern, fishing gear, an ax, a saw, a trenching tool, a tarp, canteens, extra rope, a spray cover, extra paddles, and many other small pieces of equipment. When I unloaded them at the edge of a stream and placed them next to the boat, it brought exclamations from bystanders. But the kayak holds it all and has room left over; it's all in the art of packing!

To sum up, before you choose a kayak rather than a canoe, or vice versa, be sure to compare their rated capacities. Then analyze the type of gear you plan to carry and how many persons will be taken on most trips. If you feel that capacity in terms of maximum weight is not a determining factor, consider capacity in terms of volume. If you have to carry a lot of large, heavy, bulky equipment that was originally intended for camping out of a car, lean toward the canoe. On the other hand, if your equipment is fairly lightweight and small in bulk, the kayak will be just as suitable.

## FLOTATION

Wood and wood-covered-by-canvas canoes float near or at the water's surface when they overturn. But craft made of most other materials require extra flotation to keep them buoyant when they are filled with water. In most aluminum and fiberglass canoes, flotation is provided by foamed plastic contained under the decks in bow and stern. Two flotation methods are used in kayaks: air bags stuffed under the front and rear decks or, as in the Klepper, inflated sponsons incorporated along both sides of the craft. Several canoes, notably Sportspal and MirroCraft, also run foam sponsons along the outside underneath the gunwales.

Two factors should be considered as far as flotation is concerned, and they should significantly influence whether you buy a particular canoe or kayak. Does the craft float rightside up, upside down, or on its side when filled with water? And how much passenger weight will the water-filled craft support when floating with its gunwales at water level?

It is difficult to determine the position a swamped craft will take or how much weight a water-filled craft will support prior to purchasing it. When the boat floats filled with water, the water constitutes a load in excess of its rated capacity. This impairs its stability, and it is likely to roll when you climb in, whatever position it takes originally.

In general, most canoes or kayaks that have foam or sponsons running along the gunwales tend to float upright after capsizing. Other craft may float in a variety of positions. Tests conducted by *Consumer Reports* magazine on a number of popular canoes indicated the following flotation positions: Grumman—upright; Aero-Craft Apache—upright; Old Town FG—upright; Aluma-Craft Quetico QT17—upright; Seminole 15½—upright; Smoker-Craft Standard SS17—upright; Ward's Sea King—upright; Old Town Guide—upright; Old Town Octa—upright; Chestnut Prospector Fort—upright; Indian Brand Sagamo—bottom up; Sears 61-47—upright; Quachita—upright; Indian Brand Princess—upright; Sawyer Sport—bottom up.

As far as supporting weight when swamped, wood and wood-covered-by-canvas canoes are generally inferior, relying solely on the flotation of their construction materials to hold them up. Other craft vary in ability to support weight when swamped. Some can carry gear as well as support one paddler who may climb inside to bail. The Old Town FG reportedly supports three times its hull weight when full of water—237 pounds for the 16-foot model—meaning that a paddler can climb back in and paddle the water-filled canoe to shore. Most, however, will not support a person's weight stably until some water has been bailed out.

## STABILITY

Instability is a fault that too many people attribute to kayaks and canoes. In truth, doubters would be astonished to learn how difficult it is to overturn a canoe or voyageuring kayak, even when trying to do so deliberately. (This is not to say mishaps don't happen; occasionally they do. Working as an instructor at a boys' summer camp, I helped take groups of youngsters on one canoe trip after another without an accident. Then the camp director, a burly, gruff, football-coach-and-army-sergeant type, decided to come along. I remember his ringing, "Doggone it, anyway!" as his canoe rolled like a tall pine on its way to the sawmill and can still see his sailor cap and pack of cigarettes floating away downriver while the water foamed at his waist.)

How can you judge stability? Generally, it depends on the shape of the hull. Canoes with "round" bottoms are more "tender" than those with relatively flat bottoms. Wide canoes tend to be more stable than narrow ones built for speed. Canoes with "bulges" along their waterlines offer extra stability. It is possible to make a canoe more stable simply by making it extra wide. Unfortunately, when a canoe is too wide, it is also likely to be less maneuverable. You should not have to sacrifice course holding or maneuverability for stability. With proper handling, most normally shaped canoes and voyageuring kayaks are more than stable enough to ride out even the worst conditions.

Generally, how do canoes compare with kayaks for stability? Many canoes tend to be slightly more "tender." Because the paddler sits on a high seat or kneels, his center of gravity resides about the area of his butt. This is above the water level and so makes the canoe more prone to tip. In the larger kayaks, on the other hand, the paddler sits in the bottom, placing the center of gravity about an inch below the waterline and making them very stable. Many canoes can be tipped by two paddlers sitting up high and reaching simultaneously to push a branch out of the way as they pass underneath. But most two-man flexible-skin kayaks are difficult to tip this way. In fact, the paddler is apt to lose his balance and fall out of the boat first. About the only thing likely to tip a large kayak with a wide beam is a strong wave washing it against a shoreline or an obstacle in the water.

This does not imply that all kayaks are more stable than all canoes—far from it. True, the popular voyageuring kayaks are highly stable, but this does not apply to the narrower "sport" versions. The downriver and slalom kayaks by Old Town, Vermont-Tubbs, Hauthaway, and others are built for speed and require paddlers who know their business. It is important to balance these craft almost as one would a bicycle. Leaning too far to one side can cause them to capsize.

## PERFORMANCE

The greatest advantage canoes and kayaks have over rowboats and inflatables is performance. Their swiftness and maneuverability hark back to their origins. Canoes, designed for fast transportation on shallow streams, had to be highly maneuverable to dodge snags and boulders; the kayak was fast and sleek for racing through ice-cold seas in pursuit of seals, walrus, and other aquatic animals.

Today's canoes and kayaks usually have little in common with their ancestors except the shapes of their hulls. But their hulls give them their performance.

In general performance, the kayak is usually swifter and easier to maneuver than a canoe of comparable length. This is one reason that there is a preponderance of kayaks in competitive events.

Performance in canoes or kayaks depends on factors such as beam, waterline length (referring to the length of the boat where it emerges from the water), rocker, plan shape (the shape of the boat as seen from above), draft (the depth of water required to float the craft), and the shape of the hull as seen end-on.

The following points should be considered when comparing canoes and kayaks for performance:

The longer the waterline, the faster the canoe or kayak. But as waterline length increases, maneuverability decreases.

Rocker is seldom regular; it increases sharply at bow and stern while being almost flat amidships. The more rocker amidships, the greater the turning ability. As rocker decreases, the craft tends to be faster and easier to paddle in a straight line.

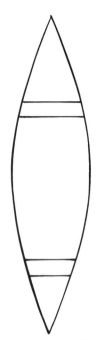

*Canoe shapes. The beam is constant, but the shape shown at top will be faster than that shown at bottom.*

*How degree of rocker is measured.*

Beam is a fairly reliable indicator of stability. The greater the beam, the less likely the craft is to capsize, but also the slower the boat will be. In the case of kayaks, wide beam limits the ability to roll.

Plan shape is important in judging performance. Most canoes are symmetrical, that is, they are shaped about the same bow and stern. But a canoe that is comparatively narrow between the middle and the ends is faster than one that is wider, even when beam is constant.

In kayaks, there are three common plan shapes: *symmetrical, fishform,* and *Swedeform.* The symmetrical design seats the paddler amidships where the beam is widest. The kayak is shaped about the same in the bow as in the stern. In a fishform kayak, the paddler sits slightly ahead of center, and the beam is greatest ahead of center. Swedeform is the reverse of fish-

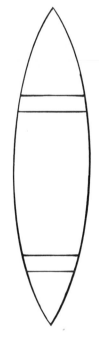

25

form. The Swedeform shape finds the paddler seated approximately amidships, sometimes a little forward of center and sometimes a little aft. The bow is pointed sharply and the beam is widest toward the stern.

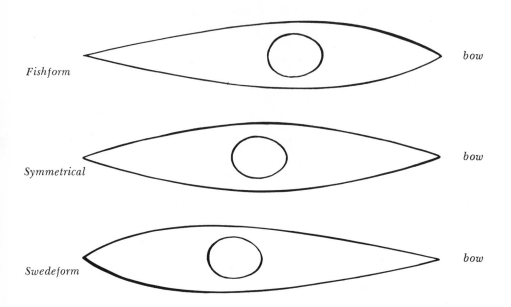

*Fishform*        *bow*

*Symmetrical*        *bow*

*Swedeform*        *bow*

Each form has definite advantages and disadvantages for specific types of paddling. The best all-around design is symmetrical, performing satisfactorily in all water no matter how white or swift. The bow tends to float over oncoming waves, while the stern floats up on waves that overtake it. A symmetrical kayak usually offers good stability for its size and type. In general, there are few disadvantages to the design.

Swedeform and fishform kayaks are constructed to offer special advantages under various conditions. The fishform is for meeting oncoming waves. The wide bow floats up on the waves and provides stability. The Swedeform kayak is tremendously fast but often unstable. It is designed for making rapid time on flatwater or downriver. Its sharply pointed bow slices into the waves and does not tend to rise, thereby saving seconds as the craft slices straight toward its goal. The paddler may get wet, but he can certainly race the stopwatch. Like the fishform, the Swedeform, at least when exaggerated, is a boat for the expert, and is not recommended as a beginner's kayak.

After looking at canoes and kayaks from the top to determine their general shapes, they must be viewed from the side. From this vantage, much can be told about their relative maneuverability. Generally, if you are not as interested in speed as in maximum maneuverability, say for slalom racing or whitewater, look for models with substantial rocker. On the other hand, if you want to travel in a stable, straight line at maximum speed, your boat should have as little rocker as possible.

*Flat bottom*

End-on shape has much to do with determining performance. Round-bottom canoes tend to be faster than flat-bottom models. The end-on view also discloses much information about the relative maneuverability of kayaks, especially the sport models.

*V-bottom*

There are four basic configurations: flat bottom, "V" bottom, round bottom, and combination. For maximum initial stability, that is, for the kayak to sustain an upright stance in the water without requiring an inordinate amount of balancing, choose a kayak with a flat bottom. Another advantage of the flat bottom is shallow draft. But there are also disadvantages. Flat-bottom kayaks often are overlooked by racing enthusiasts because they are slow and tend to turn and steer differently when the boat is upright than when it is leaning. Another disadvantage of the flat-bottom design is that such boats are vulnerable to the tossing effect of side waves.

*Round bottom*

The "V"-keel kayak requires more draft than the flat-bottomed type. It does not have as great initial stability, but as it leans it becomes ever more stable. Kayaks of this type are almost impossible to tip, but offer a sharp edge that can be assaulted by heavy water, making handling difficult on occasions. The "V" bottom steers truer than the flat-bottomed type and is also preferred for straightaway downriver paddling.

*Combination*

Next there is the round-bottomed kayak, which has no single point of stability—it requires balancing on the paddler's part to keep it upright. But it possesses the type of steering that makes it most responsive to bodily movements. As the paddler leans, he does not materially alter the shape of the hull in the water, which means the boat has very predictable steering characteristics.

Finally, the combination has elements of all the various designs and also includes tumblehome, achieved by rounded gunwales. Its shape gives it more stability than round-bottomed models and less susceptibility to attack from side waves than the flat-bottomed type. Furthermore, it does not require the draft of the V-bottom model. Most sport kayaks are of the combination type.

27

Keep in mind that all kayak hulls have some elements of all the configurations described, depending on where you look at them along their lengths. But at its widest point, a kayak does fall into one of the end-on shape categories we have discussed. If you examine the one you are thinking of buying for its plan shape, rocker, and end-on view or cross section, you can glean an idea of the capabilities it possesses and the purposes for which it was designed.

## SUMMARY: CANOES VS. KAYAKS

The question remains: What should you buy—a canoe or kayak? No one can answer definitively for you. It depends mostly on the type of paddling you intend to do.

You will be happiest with an aluminum canoe if you plan camping trips and are going to challenge a little whitewater. Fiberglass canoes are quieter in the water and will do the job almost as well, although they are more apt to scratch if the going gets rough. If, on the other hand, your canoeing is to be done in deep water or on lakes, there is no rival for the wood-and-canvas canoe. It is quiet and solid and has an unsurpassed feel of quality. If you are not afraid of periodic maintenance, it offers an unmatched canoeing experience.

Paralleling the canoes in practicality for touring and camping are the voyageuring kayaks such as the Folbot and Klepper. These can be bought in folding models that require minimum storage space and can be packed into several bags that fit into the trunk of your car. Some can also be purchased in rigid form, ready to be slung on top of a car. The flexible hull materials of these boats are sufficient for any type of boating including whitewater, and they should be considered serious rivals of the better canoes. Even for open-lake paddling these boats suffice, even though they lack keels. Because their bows and sterns are lower than those of canoes, they are much less sensitive to the wind, which is a great help on open water. Also, they are drier than canoes, owing to their covered decks.

Competition and racing kayaks should not be overlooked either as a source of excitement. They are specialized boats, not intended for the person who wants to take his family on an overnight trip. But they are fast, sleek, and sporty. There are a host of them available, many designed by winners of major competition events.

# PART TWO

# CANOES, KAYAKS, AND INFLATABLES

By now you are probably leaning toward either a canoe, kayak, or inflatable. Armed with a general idea of what type of craft you want, you should look over the selection of models available in your chosen category. Each category contains big models, small ones, fast ones, slow ones, and at least one model that should satisfy your sense of aesthetics. Again you must question yourself about how your new paddlecraft will be used. Do you plan to do little more than paddle around in the water, splashing here and there, getting wet? Or are you intent on cruising long distances? Is day cruising for you, or do you like to camp overnight? If you are a camper, how heavy is your equipment? How many persons will travel in the boat—one, two, three, or more? Are you likely to portage for long distances, or often? What type of water will you paddle? Whitewater? Lakes? Shallow streams? Do you prefer quiet fishing or strenuous competition? The answers to all these questions should have significant influence on the particular model of craft you buy, just as they had on the type of boat you chose to purchase.

The following pages contain charts listing selected craft * of all types. For each craft, pertinent specifications of dimension, capacity, and price are given. This information makes it possible to compare at a glance many representative brands. Some of the most popular boats are included, but there are also some from small, little-known companies. Following each comparison chart is a general discussion of the boats listed.

* While many paddlecraft are reviewed, they represent only a significant fraction of a varied market. Reading about these models can help if you choose to investigate models which are similar, but which have been omitted.

Remember that the following review has been compiled from manufacturers' information, personal observation, and often from my own familiarity with the boat's use. But there is no substitute for examining a boat yourself before purchasing it. Use these lists to narrow your search, then write to the companies that offer products of interest. When you send for information, ask for the name of a nearby dealer. After settling on two or three models, visit the dealer to verify their quality. Pay attention to details: finish, rough edges, gunwale design. Do not buy a canoe, kayak, or inflatable that shows sloppy workmanship. Poor attention to detail can signify poor overall construction, possibly even bad design. If there is no nearby dealer for a boat that fits your needs precisely, you have no choice but to order directly from the factory. If this is the case, be sure to check the boat thoroughly for defects as soon as you receive it.

# Selected Inflatables

The tremendous flotation ability of inflatable craft is obvious, considering that even the smallest and lightest inflatables can support almost half the weight that a full-sized canoe or kayak can. But despite fabulous flotation, these lightweight boats are at their best on small expanses of water; they are impractical for lengthy trips or campouts.

### ULTRALIGHT INFLATABLE PADDLECRAFT

The limitations of ultralight inflatables are considerable. Hard-pressed is the person who wants to carry gear in them. Of the six craft listed, only the Pioneer II and the Pack-Raft II have raised seats. In the others, should water be shipped into the boat—either tracked in or splashed over the sides—the paddler has to sit in it. Most ultralight inflatables are built to accommodate one person. Although the Pioneer II and the Pack-Raft II do carry two passengers, comfort is better with one. Most are equipped with oarlocks, so they can be rowed as well as paddled, but the oarlocks are seldom pinned. This means that the oars turn in the locks and slide in and out—an inducement to paddle. Because small inflatables are not very maneuverable and tend to rotate when paddled, they are suggested for "paddidling"—lolling half in and half out of the water—and playing. Really, they are but a step above an air mattress.

The smallest craft listed is the incredibly light Waterwalker by American Safety Equipment Corporation. The Waterwalker is little more than an inner tube with a seat slung in the hole and a pair of suspenders attached. It is intended primarily for fishing. When ready to emerge from the water, one does so with the Waterwalker around his waist like a pregnant Hula-Hoop, suspended from shoulder straps. There are lunch, or tackle, pouches mounted on the Waterwalker's surface. This remarkable "craft" is intended for use with armpit-high wading boots. It is the one paddlecraft listed in this book that is usually paddled with the feet. Plastic paddle-flippers that mount on your heels can be purchased from American Safety for about $10.95, but a pair of scuba fins usually does the trick.

The Waterwalker shares a unique inflation system with American Safety's Pack-Raft II. Both come with 4-ounce carrying cases that convert into instant inflating systems. Simply unsnap the cover from the inflation valve of the individual raft and insert the valve of the carrying case into it. Then grasp the case with both hands and shake it open so it fills with air. Quickly close the case by rolling it downward, forcing air into the raft. Repeat the process until the raft is inflated. This handy system is used in lieu of a pump.

The Pack-Raft II is the ultimate in a lightweight boat for backpackers, but makes some serious compromises to keep its weight down. It is made of neoprene-coated nylon, considerably thinner and lighter than the materials used in other boats such as the two-layer laminated PVC (polyvinyl chloride) in Gladding offerings. While its skin is adequate for open-water use, the Pack-Raft II is probably best kept away from sharp snags.

The most serious compromises of the Pack-Raft II occur in its design rather than its materials. The craft is one of the few inflatables with only one air section; the entire perimeter blows up into one big air bag. If you happen to puncture it, all the flotation vanishes. The floor is but a simple layer of

## ULTRALIGHT INFLATABLE PADDLECRAFT

| NAME MANUFACTURER* | LENGTH | BEAM | WEIGHT (LBS.) | SECTIONS | CAPACITY (LBS.) | PRICE | MATERIAL |
|---|---|---|---|---|---|---|---|
| Waterwalker American Safety | folded 1'5¼" unfolded 3'4¼" dia. | folded 5" | 2.8 | 2 | 300+ | $42.50 | Neoprene-coated Nylon |
| Back Pack Boat Gloy's | 4'8" | 33" | 4.0 | 2 | 200 | $20.00 | PVC |
| Pioneer I Gloy's | 5' | 40" | 4.84 | 2 | 300 | INA | PVC |
| Nylon Raft Recreational Equipment | 6' | 40" | 7.0 | INA | INA | $21.95 | Nylon |
| Pack-Raft II American Safety | folded 1'8" unfolded 6' | folded 7" unfolded 42" | 3.25 | 1 | 450+ | $100.00 | Neoprene-coated Nylon |
| Pioneer II Gloy's | 6'6" | 46" | 10.34 | 5 | 500 | INA | PVC |

*OR DISTRIBUTOR*

PVC = polyvinyl chloride

The Waterwalker, above, and below, American Safety Equipment's Pack Raft. (Photos American Safety Equipment)

fabric; it is not inflated. There are two cushions with the craft, both inflatable, that might offer flotation should the rest of the raft collapse, but these are not as large as the cushions in some other craft. These compromises seriously limit the general safety of the Pack-Raft. However, if used as intended, it should give good service. Its two-man capacity is hard to beat in a 3.25-pound boat.

The Gloy's boats listed come with a rope all the way around their perimeters, a valuable feature that makes them easy to handle out of the water and offers a grip when they capsize. They also have as standard equipment a kit suitable for making minor repairs.

The Nylon Raft from Recreational Equipment, Incorporated, is a true "paddidler." Since no paddles are supplied, you are left to cut out a pair of hand paddles on your own—shape

*Gloy's Back Pack Boat. (Photo Gloy's Division, Amdis Corp.)*

34

*Gloy's Pioneer I, above, and below,*
*Gloy's Pioneer II. (Photo Gloy's)*

them like ping-pong paddles if you will. Or you can cast about for a very short paddle. This boat, like the others, should be used within its limitations. Do not push it to the top of a dam expecting to reverse field and paddle away against the current. Ultralight inflatables will support you as life rafts in the worst seas, but where control and directed movement are necessary, they have critical shortcomings. Nevertheless, if you are on a tight budget and want to confine your paddling to some light playing about in the water, or want to pack a boat on your back to remote fishing holes, these little craft are worth considering.

## MEDIUM-WEIGHT INFLATABLE PADDLECRAFT

Gloy's Pioneer IV is a little more than double the weight of the Gladding Float 'n Peace, and carries about double the capacity. These boats typify the "extremes" of what can be categorized as medium-weight inflatable paddlecraft. Like most inflatables of this size, they are intended to be rowed rather than paddled. The Pioneer IV is even designed to accept up to a 2-horsepower motor. But, as is the case with most inflatables, both models lack pins in their oarlocks, making rowing somewhat difficult. The Float 'n Peace is designed for two passengers, while the Pioneer IV accommodates four safely. Moreover, Pioneer IV has inflatable seats, so that one does not have to sit in water that happens to splash over the sides. The Pioneer IV comes in a dark blue with white and blue checkered racing stripes.

Leisure Imports' Kaik 225 is both shorter and narrower than the Pioneer IV, but is rated for the same capacity. The Kaik is built for two persons and does not come with inflated seats. It is orange with blue trim. Especially desirable is the "I-beam" construction used in its floor.* Towing cleats and rope lacing are standard.

* I-beam construction refers to the way the air chambers are positioned in the floor. Three types of construction appear in the floors of inflatables; looking at the air compartments end-on, they appear as follows:

The first configuration is called "I-beam." Its obvious advantage is that punctures in the outer fabric layer do not admit water into the boat. Also, at no place is the paddler's weight brought directly against the outer layer, so that the outer layer retains maximum flexibility, minimizing the likelihood of puncture.

The Gladding Shark 100 Special is also said to accommodate four adult passengers, but the rated useful capacity of 616 pounds indicates that it would be too full if the four passengers averaged more than 154 pounds each.

## MEDIUM-WEIGHT INFLATABLE PADDLECRAFT

| NAME | LENGTH | BEAM | WEIGHT | SECTIONS | CAPAC-ITY | PRICE | MATERIAL |
|------|--------|------|--------|----------|-----------|-------|----------|
| *MANUFACTURER** | | | (LBS.) | | (LBS.) | | |
| Float 'n Peace | 7' | 50" | 13 | 3 | 330 | INA | PVC |
| *Gladding* | | | | | | | |
| Kaik 225 | 7'6" | 51" | 17 | 3 | 800 | INA | PVC |
| *Leisure* | | | | | | | |
| *Imports* | | | | | | | |
| Shark 100 | 7'11" | 48" | 17 | 4 | 616 | INA | PVC |
| Special | | | | | | | |
| *Gladding* | | | | | | | |
| Pioneer IV | 10' | 68" | 29.1 | 5 | 800 | INA | PVC |
| *Gloy's* | | | | | | | *OR DISTRIBUTOR* |

By and large, inflatables of medium size cannot be recommended to the serious paddler. In the case of the four-man models, they are too wide to be paddled comfortably. Because of this they do not accommodate a kayak paddle without the paddle rubbing along the sides. A canoe paddle can be used, but to shift it from one side of the boat to the other necessitates shifting the body from side to side at the same time. Moreover, because of the soft seating arrangements, much of the energy utilized for forward propulsion transfers, through the paddler's body, into the seats, making the craft relatively inefficient. As with other inflatables, the four-man craft are designed to provide "big flotation" in a shallow draft boat, and this they do admirably. But they are not designed to be sleek, to make time, or to cover long distances.

## INFLATABLE KAYAKS

Inflatable kayaks and canoes are the result of a surprisingly successful attempt to reshape traditional inflatables to give them the maneuverability they lack in their original form. The reshaping of the inflatable hull to the form of a kayak/canoe effects a surprising transformation in handling. Essentially, the beam is narrowed in comparison to the length, and the ends are pointed and upswept. Of all the inflatable craft, these canoes and kayaks are far and away the most likely to provide hours of inexpensive fun and are an excellent means of getting oriented to paddling as a hobby.

Pyrawa inflatable kayaks are among the most widely distributed. (L. L. Bean, Sears, and Montgomery Ward are only some of the outlets that handle them. Those interested can also write directly to the distributor: Leisure Imports, St. James, New York.) Pyrawas come in an attractive orange color, accented with blue. Three sizes are available, all with vinyl hulls that

## INFLATABLE KAYAKS

| NAME | LENGTH | BEAM | WEIGHT | SECTIONS | CAPAC-ITY | PRICE | MATERIAL |
|------|--------|------|--------|----------|-----------|-------|----------|
| *MANUFACTURER** | | | (LBS.) | | (LBS.) | | |
| Kalua I | 7'6" | 34" | 8.69 | 5 | 275 | INA | PVC |
| *Gloy's* | | | | | | | |
| Pyrawa N-2 | 7'6" | 29" | 11 | 11 | 250 | $43.00 | PVC |
| *Leisure* | | | | | | | |
| *Imports* | | | | | | | |
| Sea Eagle-260 | 8'3" | 32" | 12 | 7 | 250 | $69.95 | PVC |
| *Leisure* | | | | | | | |
| *Imports* | | | | | | | |
| Stebco B-15 | 9'5" | 29" | 12.75 | 8 | INA | $54.98 | PVC |
| *Stebco* | | | | | | | |
| Pyrawa N-4 | 9'6" | 33" | 15 | 11 | 450 | $79.95 | PVC |
| *Leisure* | | | | | | | |
| *Imports* | | | | | | | |
| Sea Eagle-300 | 9'6" | 35" | 16 | 10 | 450 | $94.95 | PVC |
| *Leisure* | | | | | | | |
| *Imports* | | | | | | | |
| Pyrawa N-5 | 10' | 36" | 19 | 11 | 550 | $99.95 | PVC |
| *Leisure* | | | | | | | |
| *Imports* | | | | | | | |
| Kalua II | 11' | 36" | 24.97 | 11 | 500 | INA | PVC |
| *Gloy's* | | | | | | | |
| Sea Eagle-340 | 11' | 37" | 21 | 10 | 600 | $119.95 | PVC |
| *Leisure* | | | | | | | |
| *Imports* | | | | | | | |
| Tahiti (Two-Man deluxe) | 11' | 34" | 23 | 11 | INA | $91.95 | PVC |
| *Sevylor USA* | | | | | | | |
| Sea Eagle-380 | 12'5" | 37" | 23 | 13 | 750 | $142.95 | PVC |
| *Leisure* | | | | | | | |
| *Imports* | | | | | | | |
| Tahiti (Three-Man deluxe) | 12'6" | 34" | 31 | 13 | INA | $119.95 | PVC |
| *Sevylor USA* | | | | | | | * OR DISTRIBUTOR |

are electronically welded at the seams. These boats can be used in salt water and are impervious to oil and other normally corrosive elements. A carrying bag and repair kit come with each boat, and double-ended paddles are available. Inflatable seats and rope-laced spray covers are featured. The three models— N-2, N-4, and N-5—seat one adult, two adults, and two adults

*The Pyrawa N-4. (Photo Leisure Imports)*

and a child respectively, although the larger models are more comfortable when no extra passengers are aboard.

Similar to the Pyrawa N-5 is the Kalua II two-man inflatable kayak. Like the Pyrawa, it features inflatable seats and tie-down decks. The Kalua is rated slightly lower in capacity, but is four inches longer than the Pyrawa. A smaller version—the Kalua I—closely rivals the small Pyrawa N-2, but outranks it in capacity by 25 pounds. It is about five inches wider, adding to its stability but detracting proportionately from its maneuverability. The Kalua I does not come with an inflatable seat as does the Pyrawa N-2, and for this reason the Pyrawa seems the better choice.

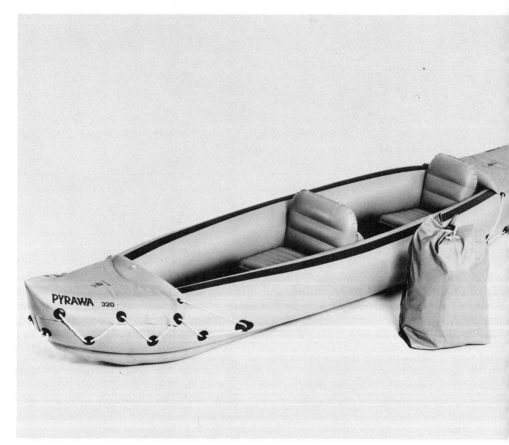

*The Pyrawa N-5. (Photo Leisure Imports)*

Sevylor also produces a two-man inflatable kayak, the Tahiti Two-Man Deluxe, that competes closely with the Pyrawa N-5 both in size and in price. Overall, the Pyrawa seems an equal-to-better purchase based on an overview of construction, valve

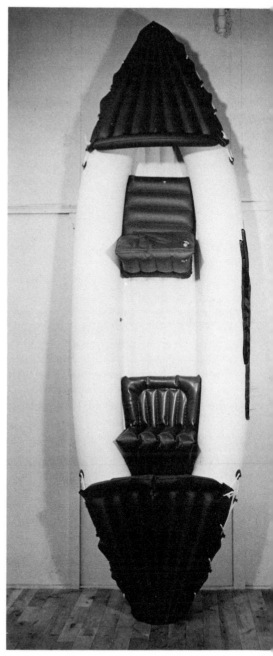

*Gloy's Kalua II.*
*(Photo Gloy's Division, Amdis Corp.)*

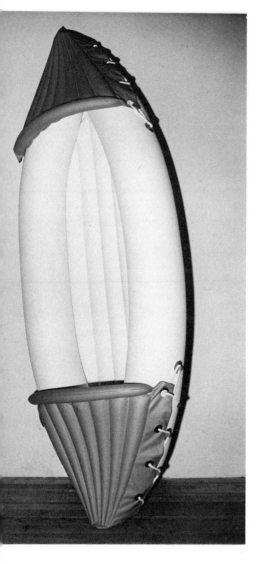

*Gloy's Kalua I.*

41

*Sevylor Two-Man K-77. (Photo Sevylor)*

design, and workmanship. But the Tahiti should not be overlooked, especially if a dealer is close by. (The Tahitis are marketed by some J. C. Penney stores, among other distributors.)

Up to this point, I have commended Pyrawa for its quality and design and compared it to competitors. There is only one inflatable craft of those reviewed that I feel might represent a *better* purchase (excluding the Sea Eagle models, which will be discussed shortly): the Stebco B-15. This is not to say the B-15 is better than the Pyrawa. It is not. But its comparatively low price is attractive. The Stebco has only one seat compared to the Pyrawa's two. But that one seat boasts a "thicker," more rigid cushion and back, which provide better support than the Pyrawa's. The Stebco's valves do not exhibit quite the same material quality as the Pyrawa's, but they are of better design. Many comparisons can be made of these craft, but briefly, the Stebco is a fine boat, especially for those who travel one-man-to-a-kayak with their gear stashed in the spot normally reserved for a second passenger.

Leisure Imports gradually is replacing its Pyrawa line with a more extensive line of Sea Eagle craft. As the accompanying chart shows, the two lines overlap, although dimensions do differ slightly among comparable craft. In the same general

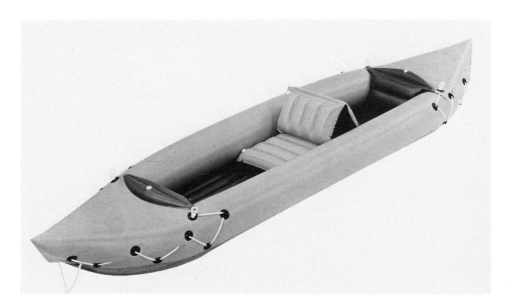

category are the Pyrawa N-5 and the Sea Eagle 340, even though the Sea Eagle is nine inches longer, five inches wider, and costs about $20 more. For $5 less than the Pyrawa N-5, one can purchase the Sea Eagle 300, nine inches shorter but three inches wider. All these models share features of quality and construction that place them among the best of their type.

Which is better, Sea Eagle or Pyrawa? It is hard to make a choice based on workmanship or material, although the distributor claims that the Sea Eagle is fabricated from somewhat thicker material. What should be noticed is that the rope lashings that secure the Sea Eagles' decks extend along the entire sides of the cockpit, a feature lacking on the Pyrawa. These lashings are helpful when it comes to tying down gear or walking the

*Stebco B-15. (Photo Stebco)*

*The Sea Eagle 340. (Photo Leisure Imports)*

craft over sand bars and through shallows. Moreover, if paddling is to be a family affair, there is no Pyrawa counterpart to the giant Sea Eagle 380, which seats three adult paddlers comfortably, or accommodates two persons with plenty of gear. While this boat is too big to be very maneuverable, it does a good job on downriver cruises where obstacles are few and the need for swift course corrections is not paramount. Given these advantages, the Sea Eagle seems the preferable line.

Competing with the Sea Eagle 380 is the Tahiti Three-Man Deluxe from Sevylor USA, Incorporated. The big Tahiti is an inch longer than the model 380 and three inches narrower, which should give it slightly better maneuverability and make it less cumbersome to paddle. While the Tahiti does not feature ropes running the full length around the cockpit, the $23 difference in price between it and the Sea Eagle makes the lower-priced Tahiti worth considering.

Inflatable kayaks and canoes are comparatively short, yet have the beams of the larger canoes and voyageuring kayaks. Their ruggedness and durability are a pleasant surprise. And the price is right—about half the cost of a comparable rigid canoe or kayak. Inflatable kayaks and canoes also make delightful second boats, allowing you to save the larger boats for extended cruises while enjoying lightness and convenience on one-day paddle trips or float trips that do not require a lot of

*The Tahiti Three-Man Deluxe.*
*(Photo Sevylor)*

*A Sevylor craft
rigged for sailing.
(Photo Sevylor)*

luggage. Of course a two-man craft can be paddled singly, with gear in the space reserved for the second passenger. This makes inflatable kayaks practical for just about any trip.

If there is any limitation to these craft, it would have to be that they are comparatively hard to mount a motor on. Also, sailing rigs are not usually available, so their versatility is limited. (Sevylor is an important exception.)

For our purposes, we have discussed fourteen representative inflatable kayaks and canoes. There are more available, as this

45

is one of the fastest-growing areas of the boating industry. If you are shopping for a craft not included here, be sure the one you buy has electronically bonded seams. If the seams are not mated exactly or if there are any separations in them, do not buy the boat. Make sure there are cleats or rings through which you can pass ropes to tie down gear. Also, be satisfied that the material used in the hull is tough, tear resistant, and not susceptible to abrasion. Where there are competing brands of inflatable canoes and kayaks alike in size and configuration, buy the higher-priced model. A few dollars extra can make the difference between years of enjoyment and irritating mishaps on the water.

In discussing the relative merits of kayaks and canoes, emphasis was placed on the touring kayaks (K-2 or two-passenger) and open canoes because they compete for approximately the same market and it was felt that the greatest number of prospective buyers would be interested in the larger models intended for family cruising. But before taking a look at selected models, you should be aware that kayaks fall roughly into five categories: two-seat touring; single-seat touring; children's; slalom sport kayaks; and downriver sport kayaks.

A major difference between touring and sport kayaks is that the former are wider. Of course this makes them less prone to tip, but, as has been stated, it also limits their speed and maneuverability. Large touring kayaks feature greater length and require more draft than the sport models. They exhibit less rocker, thereby sacrificing some turning ability for additional course-holding ability—a plus for flatwater touring. Finally, the comparatively greater capacity of touring kayaks makes them a favorite with paddlers who like to camp.

### TWO-SEAT TOURING KAYAKS (K-2)

The Super, from Folbot Corporation, is a big, rugged, comparatively heavy, and virtually untippable touring kayak. Folbot boasts that its plywood and hardwood frame is superior to that of "European" kayaks in durability. (In comparing Folbot's frame to Klepper's this writer is not sure how true the statement is. Folbot's frame does not show the quality workmanship of Klepper's even if it is "thicker.") The Super's vinyl skin is remarkable for its resiliency and ability to bounce off obstacles. The Super also allows for a choice of seating positions: the paddler can either sit on the plywood seat in the cockpit, using the normal kayak position, or he can turn the seat back onto a horizontal plane and sit on it at the level of the deck (as a rear seat) or atop the center brace. This feature is a godsend for traveling long distances because it provides a chance to change positions and stretch from time to time. It should not be used, though, when the water is rough.

The rigid version of the Super features an aluminum molding that forms a bumper outside the gunwales, covering the unsightly seams where deck joins hull. The bumper also provides effective protection at a critical point, should the boat brush against abrasive objects. If you ever "lock through" on a major river, such as the Mississippi, you'll appreciate the bumpers. They prevent the sides from being gashed when turbulent water grinds the boat against the concrete walls of the lock.

## TWO-SEAT TOURING KAYAKS (K-2)

| NAME<br>*MANUFACTURER* | LENGTH | BEAM | WEIGHT<br>(LBS.) | CAPAC-<br>ITY<br>(LBS.) | PRICE | MATERIAL |
|---|---|---|---|---|---|---|
| Family Kayak<br>*Baldwin Boat Co.* | 14' | 38" | 60 | INA | R $270 | Fiberglass |
| Glider<br>*Folbot Corp.* | 14'6" | 37" | 62 | 550 | R $229<br>K $119 | Vinyl Fiberplastic/<br>plywood &<br>hardwood frame |
| Traveller<br>*Tyne (Moor & Mountain)* | 15' | 28" | 35 | INA | INA | Fiberglass |
| Big Glider<br>*Folbot Corp.* | 16' | 40" | 82 | 750 | F $273<br>R $269<br>K $145 | Vinyl Fiberplastic/<br>plywood &<br>hardwood frame |
| Cayat<br>*Folbot Corp.* | 16' | 37" | 92 | 780 | FB $134<br>FF $219 | Wood covered with<br>glass cloth, resin |
| Kamerad W.<br>*Klepper Corp.* | 16' | 31" | 65 | INA | R $360 | Fiberglass |
| Tourer Twin<br>*Tyne (Moor & Mountain)* | 16' | 28" | 60 | INA | INA | Fiberglass |
| Tourer Open<br>*Tyne (Moor & Mountain)* | 16' | 28" | 60 | INA | INA | Fiberglass |
| Blauwal<br>*Klepper Corp.* | 16'4" | 31½" | 60 | INA | F $395 | Hypalon hull,<br>fabric decks |
| Aerius II<br>*Klepper Corp.* | 17'1" | 34" | 64 | 750 | F $480 | Hypalon hull,<br>fabric decks |
| Sports Two-Seater<br>*Tyne (Moor & Mountain)* | 17'2" | 33" | 60 | INA | INA | Flexible fabric |
| Super<br>*Folbot Corp.* | 17'6" | 37" | 79 | 720 | F $292<br>R $282<br>K $152 | Vinyl Fiberplastic/<br>plywood &<br>hardwood frame |

F = Folding; R = Rigid; K = Kit; FB = Factory Built; FF = Factory Finished; INA = Information Not Available; Prices factory direct.

The Super also features cast-metal fittings at its ends. These undoubtedly comprise the worst design element of the entire craft. They fasten onto the bow and stern with two simple wood screws that are driven into the edge of a plywood stem piece. Given this weak construction, it is important to follow good boating practice and pull the craft up on land when you leave it, or at least secure it with a rope around the center thwart. If the Folbot is secured to a tree by a painter tied to an end fitting, the fitting could separate, allowing the boat to float away.

*The Folbot Super. (Photo Folbot)*

The Super is rated to carry three adults. But don't purchase it if you intend to carry three or more people with lots of gear on camping trips. The seating configuration is definitely comfortable only for two. For paddling on quiet water over short distances and with no time limitations, the Super does accommodate two adults and three children, but this surely is not the best way to derive maximum enjoyment from it.

The Super carries an almost unbelievable amount of gear under its covered decks and because of this factor has been used in exploration trips from the arctic to the tropics. The combination of a high front deck, an almost symmetrical hull design, and a fairly wide beam gives it a tendency to ride on-

49

coming waves, plus making it exceptionally dry. But its considerable length prevents it from turning quickly—a limitation characteristic of most two-man kayaks.

On examining a Super portable (finished at the factory in rigid form), I found the factory finish not as good as I would have liked. In several places, notably the hinges that hold the flip-up seat backs, the wood screws used are too long for the plywood into which they are sunk. They stick out the back of the wood, providing potential snags for clothing or equipment. Moreover, I have seen Supers on which the fabric for the deck was cut too short, so that the trim along the gunwales masked the ragged edges poorly. These items of finish should be checked before accepting delivery of the craft if you decide to buy it, but should not deter your consideration of it: they do not affect performance, and do not offset this boat's many good points. (Knowledgeable kayakists with whom I have spoken are not overly impressed with the quality of Folbot's folding models, citing poor construction, leaks, and occasionally an oversized frame as drawbacks to this model. Some, however, recommend them enthusiastically. This indicates that the firm may have some quality control problems, and buyers should check their kayaks closely.)

Flotation bags are available as accessories for all Folbot models—at an extra cost. However, should you capsize your Super (rather unlikely under normal circumstances), these air bags provide adequate flotation but allow the kayak to spin as if on an axle. The fore-and-aft air-bag system, while common in kayaks, is not as good as that provided by the Klepper sponsons, which will be discussed shortly. Also, I believe Folbot should offer the air bags as standard equipment, while continuing to make replacements available for older models. These bags are essential to safe kayaking.

Double paddles of curved plywood are available from Folbot in a "long" version, a 9-foot version (standard), or a "junior" 8-foot version. These paddles are well shaped and long lasting. They do, however, have a ferrule in the middle that allows them to be taken apart and stored at half their normal length. This makes them easier to transport, but the ferrule may loosen after three or four years' service. They must then be repaired or they present an irritating problem —the paddle bends slightly in your hands at each stroke, or it twists out of position and requires continued adjustment of the blade angle. (This problem, it should be stated, is native to all paddles made this way and is in no way peculiar to Folbot.) Nevertheless, for the average paddler, the conveni-

ence of transporting paddles in two short sections should more than compensate for any eventual loosening of the ferrules.

    Another handy accessory of the Super is the vinyl spray cover that keeps the paddler dry in whitewater and in rainstorms. Although the spray cover is a welcome addition to a paddler's equipment, Folbot's design for its cover leaves much to be desired. Normally, on a kayak, the spray cover is a single uninterrupted piece of rubberized, or otherwise waterproofed, fabric. It fastens under the splash rails with elastic, and around the body of the paddler in the same fashion. Since these covers are often used in sport kayaks that can be rolled, the tightness of the elastic poses a finicky and critical adjustment problem, since it must not be torn from the cockpit by the twisting of the paddler or by the force of the water, yet must allow him to extricate himself without difficulty if he overturns and is unable to roll. Because the spray cover of a two-seat touring model is large and must fit around two paddlers, certain compromises must be made. The length of the cockpit means that it is not easy to slide an elastic band under a notch

*The Folbot Folding Super. (Photo Folbot)*

on the splashboards to hold the cover. The problem is compounded by the fact that two paddlers are twisting under the spray cover, and the entire cover loses its effectiveness if it pulls away from the splashguard at any point around its long periphery.

Folbot solves this problem by fastening the cover to the splashboards with snaps. Once these snaps are joined at right angles to the direction in which stress is put on the cover, they are virtually impossible to pull loose. This could endanger the paddler if a compromise were not incorporated to make his exit as easy as possible. Folbot, therefore, includes zippers that run about two feet down the center of the spray cover ahead of both paddlers. These zippers separate the cover right up to the paddlers' chests. On the one hand, they make entry and exit comparatively easy. On the other, they constitute a source of irritating leaks and necessitate extra coverage with a poncho or towel whenever the splash is more than simple spray. If water settles on the zipper, it drips through a drop at a time into the paddler's lap—something worse than Chinese water torture. And, of course, zippers are known to break at the worst times.

Other accessories available from Folbot include necessary drip rings that keep water from running down from the blades onto the paddlers' hands; comfortable, floatable back-rest pads; carrying bags for folding models; a service kit including patches and cement; flag; and a motor crossbar.

Although you may eventually want to add a motor, Supers and other kayaks are made for paddling. Attaching a motor is not recommended. For one thing, a motor must be mounted to one side and causes the kayak to list slightly. This changes the orientation of the hull in the water and results in the boat yawing strangely. It will turn well enough to the side on which the motor is mounted, but does not respond well when you attempt to turn in the opposite direction. Moreover, because as light a motor as possible must be used to keep from riding at too great an angle, the choice of engines is limited. Few lightweight outboards feature reverse or neutral gears. Picture yourself in a narrow river trying to start your motor. By the time you pull the starter rope, the wind has swung the bow toward shore. When the motor catches, it propels you at high speed toward the bank. You must slow the motor to idle, then steer away from the bank with a boat that does not respond well to steering. The experience is frustrating—especially since you must keep killing the motor in an effort to reorient the bow before restarting.

Following the Super in length, the Folbot line of two-seat touring kayaks offers the Big Glider. The materials and construction of the Big Glider and the Super are the same. Despite the fact that it is 1½ feet shorter than the Super, the Big Glider outweighs the latter by three pounds. The Big Glider is about three inches wider than the Super, yet has narrower side decks. This gives it an extra-large cockpit, which is squared at both ends and has a seat mounted in the front that pivots to horizontal, so a passenger in the bow can enjoy deck-height seating while he faces the person or persons seated in the normal paddling positions. Folbot recommends this model for two or three persons with lots of gear. The width of the Big Glider limits its maneuverability and speed, but gives it outstanding stability. This boat is available in a folding model, a rigid model, or in kit form. It is good for family camping trips, and handles fast currents too.

*Folbot's Big Glider. (Photo Folbot)*

Another boat that is a standout for family camping is the smaller Folbot Glider. This craft is 1½ feet shorter than the Big Glider and three inches narrower. Best of all, it is 20 pounds lighter. Side decks are narrow, leaving a wide cockpit that tapers to a point at both ends. It lacks the extra seat of the Big Glider. The Glider is not recommended for whitewater or open sea because of its narrow decks. But it is comparatively light, very stable, and carries a lot of gear. It can be purchased in rigid form or as a kit; it is not available as a folding boat.

The last two-seat design from Folbot is the Cayat. This

model is not of the same construction as those we have been discussing. Rather, its hull, decks, and frame are all made of wood. The hull is covered in fiberglass, while the deck is varnished with resin. This kayak carries as many as four passengers or fewer passengers and more gear. At 92 pounds, it is best used for sailing and is promoted for this sport. It accepts outriggers that turn it into a trimaran with stability not found in sailing kayaks that utilize leeboards. When it comes to paddling downriver or camping, the Cayat is somewhat heavy.

For a well-crafted and well-designed folding two-seat kayak, it is hard to beat the well-established Klepper Aerius II. Klepper has been in the folding-boat business since 1907 and solid, dependable Klepper boats have seen service all over the world. The record stretches on and on—crossing the English Channel, sailing from Germany to Egypt and India, Greenland and North and South Pole expeditions, Atlantic crossings in 1928 and 1956, expeditions to the Andes, and many other odysseys. Those who buy an Aerius II join a long tradition of adventurers and acquire a craft with one of the proudest names in boating.

A glance over the Aerius II frame reveals careful craftsmanship. It is designed to be assembled or disassembled in fifteen to thirty minutes, with no tools. Alloy snaplock fittings that cannot rust or corrode even in salt water are used throughout, and no small parts need be kept with the assembly.

The frame is incredibly strong, and attention to finishing is evident. It is constructed of mountain ash that has been dried for three years. The wood is tough but flexible. Crossribs are constructed of nine layers of cross-laminated Finnish birch. Unlike the Folbot, the hull and deck of which are fashioned of one material, the Aerius II boasts a hull and deck of different materials. The deck is waterproof fabric—long hemp and long-staple cotton. All Klepper decks are distinctively deep blue. The silver-gray bottom of the Aerius II, it is claimed by the manufacturer, may last fifteen years before it has to be replaced. The hull material is Hypalon, a tough rubber-and-long-hemp laminate, which provides flexibility and toughness.

A particularly outstanding design feature of the Aerius II is its use of air sponsons that run along the gunwales. The sponsons are long tubes that are integrated into the deck and hull, and which run virtually from bow to stern. They provide excellent flotation and, positioned as they are, maximize stability. The Klepper supports its passengers and gear when submerged, unlike the Folbot Super, and, because the sponsons are placed along the sides instead of in the bow and stern, they tend to keep the kayak righted when swamped, instead of permitting it to roll. Less obvious advantages of the sponson system are that the Aerius need not rely on metal or plastic molding to hide the joining of deck and hull, and that the sponsons serve as bumpers. A rigid "bumper" of aluminum, stainless steel, or wood along the gunwales may protect a kayak's skin, but can be gouged if it collides with an abrasive surface, damaging the look of the boat. When air sponsons strike against such a surface they bounce away, accepting few scars.

Only two disadvantages are manifest in relation to the air sponsons on the Aerius II, but the safety and stability they provide more than compensate for both. One disadvantage is that a pump for inflating the sponsons may be desirable and this takes up a small amount of luggage capacity. The other disadvantage is that a small amount of cargo space is inherently lost because of the presence of the sponsons. Of course, this can be overcome by carrying light, compact gear, not overpacking, and placing the gear in the craft properly.

Folded, the Aerius II packs into three bags for easy transportation and storage.

Accessories offered for the Aerius II and other craft by Klepper include a sailing rig, incorporating a rudder assembly with foot control and cables. In this and in the fittings that accommodate the rudder, Klepper has a definite advan-

*Klepper's famous Aerius II, one of the most versatile kayaks of all. (Photo Klepper)*

tage over Folbot. On the Folbot tiller assembly a free hand must be used to steer. Moreover, the fixture that holds the Folbot's rudder is cast aluminum and is held to the back of the boat by two small wood screws. (Before sailing you should sink a bolt right through the side of the fixture—through the stem itself—and out the fixture's other side.) The Aerius II replaces this flimsy construction with durable Hypalon rings that are part of the hull itself. A pin holds the rudder in place. In all ways, Klepper's rudder is better designed.

Another Klepper accessory superior to its Folbot counterpart is the spray cover. Klepper's closes the cockpit to splash and rain, and does so tightly because it has no zippers. It fastens to the splashrails with clips and closes tightly around the paddler's chest with snaps and string. It is harder to enter than Folbot's but performs the job for which it was intended —keeping the paddler dry. This fine spray cover costs more than Folbot's, but it certainly is more functional.

Other accessories for the Klepper Aerius II include a foot bellows for inflating sponsons, an inflatable seat cushion, a seat back, inflatable clothing and camera bags, a collapsible two-wheeled cart for rolling the kayak to and from the water,

*Klepper Aerius II rigged for sailing. (Photo Klepper)*

and an air mattress that can be used in your tent or propped up in such a manner as to make a good seat when sitting around a campfire.

The accompanying Two-Seat Touring Kayak chart shows a difference of $188 between the Folbot Super and the Klepper Aerius II; while the Aerius definitely is more expensive, it does not cost as much more as this disparity in price might lead you to believe. Included in the price of the Aerius are the air sponsons, air cushions for the seats, padded cushions for the back rests, utility bags with zippers, two double-bladed touring paddles with drip rings, flag with flagstaff, packbags, rudder bracket, and mast bracket. Nearly all these accessories or their equivalents are "extras" with the Folbot and Klepper will sell kayaks without the equipment, if buyers so desire.

A second two-seat touring kayak from Klepper is the Blauwal, which is nine inches shorter and three inches narrower than the Aerius II. It accepts the same accessories and is constructed the same way. The most significant difference between the two craft is that the Blauwal lacks sponsons and its flotation is provided by air bags stuffed under the fore and aft decks. This, also, is a rugged and seaworthy craft. It comes with similar accessories to those found on the Aerius, minus the flotation bags, which must be purchased at extra cost.

Klepper also supplies a rigid fiberglass K-2 kayak—the Kamerad W. Although rigid two-seaters are offered by several other companies, the klepper is representative. The Kamerad has four short flotation tubes, rudder bracket, mast bracket, and comes in red with a white hull, or blue with white. Paddles, cushions, and rudder are extra. The sleek fiberglass hull is easy to clean, and, because of its rigidity, problems of sand working between ribs and skin are eliminated.

Another fiberglass two-seater is the Family Kayak from Baldwin, a company that recommends this boat as a general-purpose craft for campers. Baldwin also claims that it is stable and easy to portage. Its molded seats are raised about five inches from the floor, not high enough to impair stability, but the usual rule of thumb is that the lower the seats the better, and it would seem preferable to mount them closer to the floor.

Moor & Mountain markets a line of kayaks built by Tyne Canoe Company of Middlesex, England. In their two-seat touring category are four models: the Traveller, Tourer Twin, Tourer Open, (all rigid), and the folding Sports Two-

Seater that competes with the Klepper Aerius II and the Folbot Super. These Tyne models range from the symmetrical to the slightly fishform in configuration, so they should handle facilely situations in which waves are encountered from the bow.

The Traveller, a short 15-footer, is suggested for touring by one adult and a child or by an adult alone with gear packed into the front cockpit hatch to provide proper balance. The Tourer Twin features a dual cockpit, that is, the deck closes over the middle of the boat between paddlers. Tyne recommends this model for estuary paddling, and does not recommend any of its two-passenger kayaks for whitewater paddling. The Tourer Open is similar to the Twin except that the dual cockpits are replaced by a single cockpit. This provides greater access to gear and more flexibility in seating arrangements, elements usually preferred by beginners. The folding Sports Two-Seater is the narrowest and lightest of the 17-foot folding kayaks described. Its construction is good, and it should provide hours of excellent paddling for its owner, while its break-folding feature eliminates any problems in storage.

## SINGLE-SEAT TOURING KAYAKS (K-1)

When in the market for a single-seat touring kayak—one that can be taken on extended trips, carrying gear under the decks—you encounter a wide variety of offerings. Models range from the giant Folbot Explorer to the diminutive Tyne Perfect Single Seater. These kayaks can be obtained in all the popular construction materials.

From Folbot come two likely models—the 17½-foot Explorer and the 15-foot Sporty. Both are constructed the same way as the Folbots discussed under two-seat touring kayaks, and both accept basically the same accessories. Due to the Explorer's weight (95 pounds), it is not, in my opinion, suitable for one man to portage. It is, however, a wise investment for extended trips if a great deal of gear, or if heavy, instead of lightweight, camping gear is used. If your trips are over open water or down major rivers, such as the Ohio or Mississippi where no portages are required, the Explorer is appropriate. Its wide beam makes it stable in rough water, and its length allows you to sleep inside it should you ever have to do so.

The Sporty is a wiser choice for average paddlers. It is fairly light, has good capacity and totes a suitable amount of gear. Moreover, it is stable and does not require the mastery of technique that some of the smaller touring kayaks do.

Competing head to head with the Sporty is the Aerius I from Klepper Corporation. The Aerius I is also 15 feet long, and measures only one-half inch narrower than the Sporty. Like its big brother, the Aerius II, it has inflatable sponsons running along its gunwales, and the same advantages and disadvantages attend its design and construction. Although the Aerius I is more sophisticated, the comparatively low price of the Sporty makes it, in my opinion, an equally good buy for the beginner. Should you require a folding model, prefer the Klepper; but if you can use a rigid model, save your money by investing in the Folbot. If you are handy, the kit for the Sporty is a terrific buy.

Tyne also offers a superb folding kayak, the Perfect Single-Seater, which at only 12 feet 6 inches long weighs in at a light 40 pounds. It is fairly narrow, having a 26-inch beam, and exhibits a slightly fishform hull so that it should function especially well when directed into oncoming waves.

Tramp S is a whitewater kayak that Klepper claims is also suitable for touring on sea and lake. Among the Klepper fiberglass kayaks it is touted as the best model for taller people, partly due to its comparatively large cockpit. The Tramp S is available with a red deck and a white hull or with a blue deck and a white hull.

Another rigid fiberglass single-seater from Klepper, suitable for touring, is the Bummler. This stable, roomy kayak for long trips is, like the Tramp S, designed for larger people. It is equipped with a plastic contour seat, adjustable footrest, rudder bracket, and is available in the same colors as the Tramp S.

Let me caution at this point that the Tramp S, Bummler, and many of the rigid models described in the following paragraphs cannot be considered the best kayaks for begin-

*Klepper Aerius I, an agile, seaworthy craft. (Photo Klepper)*

ning paddlers who are enthusiastic about camping. While these boats can be used for overnight paddle camping, they compel investment in the very lightest equipment—and carry precious little of it. On the other hand, if you would eventually like to try serious whitewater, or even competition, examine them. They force you to master the basic strokes and balancing techniques necessary for entering competitive events. By starting out with heavier, more stable kayaks, you tend to develop many paddling habits not suitable to the

## SINGLE-SEAT TOURING KAYAKS (K-1)

| NAME<br>*MANUFACTURER* | LENGTH | BEAM | WEIGHT<br>(LBS.) | CAPAC-<br>ITY<br>(LBS.) | PRICE | MATERIAL |
|---|---|---|---|---|---|---|
| Perfect Single-Seater<br>*Tyne (Moor & Mountain)* | 12'6" | 26" | 40 | INA | INA | Flexible fabric |
| Minitouring Kayak<br>*Hauthaway Kayaks* | 13'1½" | 24" | 25 | INA | R $260 | Polyester<br>fiberglass |
| River Chaser<br>*Hollowform* | 13'2" | 24" | 35 | INA | R $129.95 | "Marlex" plastic |
| Senior<br>*Tyne (Moor & Mountain)* | 13'9" | 24" | 35 | INA | INA | Fiberglass |
| Whitewater<br>*Tyne (Moor & Mountain)* | 13'10" | 24" | 37 | INA | INA | Fiberglass |
| Ninevah<br>*Vermont Tubbs* | 14' | 25" | 32 | 225 | R $240<br>K $175 | Fiberglass |
| Tramp S<br>*Klepper Corp.* | 14' | 25" | 40 | INA | R $295 | Fiberglass |
| Downriver Touring<br>Kayak<br>*Hauthaway Kayaks* | 14'8" | 24" | 34 | INA | R $280 | Polyester<br>fiberglass |
| Downriver Touring<br>Kayak<br>*Old Town* | 14'8" | 24½" | 35 | INA | R $310 | Vinyl/ABS<br>sandwich |
| Bummler<br>*Klepper Corp.* | 14'9" | INA | 50 | INA | R $295 | Fiberglass |
| Sportsman<br>*Tyne (Moor & Mountain)* | 14'9" | 24" | 38 | INA | INA | Fiberglass |
| Sporty<br>*Folbot Corp.* | 15' | 32" | 59 | 470 | R $209<br>F $215<br>K $115 | Vinyl Fiber-<br>plastic/plywood &<br>hardwood frame |
| Aerius I<br>*Klepper Corp.* | 15' | 31½" | 55 | INA | F $380 | Hypalon hull,<br>fabric decks |
| Explorer<br>*Folbot Corp.* | 17'4" | 38" | 95 | 720 | F INA | Vinyl Fiber-<br>plastic/plywood &<br>hardwood frame |

lighter craft. Before investing in a single-seat touring kayak, a fundamental decision must be made: what style of paddling do you intend to pursue?

Five of the six remaining rigid fiberglass touring kayaks discussed make use of Swedeform hulls. The first of these is Old Town's Downriver Touring kayak. This kayak is similar to another Old Town model—labeled the Downriver and designed by Bart Hauthaway—except that it has greater volume to accommodate more equipment. The Downriver Touring kayak was also designed by Bart Hauthaway, who coached the 1972 Olympic kayak paddlers on an individual basis and was himself a member of the United States World Championship team in 1965. The Downriver Touring kayak is designed for maximum speed in whitewater competition and downriver touring. Old Town also claims that this boat is good in extended open-water cruising. The craft comes with a molded seat, foam knee braces, and a five-position adjustable foot brace. Also featured are bow and stern grab loops.

Two other Bart Hauthaway kayaks are marketed by Hauthaway: the Downriver Touring Kayak (yes, that's the same name as the Old Town model, but is a different craft) and the Mini-touring Kayak. The latter is a small touring sport kayak designed for paddlers up to 150 pounds. Like the larger models in this category, it comes equipped with molded seat and leg braces, a five-position adjustable foot brace, and grab loops. The larger Downriver Touring kayak is very similar in dimension and configuration to the Old Town model, but there is a price advantage favoring the Hauthaway model, which is (like its Old Town counterpart) slightly Swedeform and comes with molded seat, leg braces, a five-position foot brace, and grab loops.

Another attractive craft in the single-seat touring kayak class is the relatively short Ninevah single-seater of rigid fiberglass construction introduced by Vermont Tubbs Incorporated. This craft has substantial rocker that should make it very maneuverable and boasts a high front deck for a kayak of its type, which should make it dry when traveling into waves. The Ninevah is said to have sufficient room to accommodate large paddlers and is suggested by the manufacturer for wilderness trips. (Prototypes of the craft were tested on trips through the Grand Canyon.) This shimmering, iridescent green kayak with its red and white stripes should merit careful consideration, assuming you are interested in competition and whitewater as well as touring.

A slightly Swedeform kayak that can be used for touring,

*The Hollowform River Chaser, a sport kayak that can also be used for touring. (Photo Hollowform)*

yet will serve for slalom racing too, is the River Chaser, manufactured by Hollowform Incorporated. Unlike most fiberglass models, which are molded in halves and joined at the gunwales, the River Chaser is molded in one piece from cross-linked plastic. This means that both the inside and outside are finished smoothly. The craft features grab loops, an adjustable foot rest, and a foam seat than can be carved for a custom fit. It is certainly worth looking into.

From Tyne Canoe Company, whose products are distributed through Moor & Mountain, the Massachusetts outfitter, come three fiberglass kayaks specifically designed for touring, and they too should give fairly good performance in whitewater. The Senior is a general-purpose model for quiet water where its shape (generally symmetrical) gives optimum performance. Tyne suggests other kayaks for use in open sea or rough water. For estuary work or paddling large rivers the long-keeled, flat-rockered Sportsman is designed to take the waves of open water. The Whitewater is for the kayakist who wants to tackle fast-moving rivers and carry camping gear at the same time. Designed for maneuverability, it is suggested by the manufacturer for rapid-river touring or challenging coastal breakers.

## SPORT KAYAKS

Having discussed touring kayaks, we come now to sport models. These kayaks, along with smaller touring models, introduce a new way of relating to the water. Unlike most other boats, which are designed to introduce a barrier between their passengers and the water, sport kayaks permit paddlers to conquer the waves while remaining close to them. No other boat permits such close communication with the aquatic element as does the lightweight kayak. You cannot depend completely on these boats to remain upright. Rather, they are effectively balanced by means of bodily movement and paddle use. The kayak becomes an extension of the paddler, permitting maximum speed and maneuverability. Once the necessary strokes and balance and the famous art of esquimautage (rolling the kayak and coming upright again)

*Executing the Eskimo Roll, one of the most dramatic maneuvers in kayaking. (Illustration from Old Town)*

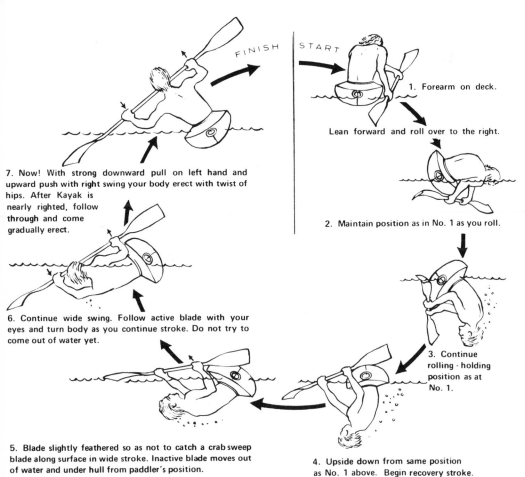

FINISH — START

1. Forearm on deck.

Lean forward and roll over to the right.

2. Maintain position as in No. 1 as you roll.

3. Continue rolling - holding position as at No. 1.

4. Upside down from same position as No. 1 above. Begin recovery stroke.

5. Blade slightly feathered so as not to catch a crab sweep blade along surface in wide stroke. Inactive blade moves out of water and under hull from paddler's position.

6. Continue wide swing. Follow active blade with your eyes and turn body as you continue stroke. Do not try to come out of water yet.

7. Now! With strong downward pull on left hand and upward push with right swing your body erect with twist of hips. After Kayak is nearly righted, follow through and come gradually erect.

are mastered, paddlers can assault the most difficult waters and thread their way among boulders and snags that turn water to white foam.

These kayaks are for thrills and should be considered by those who intend to enter competitive events. They are expensive considering that they carry only one passenger, weigh very little compared to larger touring kayaks, and are limited in cargo space. On the other hand, they do represent the ultimate in a lightweight craft.

Because this guide is intended primarily for those interested in camping and touring, I will not dwell at length on sport kayaks. Furthermore, most kayaks in this category are built according to a formula, making them very similar in size, form, and, as happens, in construction materials. What is said of one is generally true of another.

## DOWNRIVER KAYAKS

The longer the waterline of a sport kayak the better it holds course. Thus when discussing downriver kayaks, it is interesting to note that the models by Baldwin Boat Company are comparatively short in length, approximating the length of most slalom models.

The comparatively low prices of the Baldwin models, however, make them good buys in this category. The price of a kit is especially attractive and the handyman can build a very adequate boat from it. The Downriver K-1 Competition model is symmetrical in design, and its low profile is said to make it handle effortlessly even in high crosswinds. Except for the most serious competition, the Economy version of the Baldwin Downriver is probably a better bet. Only six pounds in weight is gained by opting for this version, yet it is still light enough for easy handling and good maneuverability. Accessories for Baldwin kayaks include paddles with an ash shaft and curved fiberglass blades, or with a fiberglass shaft and curved blades. When ordering, you must specify whether you prefer a right- or left-handed grip. A spray skirt and a helmet are also offered.

Not much information is available on the newly introduced Klepper Blizzard at this writing. Nevertheless its weight is very low, and its dimensions are typical for a boat of this category. Given Klepper's long-standing reputation for quality and durability, it should be one of the fastest and easiest to handle in its class.

The Downriver Kayak offered by Old Town is *designed* by Bart Hauthaway. This makes a comparison of the Bart

Hauthaway *marketed* Downriver and the Old Town model worthwhile. Both are 14 feet 8 inches long and 24 inches wide. The Old Town weighs 33 pounds, 3 pounds more than the Hauthaway model. Probably the most significant difference is that the Hauthaway model is priced lower than Old Town's Downriver. Even with the price difference, it is always a good idea to shop for a boat at a dealer's showroom so you can examine it. Since Hauthaway does not have the number of dealers Old Town does, you probably are better off seeing what kind of a deal you can make with a store that carries Old Town. On the other hand, if you purchase factory direct, the Hauthaway model would seem to be the better investment.

Three downriver models from Kayak Specialities Incorporated may interest those who are experts in handling kayaks. They are the K-1 Slender, the Fenja 65, and the Fenja 85. The K-1 Slender is considered fast with good stability. It is made of fiberglass with urethane foam embedded in the hull and sports a protected rudder that aids in steering during crucial maneuvers, yet which should remain undamaged if the kayak is taken through shallow water. The Fenja 65 and 85 are Swedeform fiberglass models that sport the same type of rudder and steering assembly as the Slender. The 85 incorporates the same

## SPORT KAYAKS: DOWNRIVER

| NAME<br>*MANUFACTURER* | LENGTH | BEAM | WEIGHT<br>(LBS.) | CAPAC-<br>ITY<br>(LBS.) | PRICE | MATERIAL |
|---|---|---|---|---|---|---|
| Downriver K-1<br>Competition<br>*Baldwin Boat Co.* | 13′2″ | 24″ | 30 | INA | $240<br>K $165 | Fiberglass |
| Downriver K-1<br>Economy<br>*Baldwin Boat Co.* | 13′2″ | 24″ | 36 | INA | $190<br>K $125 | Fiberglass |
| Blizzard<br>*Klepper Corp.* | 14′8″ | 24″ | 28 | INA | $310 | Fiberglass |
| Downriver<br>*Bart Hauthaway* | 14′8″ | 24″ | 30 | INA | $270 | Fiberglass |
| Downriver<br>*Old Town* | 14′8″ | 24″ | 33 | INA | $305 | Fiberglass |
| K-1 Slender<br>*Kayak Specialties* | 17′¾″ | 20″ | 35 | 280 | $298 | Fiberglass |
| Fenja 65<br>*Kayak Specialties* | 17′¾″ | 20½″ | 33-35 | 100-200 | $337 | Fiberglass |
| Fenja 85<br>*Kayak Specialties* | 17′¾″ | 20½″ | 33-35<br>26 | 150-200 | $337 | Fiberglass<br>Foam |

underwater body as the 65, but its decks arch higher to accommodate larger passengers.

## SLALOM KAYAKS

Slalom kayaks are built within the constrictions of a formula. It is interesting that of all listed here only the Folbot Racer is 25 inches wide. All other models are 24 inches, with the exception of those from Easy Rider. Lengths range from a short 13 feet for the Hauthaway models to a long 15 feet for the Racer. Of course the nature of a slalom kayak is to have a relatively short waterline and increased rocker compared to downriver models. Thus, the average slalom model has a length almost 16 inches less than the average downriver model included in these charts.

As in the case of the downriver kayaks, the Baldwin slalom models seem to represent good value at moderate price. Their weight is average for this type of craft. Also the option of a kit for each model can save money if you are handy. If you intend to get into racing or whitewater, the Klepper Loisach or any of the Hauthaway, Old Town, Vermont Tubbs, or Tyne models are excellent choices. The Easy Rider models also represent good purchases. Be sure when negotiating the purchase of one of these craft to check the maximum weight of the paddler it is intended to carry.

The Folbot models in this category are reported to have won their share of races, but their comparatively high weight (and, in the case of the Racer, its extra length) tends to negate the many other fine features of the craft. After all, for the slalom, you are looking for the boat that will get through the gates as rapidly, agilely, and surely as possible. No time can be lost trying to muscle an extra few pounds, or a foot of extra length, through its paces.

In general when buying a sport kayak, either downriver or slalom, look carefully at the cockpit area. The seat should be

*Bart Hauthaway's Slalom kayak. (Photo Bart Hauthaway)*

*Old Town's Slalom kayak. (Photo Old Town)*

form-molded to give support at the hips. Try the kayak to make sure the seat is comfortable; it can become excruciating to sit in a non-accomodating seat during tense competitive events.

If you plan to race, ask to test a demonstrator model and

*The Klepper Loisach. (Photo Klepper)*

67

demand that the kayak respond to every dip and insinuation of the paddle. Every bodily movement should transfer directly to it. For this to happen, it must have a properly fitting seat, hip braces, knee braces, and foot braces. Sport kayaks often have back supports (seat backs) built into the cockpits. In this type of craft, however, most serious paddlers use the back rests only between sprints; they do not lean against them when paddling.

## SPORT KAYAKS: SLALOM

| NAME MANUFACTURER | LENGTH | BEAM | WEIGHT (LBS.) | CAPAC-ITY (LBS.) | PRICE | MATERIAL |
|---|---|---|---|---|---|---|
| Olympic Slalom Bart Hauthaway | 13' | 24" | 26 | INA | $260 | Fiberglass |
| Minislalom Bart Hauthaway | 13' | 24" | 24 | INA | $260 | Fiberglass |
| Slalom Bart Hauthaway | 13' | 24" | 29 | INA | $275 | Fiberglass |
| Slalom Old Town | 13'1½" | 24" | 31.5 | INA | $300 | Fiberglass |
| Minislalom Old Town | 13'1½" | 24" | 28.5 | INA | $290 | Fiberglass |
| Snapper Old Town | 13'1½" | 24" | 37 | INA | $345 | Fiberglass |
| Augsburg I Easy Rider | 13'2" | 23¾" | 32 | 180 | $255 | Fiberglass |
| Augsburg II Easy Rider | 13'2" | 24¼" | 32 | 270 | $255 | Fiberglass |
| Slalom Tyne (Moor & Mountain) | 13'2" | 24" | 32 | INA | INA | Fiberglass |
| Slalom K-1 Competition Baldwin Boat Co. | 13'2" | 24" | 28 | INA | $240 K $165 | Fiberglass |
| Slalom K-1 Economy Baldwin Boat Co. | 13'2" | 24" | 33 | INA | $190 K $125 | Fiberglass |
| Neshobe Vermont Tubbs | 13'2" | 24" | 30 | INA | $240 K $170 | Fiberglass |
| Loisach Klepper Corp. | 13'3" | 24" | 25 | INA | $310 | Fiberglass |
| Scout Folbot Corp. | 13'4" | 24" | 36 | 250 | $232 | Fiberglass |
| Munchen 72 Klepper Corp. | 13'9" | 24" | 40 | INA | $295 | Fiberglass |
| Racer Folbot Corp. | 15' | 25" | 44 | 300 | $278 K $209 $240 K $132 | Fiberglass or vinyl |

## CHILDREN'S KAYAKS

One healthy way to interest your offspring in a vigorous, healthy hobby is to make a present of a kayak. Even if you do not expect your son or daughter to become an Olympic star at some remote time, keeping him or her occupied on the water has many benefits for both physical and spiritual development. And if you are a member of a paddling family, there may come a time when you want to expel junior from the family K-2 to make room for a younger brother or sister— or for a little more luggage.

Whatever your reason, there is a kayak for junior. And again, your own philosophy of kayaking determines which model is best for him. The small Folbot Junior is comparatively heavy for a touring craft of its size, but it is also wide, giving good stability so that the child will have no particular problem with tipping over. The other models listed here are sport models—scaled-down versions of popular Old Town, Hauthaway, Tyne, and Kayak Specialties models. They are not specifically listed as children's kayaks, but are rated to take passengers only up to 100 pounds in most cases. These are fine kayaks if you want your boy or girl to learn how to handle a kayak correctly. He or she can learn to get the best performance, speed, and maneuverability out of the boat, and can learn the art of esquimautage.

A word of caution about children's kayaks: *do not purchase them until your child knows how to swim well* and, if at all possible, enroll the child in a kayaking course taught by a professional. The sport models especially require swimming as a prerequisite to their use, but any kayak can have its bad moments. Moreover, most children are playful and enjoy swamping their craft and climbing aboard again.

### CHILDREN'S KAYAKS

| NAME<br>*MANUFACTURER* | LENGTH | BEAM | WEIGHT<br>(LBS.) | CAPAC-<br>ITY<br>(LBS.) | PRICE | MATERIAL |
|---|---|---|---|---|---|---|
| Junior<br>*Folbot Corp.* | 10' | 28" | 32 | 220 | $119<br>K $59 | Vinyl Fiberplastic<br>over wood frame |
| Junior Slalom<br>*Bart Hauthaway* | 11' | 21" | 21 | INA | $195 | Fiberglass |
| Streaker<br>*Old Town* | 11' | 22" | 22.5 | INA | $250 | Fiberglass |
| Junior<br>*Tyne (Moor & Mountain)* | 11'3" | 21" | 30 | INA | INA | Fiberglass |
| Menja<br>*Kayak Specialties* | 13'6" | 19" | 23 | 65-110 | $263 | Fiberglass |

# CHAPTER
# 6
## Selected Canoes

Hundreds of canoe models are available today, and somewhere among them should be one that fits your physical and budgetary needs. For the average person about to embark on a hobby of paddling, the 16- or 17-foot models undoubtedly represent the best selections. Canoes over 17 feet have immense capacities for cargo, but are more than a beginner need propel. A 16- or 17-footer should be sufficiently light for two persons to carry, and can be carried alone if necessary. It will tote enough luggage for extended camping trips.

If you plan to canoe alone, you may want to look at the smaller, ultralightweight canoes. A word of caution, however: some ultralight models lack thwarts. Thwarts are extremely handy for lashing down gear and capsizing can be tragic if gear is not lashed.

Once again ask yourself what type of water will be paddled most of the time. Will there be many portages and, if so, over what type of terrain? Will you camp overnight or simply do day cruising? How many other paddlers or passengers will you carry most of the time? How much equipment will be lugged along, and how heavy and bulky is it? Finally, all other factors

*Easy portageability is the goal of the Ultralight Pack Canoe, a boon to fishermen. (Photo Sportspal)*

being equal, choose a canoe that satisfies your personal sense of aesthetics. Many larger canoe manufacturers produce numerous models in a variety of materials, configurations, colors, keel types, and lengths. It is worthwhile to review the following charts and discussions thoroughly before selecting the model or models you think best suited.

Once you choose a likely model, visit a local dealer or write for information directly to the factory that makes the model. In almost all cases you will receive a beautifully illustrated brochure extolling the virtues of the craft. Review it carefully before rushing out to buy. The worst way to purchase a canoe is to start shopping a week before a major trip. You will get a more satisfactory craft at a better price by taking time to think, plan, and shop carefully.

## ULTRALIGHT PACK CANOES

If you plan to do most of your paddling alone or foresee many lengthy portages, examine the canoes in the ultralightweight (under 40 pounds) class closely. For purposes of categorizing, I have lumped together a variety of canoes that weigh 40 pounds or less and arranged them according to their ascending weights. They range in size from the diminutive Sportspal Papoose at 8 feet long, to the Hauthaway Ojibway at 13½ feet long, and from the featherweight Companion by Vermont Tubbs to the 40-pound Ojibway. All these canoes are made of fiberglass or plastic laminate with the exception of the Sportspal models, which are constructed of ultralightweight aluminum alloy only .023-inch thick (as opposed to the .050-inch thickness of most other aluminum canoes.)

The extensive line of canoes from Old Town features two

*The two-man Carleton Pack Canoe. (Photo Old Town)*

*The Sportspal 12-footer. (Photo Sportspal)*

## ULTRALIGHT PACK CANOES

| NAME<br>*MANUFACTURER/DISTRIBUTOR* | LENGTH | BEAM | DEPTH | WEIGHT<br>(LBS.) | PRICE | MATERIAL |
|---|---|---|---|---|---|---|
| Companion<br>*Vermont Tubbs Inc.* | 10'4" | 26" | INA | 16 | INA | Fiberglass |
| Rushton<br>*Old Town* | 10'6" | 27" | 10" | 18 | $225 | Fiberglass |
| Rushton<br>*Bart Hauthaway* | 10'6" | 27" | 10" | 18 | $195 | Fiberglass |
| Papoose<br>*Sportspal* | 8' | 37" | INA | 20 | $185 | Aluminum |
| Verity<br>*Moore Canoes* | 12' | 25" | 10½" | 25 | $200 | Fiberglass |
| Scout 13<br>*Easy Rider* | 13' | 32" | 12½" | 40 | $260 | Fiberglass |
| Pack Canoe<br>*American Fiber-Lite* | 10'6" | 26" | 11" | 29 | INA | Fiber-Lite |
| Sportspal<br>*Sportspal* | 12' | 44" | INA | 29.5 | $295 | Aluminum |
| Guide's Model<br>*Bart Hauthaway* | 11' | 33" | INA | 32 | $260 | Fiberglass |
| Hunter's Canoe<br>*Bart Hauthaway* | 11' | 33" | INA | 32 | $275 | Fiberglass |
| Carleton Pack Canoe<br>*Old Town* | 11'11" | 32" | 12½" | 35 | $250 | Fiberglass/balsa<br>sandwich |
| Woods Canoe<br>*Bart Hauthaway* | 12' | 32" | INA | 35 | $280 | Fiberglass |
| Chipewyan Pack<br>Canoe<br>*Old Town* | 11'11" | 32" | 12½" | 40 | $285 | Vinyl/ABS foam<br>sandwich |
| Sportspal<br>*Sportspal* | 14' | 44" | INA | 40 | $334 | Aluminum |
| Ojibway<br>*Bart Hauthaway* | 13'6" | 32" | INA | 40 | $320 | Fiberglass |

*The Rushton.*
*(Photo Old Town)*

lightweight pack canoes, the Carleton and the Chipewyan, weighing 35 and 40 pounds respectively. The primary difference between the two (they feature virtually the same specifications) is that the Carleton is constructed of a fiberglass-balsa sandwich using all-cloth construction, whereas the Chipewyan is a vacuum-formed vinyl-ABS-foam sandwich. Both feature vinyl rails and acrylic-ABS decks and seats. The Carleton features a shallow shoe keel (i.e., a wide flat strip that protects the bottom but lets the canoe sideslip in fast water), while the Chipewyan is keelless. Both canoes feature flotation under their decks, both have one thwart, and both accommodate a single paddler. Like all pack canoes, both are designed for easy paddling and portaging. Old Town also markets the Hauthaway-designed Rushton, which is described fully in this section as a Hauthaway model.

From Sportspal come three unconventional lightweight craft: the Papoose and the Sportspal 12 and 14 foot models. As mentioned, these canoes use ultralightweight aluminum alloy for their hulls. Seats, lining, and thick sponsons that run down the sides are made of Dow Chemical Company's high flotation "Ethafoam," a lightweight, closed-cell plastic foam. Colors of these models include birch bark, olive drab, and dark red, all of which are accented by the black Ethafoam.

The short lengths listed for the Sportspal models belie their workhorse carrying capacities. The 8-foot Papoose is said to carry 200 pounds, the 12-foot Sportspal 600 pounds, and the 14-foot Sportspal 850 pounds. The reason they carry such heavy loads is their exceptionally wide beams. A glance at the specifications tells you they feature a distorted shape that makes them extremely stable. But they do not provide the speed and ease of paddling that a canoe of their weight would have if it had a more conventional configuration.

The models from Sportspal have, as standard equipment,

*The Sportspal 14-footer. (Photo Sportspal)*

two foam seats (the Papoose has one), two wooden paddles, two carrying handles, a motor mount on the two larger models, detachable foam sponsons, a towing eye fore and aft, an anchor or towing cord, and a waterproof match holder. Optional accessories include a sail kit, a folding anchor, and carriers. These unconventional craft are expensive considering their comparatively short lengths, but they represent a valid investment if you require a small, very stable, safe, extremely light craft that carries more than its share of gear when called upon to do so.

If you want a canoe with a little more length, take a close look at the Verity from Moore Canoes Inc. This low-ended canoe has a carrying capacity of 304 pounds (with a 6-inch freeboard—the distance from the gunwale at its lowest point to the water). It is fiberglass with aluminum trim. Its seat, which normally lies near the floor, is removable to permit paddling from the kneeling position.

Bart Hauthaway supplies five extremely light canoes in the lightweight category. First is the Guide's Model Pack Canoe described by the manufacturer as a practical, general-purpose model for solo use but capable of carrying two paddlers. The canoe has one seat and a thwart far forward. Boxed inwales (the inner part of the gunwales) are filled with foam and further flotation comes from Dow Ethafoam under the seat and decks. The Guide's Model features grab loops fore and aft (watch out that these don't snag where trees overhang the watercourse), and is available in two-tone colors with a white hull, red, orange, yellow, green, or blue topsides, or in solid colors.

The same general characteristics apply to the Woods Canoe

*Moore's Verity
canoe. (Photo
Moore Products)*

as to the foot shorter Guide's Model Pack canoe, except that the Woods has two thwarts and no seats. Its hull is reportedly fast, holds course well, and maneuvers easily. The colors for this canoe are marsh green and light gray, but others are available on request.

Third in the Hauthaway line is the Hunter's Canoe, almost identical to the Guide's Model except that it has a gun boot that holds a rifle or shotgun firmly in position, with its barrel pointing over the gunwale. This is designed to eliminate a problem that often occurs when hunting from a canoe: that of having the gun turn upside down or slip into the bilge. Colors for this model are marsh green, duck-boat brown, and "dead grass."

The Ojibway from Hauthaway is a sport canoe, suitable for competition slalom events. Its rockered hull makes it maneuverable in whitewater. Features for the Ojibway are generally the same as those found in the other Hauthaway canoes except that it has extreme tumblehome, resulting in partially covered side decks. In addition to its use in whitewater and competition, this model is at home on lake, river, or stream. It features two thwarts and no seats.

Finally, Hauthaway produces the 18-pound Rushton. This canoe is derived from an 1880 design by Henry J. Rushton dubbed the "Wee Lassie." The original canoe was built of wood to lightweight specifications and cost only $27.50. No attempt is made by either Hauthaway or Old Town to emulate the original price, but in all fairness the craft has been improved substantially by using space-age materials. Fiberglass is used for the hull and Ethafoam forms the seat and fills in under the decks for flotation. The Rushton's single thwart is curved and runs immediately behind the paddler, forming a back or butt rest. The boat is propelled with a single-blade paddle. The designer supposedly intended to use the boat for fall hunting, and the coolness of the weather at that time of year caused him to eschew the drip from double-blade (or kayak) paddles. The requirement for paddling with a single blade led to the curved thwarts. For getting into the back-waters smoothly, swiftly, quietly, with a boat that offers maximum portability, it is hard to beat the Rushton. The manufacturers' listed prices give the advantage to Hauthaway.

Canoe manufacturers are always experimenting with new materials, attempting to develop better hulls. One of the latest efforts in this quest is a nicely finished little Pack Canoe from American Fiber-Lite. The hulls of the various craft from this firm are fashioned in one piece from Fiber-Lite, a plastic material that approximates wood in its specific gravity. The Fiber-Lite is covered with a tough coat of epoxy for protection against scrapes. But should the coating wear off, the material soaks up water just as wood does. This is not a major problem, but it compels at least minimum maintenance. On the other hand, Fiber-Lite does not rot as wood does. While tensile and flexural strengths are rated at about half those of conventional fiberglass, stiffness and impact strength are rated equal. Since neither tensile nor flexural strengths are apt to be tested severely under normal circumstances, the hull should be practically as durable as one of fiberglass. Abrasion resistance, on the other hand, is like that of wood, and this must be judged a disadvantage compared to fiberglass. If you run over stumps and stones, expect some gouges and wear. A solid plus in favor of this canoe is that Fiber-Lite tends to minimize sound transfer and provides the feeling of a "solid" ride that is better than that of other canoes in its class.

Overall, the Fiber-Lite Pack Canoe is nicely finished with aluminum gunwales and one aluminum thwart. A block of foam attached to the floor serves as a raised seat, making the boat ideal for paddling kayak-style with a double paddle. Furthermore, since Fiber-Lite floats like wood and expanded foam is incorporated in the hull for additional flotation, this canoe provides good buoyance if and when it capsizes.

The last boat in the ultralightweight pack-canoe category is Easy Rider's Scout 13. This canoe is relatively heavy for its category, but it provides extra space and can comfortably carry extra gear or a child in addition to an adult. Scout 13 is constructed of fiberglass reinforced with DuPont Kelvar 49, an organic reinforcing fiber said to provide extra strength. Its

*American Fiber-Lite's Pack Canoe. (Photo American-Fiber-Lite)*

two flattened thwarts serve as seats. The wrap-over design along the gunwales results in narrow decks that should keep the boat relatively dry in choppy water. Like many other small canoes, it can be paddled with a single paddle from a kneeling position or with a double paddle from a sitting position.

While the canoes in the ultralightweight (under 40 pound) category cannot be recommended for family overnights, they have use for the paddler who likes to solo. If he hunts ducks or geese, or fishes in out-of-the-way backwaters, he should not overlook these models. Chances are, if a person starts to paddle using a larger canoe, he may eventually want a lightweight model for a second boat.

## CANOES 11 FEET LONG AND UNDER

When considering canoes heavier than those included in the ultralightweight classification, it helps to arrange them by order of length rather than weight. Thus all the ensuing charts will be arranged according to the length of the canoes from shortest to longest.

The Aero-Craft Fox 11 by Browning is an excellent canoe for fishermen who like to solo or who occasionally take children or lone companions on their trips. It is also a great little craft for youngsters. Its wide beam gives it good stability and its foam side sponsons make it safe and unsinkable. Another nice touch is the use of nonskid paint on the canoe's bottom. While the Fox 11, at 47 pounds, does not provide the easy portaging

77

## CANOES 11 FEET LONG AND UNDER (BUT OVER 40 POUNDS)

| NAME<br> *MANUFACTURER* | LENGTH | BEAM | DEPTH | WEIGHT<br>(LBS.) | PRICE | MATERIAL |
|---|---|---|---|---|---|---|
| Trapper<br> *Old Town* | 11' | 36" | 13" | 44 | $670 | Wood/Canvas |
| Lightweight<br> *Old Town* | 11' | 36" | 13" | 47 | $640 | Wood/Canvas |
| Aero-Craft Fox 11<br> *Browning* | 11' | 39½" | 12" | 47 | $205 | Aluminum (.050 ga.) |

ga. = gauge

that canoes in the ultralightweight category do, it is light enough to be borne easily—two youngsters can do it.

For those who want top quality and aesthetic reward from a small canoe, two Old Town entries should more than fill the bill. They are the Lightweight Canoe and the Trapper. The former is made of wood and canvas and the Trapper of wood gunwales, seats, thwart, ribs, and sheathing, but with a rein-forced plastic covering. Both craft are costly considering their limited size. Both feature two seats and a thwart amidships; they have low bows and sterns, so they are comparatively easy to maneuver on windy days. Although the Trapper costs slightly more than the Lightweight, the added durability of its plastic hull and the fact that its skin can save appreciable maintenance over the years make it worth investigating. These craft are offered in various colors, but both come standard in traditional dark green. The fact that the Trapper weighs three pounds less than the aluminum Fox II discredits the often-made assumption that wood canoes must be heavier than those made from other structural materials.

## CANOES 11 FEET 1 INCH TO 13 FEET LONG

Listed here are six canoes 12 feet long and five 13-footers. Three of the 12-footers (from Trailcraft) are available in kits, and all of these are wood-and-canvas canoes. In the 11-to-13-foot category, canoes incorporate extra weight that was slashed in designing the ultralightweight pack canoes. These larger canoes are still light enough for one man to portage, but most are not nearly as easy to carry as are the smaller canoes. Eleven-to-13-footers are highly suitable for paddlers who usually solo, but who want to travel with companions occasionally. They are also excellent second boats for family travel.

From the Mississippi River town of Wabasha, Minnesota, comes an entry from Dolphin—the 12-foot Scout. This attrac-tive fiberglass canoe wears a host of pleasing colors—snow white, saturn red, limekist green, sun yellow, harvest wheat.

The Scout features a single hardwood thwart and a vinyl-covered seat. With its 35-inch beam, the Scout is very stable, and its light weight makes it easy to portage. The deep full-length metal keel gives it good course-holding ability for its size and suggests a superiority on open water. These fine characteristics are at least partly offset by a bow and stern that are highly upswept. This makes the canoe sensitive to wind and could mean trouble on breezy days. If aesthetics are important and you like the poetic exaggerated "canoe shape," the Scout is worth considering. For gentle, enjoyable paddling in calm waters it provides maximum enjoyment.

The 13-foot Grumman canoe gets top marks as suitable for the man who likes to paddle alone and who must make occasional portages. It can be bought in standard weight, with a skin of heat-tempered aluminum alloy that is .050 inch thick or in a lightweight version that has a skin .032 inch thick. The heavier model features a standard-depth keel while the light-

CANOES 11 FEET 1 INCH TO 13 FEET LONG

| NAME<br>*MANUFACTURER* | LENGTH | BEAM | DEPTH | WEIGHT<br>(LBS.) | PRICE | MATERIAL |
|---|---|---|---|---|---|---|
| Scout<br>*Dolphin* | 12′ | 35″ | 10″ | 47 | INA | Fiberglass |
| Cub B 12<br>*Trailcraft* | 12′ | 28″ | 12″ | 60 | K $24.50 | Wood/canvas |
| Cub C 12<br>*Trailcraft* | 12′ | 28″ | 12″ | 60 | K $59 | Wood/canvas |
| Crossbreed<br>*Trailcraft* | 12′ | 40″ | 15″ | 80 | K $129 | Fiberglass |
| Pelican EPP-12-SB<br>(SS)<br>*Eskay Plastics* | 12′ | 43″ | INA | 55 | INA | HMW polyethylene |
| Sport Canoe<br>*American Fiber-Lite* | 12′ | 36″ | 13½″ | 55 | INA | Fiber-Lite |
| 13-foot Lightweight<br>*Grumman* | 13′ | 35 3/8″ | 12 7/8″ | 44 | $249 | Aluminum (.032 ga.) |
| 13-foot Standard<br>*Grumman* | 13′ | 35 3/8″ | 12 7/8″ | 58 | $235 | Aluminum (.050 ga.) |
| Ojibway<br>*Old Town* | 13′ | 31¾″ | 11½″ | 45 | $425 | Fiberglass/balsa<br>sandwich |
| Lightweight<br>*Old Town* | 13′ | 36″ | 13″ | 53 | $650 | Wood/canvas |
| Trapper<br>*Old Town* | 13′ | 36″ | 13″ | 50 | $680 | Wood/plastic |

ga. = gauge; K = kit; INA = Information Not Available

weight craft has a shallow-draft keel for whitewater. Extra ribs are included to reinforce the whitewater model. As is typical of all Grumman canoes, flotation consists of foam-filled sections in both bow and stern.

Grumman cautions the buyer that the lightweight version dents more easily than the standard, and that after a time the cosmetic appearance may suffer. With proper care, this should not present an inordinate problem, and a few skin blemishes certainly should not affect performance or usefulness. The difference in price between the lightweight and the standard is small, but favors the standard. Price notwithstanding most paddlers may prefer the lightweight. The exception should be those who canoe on open water or lakes where holding course takes precedence over maneuverability. Here, both the extra weight and deeper keel of the standard are of value.

The Grumman 13-footer's profile is a good compromise between the high-ended designs of canoes that attract buyers more by aesthetics than practicality, and canoes whose ends are kept as low as possible for racing purposes. The Grumman bow is sufficiently high to cut through waves and hold out water; it is low enough to allow reasonable handling in the wind.

The Grumman 13-footer features one thwart, roughly amidships, and two aluminum seats. Grumman's outstanding reputation as a builder of canoes need not be elaborated; when you buy a Grumman, you buy the canoe preferred by a host of outfitters. These canoes are maneuverable, stable, and have few shortcomings. Accessories available from Grumman at extra cost include paddles, vinyl gunwale covers, wood-slat floorboards, a rowing attachment, a carrying yoke, styrofoam outriggers, an outboard motor bracket, seat cushions, and an extra passenger seat.

Old Town Canoe Company builds three 13-foot canoes: the Ojibway of a fiberglass-balsa sandwich, the Lightweight, and the Trapper, the former constructed of wood and canvas, the latter of wood and plastic. The Ojibway is unconventional, with extreme tumblehome (wrapover of the hull at the gunwales) that gives it decks almost like a two-passenger kayak. It has one seat molded into the rear deck and another provided by a flattening of the thwart. The Ojibway lacks a keel, making it suitable for slalom or wildwater, but it also holds its own on lake, river, or stream. Foam flotation is packed under the gunwales, and grab loops are provided at both bow and stern, a feature of mixed value since the loops can snag on overhanging branches when the craft is used on rivers. Standard colors are a white hull and red decks. The Lightweight and Trapper from Old Town were discussed in the 11-foot-and-under category, and the 13-footers are simply larger versions. While the Trapper is more expensive, its cost is usually offset by maintenance savings later on.

The Pelican EPP-12-SB is an interesting, perhaps unique, little square-stern. It is something of a platypus among canoes, a hybrid of several other craft. With its pregnant 43-inch beam, it bears kinship to the models from Sportspal, but its plastic (high-molecular-weight polyethylene) construction makes it heavier in proportion to its size. Like the Sportspal models, it features Ethafoam sponsons along the sides under the gunwales, and also has an inner lining of Ethafoam reinforced by aluminum ribs. Its seats are padded. Carrying handles are molded into bow and stern. The safe capacity is rated by the manufacturer at a whopping 800 pounds. Generally, the Pelican EPP-12-SB should be considered more appropriate for motoring than paddling because of its width-length ratio. But for family paddling fun, it is light and can tote either a big cache of gear or several children.

The American Fiber-Lite offering in this category, the 12-foot Sport Canoe, shows the same fine finish as the company's 10½-foot Pack Canoe described in the section on ultralights. However, in place of a foam pad mounted on the floor of the Pack Canoe, this model boasts two wood-slat seats. The hull material floats like wood, and additional foam flotation is provided. For a discussion of hull properties, see the comments on the Fiber-Lite Pack Canoe.

*American Fiber-Lite's Sport Canoe. (Photo American Fiber-Lite)*

81

If you are dextrous with your hands and with tools, you can save a lot of money by buying a kit and building your own canoe. From the flat prairies of Kansas come Trailcraft canoe kits. Two wood-canvas kits and one fiberglass kit are available for 12-footers in the Trailcraft line. For the wood-canvas Cubs, a starter kit is available for approximately $25 and a full kit for under $60. The other 12-footer is the fiberglass Crossbreed, a versatile square-stern.

The full kit for the Cub includes two exterior plywood curved-end pieces, two mahogany deck pieces, two mahogany gunwales, two mahogany gunwale trim pieces, plywood ribs, a keel, twenty-six mahogany stringers, thwarts, mahogany slats for floorboards, marine glue, canvas, hardware, canoeing manual, decals, and instructions. The starter kit contains everything in the full kit except the wood parts: i.e., it omits stringers, gunwales, keel, and floorboards.

The Crossbreed is similar in construction to the double-ended fiberglass canoe kits from Trailcraft. If properly done, the handmade Crossbreed is a nicely finished craft with foam flotation. It is wide, at 40 inches, making it an interesting transitional craft, somewhere between a rowboat and a canoe; hence its name. This is suitable for the person who has little money to invest and wants to do serious camping in areas where portages are not common. It can carry two people and gear, and is very stable. Of course, a motor can be attached for fishing and cruising.

Trailcraft claims that to assemble its fiberglass kits only a

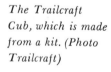

*The Trailcraft Cub, which is made from a kit. (Photo Trailcraft)*

few C-clamps, one or two paintbrushes, and a drill are needed. But a word of caution about any kit. Assembly is always billed as "simple" by the advertising brochures. It may, however, be difficult, especially if you are not familiar with tools, wood, or fiberglass. If you do buy a kit, read the instructions fully *before* starting to build. Ask any questions that come to mind of someone who knows about construction, preferably about boat building. Do not plod blindly ahead and make costly mistakes that can ruin the kit.

Accessories for the Trailcraft line include webbed seats, bow and stern handles, paddles, and finishing accessories for covering the wood-canvas model with a permanent layer of fiberglass. Also available is a fiberglass repair kit.

## CANOES 13 FEET 1 INCH TO 15 FEET 6 INCHES

Canoe builders, like other manufacturers, adjust the extent of their model coverage according to their company sizes and marketing positions. Thus, some very large canoe companies are represented in almost every size category; they make canoes in all dimensions, of all materials, and in many configurations. But their smaller counterparts, although offering canoes of excellent quality, must limit offerings to the most popular categories. Their relatively small company size and advertising budgets preclude tooling for limited-production models, so they stick with what the "average" canoeist is sure to be looking for.

The 13-feet-1-inch to 15-feet-6-inch category is that in which many canoe manufacturers start offering selections. This category covers a vast number of craft manufactured by a large number of canoe makers. The reason is that canoes measuring 14 or 15 feet are extremely versatile. For the occasional paddler they offer capacity for two persons plus their gear, while remaining fairly light for portaging or slinging atop a car. Most canoes of this length are wide enough for good stability yet hold course reasonably well. They are superb for youngsters learning to paddle. For these and other reasons, this category is very popular.

A general suggestion is to prefer the 16- and 17-foot canoes if planning to transport more than one person most of the time. Then look to a canoe of the 13-feet-1-inch to 15-feet-6-inch category as a useful second craft, one that can be manned alone when fishing, hunting, or touring. It is more convenient to move from a larger canoe to a smaller one than vice-versa. In other words, it is better to be over-canoed than under-canoed.

Listed here are 43 canoes that measure between 13 feet 1 inch and 15 feet 6 inches, and these are but a sample of the market. Every popular construction and material is represented, as well as some that must be considered exotic. Weights range from a low of 42 pounds to a high of 12 pounds. (Two Easy Rider C-1 models are included at 35 and 36 pounds. These have been listed by length rather than by weight because they are specialized competition craft rather than ultralight pack canoes.) Prices range from approximately $70 for a Trailcraft kit to around $700 for the fiberglass-over-wood Old Town Trapper. There is something here for everybody, suitable to all tastes and budgets. Literature is usually available from any of the companies to help the shopper decide which canoe to buy.

In the 13-feet-1-inch to 15-feet-6-inch category fall two whitewater slalom canoes from Old Town. At a glance it may be difficult to distinguish them from kayaks. The first is the Wenatchee, a canoe with a fully covered deck and a small cockpit that accommodates one paddler. The craft is of fiberglass-balsa-sandwich construction and is said to have ample space under its decks for storage so that it can be used for river cruising. But the boat's primary purpose is competition. The most significant difference between the Wenatchee and a kayak is that the paddler kneels in the former rather than sitting on the floor. The second, and larger, whitewater slalom canoe is the Potomac. It has cockpits in each end to accommodate two paddlers. Center space is available under the covered deck for gear or an additional flotation bag. Cockpit-rim seats are standard, and pedestal or strap seats come on special order.

For those not as concerned with competition, there are three 14-footers from Old Town, all constructed of one or another type of fiberglass. The Carleton features two seats and one thwart. It is fashioned of reinforced fiberglass-balsa sandwich with rigid vinyl rails and ABS seats and decks. It has no keel unless you order one specially.

Like the Carleton, Old Town's Chipewyan has two seats and a single thwart with foam flotation under the decks. Its hull is formed from a single sheet of vinyl-ABS-foam that is very tough and provides its own flotation. Old Town recommends the craft for use in all kinds of water. Since the boat has no keel, it would strongly suggest use for whitewater.

The 14-foot F.G. from Old Town uses a fiberglass-balsa-sandwich hull, said to be so rugged as to need no ribs. It has two seats but no thwart, a design concept that may maximize cargo space but limits the ability to lash belongings. Its strongest

## CANOES 13 FEET 1 INCH TO 15 FEET 6 INCHES

| NAME MANUFACTURER | LENGTH | BEAM | DEPTH | WEIGHT (LBS.) | PRICE | MATERIAL |
|---|---|---|---|---|---|---|
| Wenatchee *Old Town* | 13'2" | 33" | 13½" | 42 | $385 | Fiberglass/balsa sandwich |
| Winner C-1 *Easy Rider* | 13'2' | 27½" | INA | 35 | INA | Fiberglass |
| Munich C-1 *Easy Rider* | 13'2" | 28¼" | INA | 36 | INA | Fiberglass |
| Pawnee 13 *Browning (Aero-Craft)* | 13'4" | 36" | 13" | 57 | $210 | Aluminum |
| Carleton *Old Town* | 14' | 36" | 12" | 69 | $290 | Fiberglass/balsa sandwich |
| Chipewyan *Old Town* | 14' | 36" | 12" | 58 | $335 | Vinyl/ABS sandwich |
| F.G.-14 *Old Town* | 14' | 36" | 12" | 69 | $370 | Fiberglass/balsa sandwich |
| Scout S14 *Trailcraft* | 14' | 31" | 13" | 65 | K $69 | Wood/canvas |
| Trailpacer *Trailcraft* | 14' | 32" | 12" | 70 | $139 | Fiberglass |
| Trailfinder *Trailcraft* | 14' | 32" | 12" | 70 | $149 | Fiberglass |
| Skimmar *Aero-Nautical* | 14' | 36" | 12" | 72 | $225 | Fiberglass |
| Allagash *Bart Hauthaway* | 14' | 32½" | INA | 45 | $325 | Fiberglass |
| Battenkill *Vermont Tubbs* | 14' | 35" | 11½" | 48 | $315 | Fiberglass |
| SS15 *Trailcraft* | 15' | 32" | 13" | 85 | K $79 | Wood/canvas |
| Quetico 15 *Alumacraft Boat Co.* | 15' | 37¼" | 23½" | 64 | $242 | Aluminum (.040 ga.) |
| Navaho-15 *Browning (Aero-Craft)* | 15' | 36" | 13" | 69 | $215 | Aluminum |
| CST 15 Core-Craft *Bemidji Boat Co.* | 15' | 35" | 13" | 65 | $279 | Fiberglass |
| 15-foot Lightweight *Grumman* | 15' | 35½" | 12 1/8" | 55 | $255 | Aluminum (.032 ga.) |
| 15-foot Standard *Grumman* | 15' | 35½" | 12 1/8" | 69 | $239 | Aluminum (.050 ga.) |
| 15-foot *Grumman* | 15' | 36 1/8" | 13 1/8" | 74 | $264 | Aluminum (.050 ga.) |
| 15-foot Square Stern *Grumman* | 15' | 36 1/8" | 13 1/8" | 77 | $269 | Aluminum (.050 ga.) |

(CONTINUED ON NEXT PAGE)

## CANOES 13 FEET 1 INCH TO 15 FEET 6 INCHES (continued)

| NAME<br>   *MANUFACTURER* | LENGTH | BEAM | DEPTH | WEIGHT<br>(LBS.) | PRICE | MATERIAL |
|---|---|---|---|---|---|---|
| T-15<br>  *Michi-Craft* | 15′ | 36″ | 13″ | 69 | $220 | Aluminum |
| FT-15<br>  *Michi-Craft* | 15′ | 36″ | 13″ | 69 | $235 | Aluminum |
| FW-15<br>  *Michi-Craft* | 15′ | 36″ | 13″ | 69 | $265 | Aluminum |
| S-15<br>  *Michi-Craft* | 15′ | 36″ | 13″ | 69 | $207 | Aluminum |
| F-3685-21<br>  *Mirro Craft* | 15′ | 35″ | 13″ | 79 | $240 | Aluminum (.051 ga.) |
| 4020<br>  *MonArk Boats* | 15′ | 35″ | INA | 65 | $240 | Aluminum |
| Sea Nymph<br>  *Stanray Corp.* | 15′ | 37″ | 12″ | 75 | INA | Aluminum (.051 ga.) |
| Lightweight<br>  *Old Town* | 15′ | 35½″ | 11½″ | 58 | $660 | Wood/canvas |
| Trapper<br>  *Old Town* | 15′ | 35½″ | 11½″ | 55 | $690 | Wood/canvas |
| Featherweight<br>  *Old Town* | 15′ | 35½″ | 11½″ | 46 | $680 | Wood/canvas |
| 15-foot<br>  *Ouachita* | 15′ | 35½″ | 12″ | 62 | $202.63 | Aluminum (.051 ga.) |
| Flambeau<br>  *Fiberglass Engineering* | 15′ | 34½″ | 12½″ | 70 | $189 | Fiberglass |
| Swing<br>  *Easy Rider* | 15′ | 31½″ | INA | 46 | INA | Fiberglass |
| Scout 15<br>  *Easy Rider* | 15′ | 34″ | 13″ | 60 | INA | Fiberglass |
| EP-15<br>  *Eskay Plastics* | 15′ | 38″ | 14″ | 68 | INA | ABS |
| EPP-15<br>  *Eskay Plastics* | 15″ | 37″ | INA | 60 | INA | HMW Polyethylene |
| EPP-15-SB (SS)<br>  *Eskay Plastics* | 15′ | 38″ | INA | 60 | INA | HMW Polyethylene |
| Scout<br>  *Quapaw Canoe* | 15′ | 33″ | 13″ | 72 | INA | Fiberglass |
| Sportcanoe<br>  *Grumman* | 15′3″ | INA | INA | 112 | $349 | Aluminum (.050 ga.) |
| Potomac<br>  *Old Town* | 15′6″ | 32″ | 13½″ | 55 | $425 | Fiberglass/balsa<br>sandwich |
| Square-Stern<br>  *Ouachita* | 15′6″ | 33″ | 13″ | 77 | $217.67 | Aluminum (.051 ga.) |
| Scout<br>  *Astra Boats* | 15′6″ | 38″ | 12″ | INA | $280 | Fiberglass |

feature is flotation. Expanded foam under the gunwales and decks allows the F.G. to support up to three times its hull weight when full of water. Should you ever capsize, this makes it possible to remain in the water-filled canoe along with your gear. While it may not be easy to paddle under these conditions, bailing will be easy and thus the safety factor enhanced.

Also from Old Town come three wood-constructed canoes 15 feet long. They are offered in the Lightweight and Trapper lines, with all the characteristics discussed for these models under the categories that include 11- and 13-foot canoes. The third model is the Featherweight, a 15-footer that cuts 9 pounds off the weight of the fiberglass-coated Trapper and 12 pounds off the weight of the canvas-covered Trapper. The Featherweight falls between the Lightweight and Trapper in price, and is ideal for wood-and-canvas buffs who must portage. Like the other two models, the Featherweight features two seats and a single thwart amidships.

Easy Rider builds four canoes in this category. The first, the Scout 15, is a 15-foot version of the Scout 13. The construction is the same as for the canoe discussed in the 11-feet-1-inch-to-13-feet section. The 15-foot version is suggested for those who want to carry bigger loads, and is a better model for use by two adults. The other three canoes from Easy Rider are competition craft, designed to resemble kayaks in appearance. They are competitive with the Old Town Wenatchee and Potomac. The Easy Rider Winner C-1 is hailed by its manufacturer for speed and maneuverability in the slalom. It includes a molded bucket seat, knee straps and pads, and recessed bow and stern grab loops. The Munich C-1 is perhaps better for rough water and would be preferable for a beginner. It features more volume than the Winner C-1, making it the choice of those who want to solo carrying lightweight camping gear. The last of the three-decked canoes from Easy Rider is the Swing, a two-man model with lots of volume under the decked-over center. It has good stability and features many of the same features as the Winner and Munich.

Trailcraft offers four kits in the 13-feet-1-inch-to-15-feet-6-inch category—two wood-and-canvas models and two fiberglass models. The kits include the Scout S14, a 14-foot wood-canvas model, and the Square-Stern SS15, which is 15 feet in length.

The fiberglass canoes are the Trailpacer and Trailfinder, both 14 feet long. The Trailpacer features mahogany trim, while the Trailfinder has fiberglass trim. A description of what is included in the kits for these boats appears in the discussion of canoes 11- to 13-feet long. Once again, these kits permit you to own a canoe of good quality for about half the price of a factory-finished model.

A good fiberglass 14-footer is the Skimmar by Aero-Nautical Incorporated. Its general shape gives it good control when the wind arises, since it has a relatively low upsweep at bow and stern. Its flat bottom makes it stable and safe. It also features two foam-filled flotation tanks. Seats and end-caps are made of fiberglass, while the gunwales and the single center thwart are fashioned of aluminum. The end-caps serve as carrying grips. Standard colors for the Skimmar include horizon blue, yellow, marsh green, and orange.

Bart Hauthaway also offers a lightweight fiberglass canoe: the Allagash. At 45 pounds, this is the lightest 14-footer covered here. It has two seats and a single thwart amidships to facilitate carrying. Its comparatively narrow beam makes it easy to handle, but its rockered hull, while enhancing maneuverability, sacrifices some course-holding ability. Ethafoam under the seats and decks provides added flotation, and boxed inwales filled with PVC foam are a further help in this regard. Grab loops appear fore and aft. The Allagash is offered in green-gray, and other colors on request.

The Battenkill from Vermont Tubbs is perhaps more canoe than a beginner need pay for, but if he wants a superb quality 14-footer, this may be it. Like the larger canoes from this manufacturer, it is made from fiberglass, with traditional-appearing ash gunwales, thwarts, and rawhide woven seats. Expanded polyurethane provides the extra flotation, and bow and stern receive added reinforcement. Capacity for the Battenkill is rated at 675 pounds. A center keel and two half keels enhance course holding.

An impressive 15-footer is the fiberglass offering from Bemidji Boat Company, the Core-Craft CST 15. Although this model has a higher upsweep to its bow and stern than may be preferable, it offsets its sensitivity to wind with a triple keel running along its underside. Not only does the triple keel improve course holding, it also reinforces the bottom. The CST 15 features two slightly contoured seats and a single thwart. It has excellent flotation, and reportedly supports three adults when full of water. At its gunwales, a fiberglass strip is rolled so that a flange extends past the side of the canoe, resulting in a small splashguard that prevents water from shipping over the side. The inwale, on the other hand, is tight to the side of the craft, meaning that it catches little water or sand when you empty water from the innards by turning the boat on its side or upside down. This is a handy feature, both for bailing the craft while swimming alongside it or for emptying it of debris after a trip.

The guarantee on the Core-Craft CST 15 is among the best available. To begin with, there is a lifetime guarantee against breakage due to defects in materials and workmanship. Further, there is an *unconditional* one-year guarantee against *any* breakage in normal use. Finally, there is a lifetime guarantee against any puncture beneath the waterline. This surpasses any other warranty I have examined. As with any guarantee, you should consider what must be done to take advantage of it. To have the canoe repaired, it must be sent prepaid to its Minnesota source. This means delay, having the boat out of the water when you may want to use it, and the extra cost of shipping charges. This is true of other warranties too. There is no substitute for proper use and maintenance. Nevertheless a good guarantee *is* reassuring.

The Oswego Flambeau from Fiberglass Engineering of Wyoming, Minnesota, is a very high-styled square-stern model, with a deep "V" stern. It features two seats and a carrying yoke with pads. Along the sides, under the gunwales, runs an Indian design similar to the one that appears on Quetico canoes. Capacity of the Flambeau is a healthy 800 pounds, and the craft weighs only 70 pounds.

Three 15-foot Pelicans are offered by Eskay Plastics. The first, the EP-15, is constructed with a double hull of ABS and a layer of styrofoam between the hulls. Ribs are molded into the inner hull to add a flavor of tradition, and still function somewhat as they did on the birchbark canoe—they add strength to the hull. Since this is a double-hulled craft and does not submit to much handyman alteration, Eskay has anticipated some problems that might occur. For example, a wood-reinforced mounting is molded into the craft so that a small electric motor can be mounted. It appears difficult, perhaps even impossible, to mount a motor bar, however; there is no flange at the gunwales on which to anchor it. One excellent feature of the two-seat, single-thwart canoe is the rub rail that runs around its entire perimeter, which helps eliminate unwanted scratches. Maximum capacity is rated at 800 pounds.

The other two craft entered by Eskay Plastics in this 13-feet-1-inch-to-15-feet-6-inch category are the EPP-15 and the EPP-15-SB. The SB is simply a square-stern version of the EPP-15. These craft share many characteristics with the 12-foot EPP-12-SB described earlier. They are constructed of high-molecular-weight polyethylene and carry an interior Ethafoam lining as well as Ethafoam sponsons under their gunwales. The boats are wide and stable, but do not feature quite the exaggerated shape that the EPP-12-SB does. Grab handles are molded into the decks for easy two-man portaging, and seats are padded (needlessly, in my opinion). The interior Ethafoam is supported and held in place by aluminum ribs. The 15-foot Pelicans can carry large loads, and are rated for a safe capacity of over 800 pounds. The Pelicans will do better in open water than on narrow, tree-lined streams, because their sponsons tend to catch against obstructions rather than slide by. The sponsons, can, however, be removed. All told, these appear to be suitable canoes for families.

Despite the high-powered talent that goes into designing canoes, it seems that some manufacturers indulge in oversights on the drawing board. They adopt designs that, for one reason or another, leave something to be desired. This is the case with Quapaw's 15-foot Scout. The Scout is an attractive craft made of reinforced fiberglass, with moderate upsweep at the bow and stern and well-finished aluminum gunwales and thwarts. In most ways it appears to be as good a buy as any similar craft discussed here. But the Quapaw designers chose to insert expanded foam flotation under the seats rather than in the bow and stern. The result is that the paddler is virtually forced to sit when paddling: the fact that the seat extends to the floor makes it impossible to kneel. Since the safest position (after sitting on the floor) is kneeling, the design poses a serious drawback. In most other ways, this craft is acceptable. Its one-piece hull, for example, is durable, and it has sufficient flotation to hold three passengers when full of water.

Four 15-foot aluminum canoes are available from Grumman, one of which is a square-stern rated at 715-pounds capacity. This model has spray rails running along its sides at the waterline to keep the paddler dry when under power and accepts up to a 5-horsepower outboard motor. It has two thwarts, two seats, a rolled-over aluminum deck that also functions as a carrying handle, and six ribs reinforcing its stretch-formed hull of .050-inch-thick tempered aluminum alloy. Flotation blocks are contained in the bow and under the rear seat.

The three double-ended models from Grumman are all rated for 720 pounds capacity and differ from one another in the gauge of aluminum used for fabrication, in the number of reinforcing ribs, and in the types of keels provided. The 15-foot Standard has three reinforcing ribs, is made of .050-gauge aluminum alloy, and weighs 69 pounds. It features a standard 1-inch-deep keel. It is also offered for whitewater use with a shallow-draft keel $\frac{5}{8}$ inch deep. The whitewater model receives extra reinforcement—having five ribs—and weighs 74 pounds. The shallow keel makes it more maneuverable laterally, and the extra reinforcement makes it more damage-resistant as it pounds over rocks.

Finally there is the Lightweight, made of .032-inch-thick aluminum alloy reinforced with five ribs. It weighs a light 55 pounds, making it easy to portage and to loft. Grumman warns that the Lightweight, while it should be adequately puncture-proof, dents more readily than the standard model. This does not affect performance appreciably, but it could mar cosmetic appeal after a while. Ordinarily, it is better to buy the most rugged canoe available, which means that the nod goes to the standard models. But if you need an extra-light canoe, the Lightweight represents a sound investment.

Grumman's Sportcanoe (15 feet 3 inches) is a relatively heavy craft, but it is really half rowboat and half canoe. It is about 8 inches wider than even the widest double-end canoe and is therefore very stable. While the Sportcanoe is not best on rivers and streams, it is nonetheless a fine boat, especially for hunting and fishing. It takes up to a 5-horsepower motor.

Among the canoes most respected by professionals, the Alumacraft models rank right behind the Grummans, and many outfitters include them in their inventories. The smallest Alumacraft is the Quetico 15, a 15-footer that accommodates two comfortably, yet is responsive when paddled solo. This aluminum canoe features two seats, two thwarts, and a built-in carrying yoke positioned admidships that functions as a third thwart. Four ribs reinforce the hull, which consists of two halves of stretch-formed .040-gauge aluminum alloy. Gunwales are extruded aluminum that has been heat-treated for maximum strength. The keel on the Quetico 15 is $\frac{5}{8}$ inch deep and is known in Alumacraft jargon as the "Cruising Keel." The standard Alumacraft keel, not available on this model, is 1 inch deep and is designed to keep the canoe on course on open water in a wind. The Quetico 15, however, is built for responsive lateral movement and maximum control in fast water. Styrofoam flotation is included in the Quetico 15, locked into bow and stern by aluminum bulkheads. Its carrying capacity is a whopping 840 pounds B.I.A. rated.* Unfinished aluminum

---

* B.I.A.: Boating Industry Association. The B.I.A. has established standards for rating canoe capacity. The B.I.A. designation helps the buyer compare canoes on the same basis. Unfortunately, some canoe manufacturers rate their own canoes for "safe" maximum capacity. Not all capacities shown in this book are B.I.A. although I have used them where possible.

is the standard color for all Alumacraft canoes, and Indian trim (consisting of a handsome interlocking triangle design running immediately beneath the gunwales) is also standard. Optional are painted hulls of red, yellow, green, or camouflage for the hunter. If you are looking for a versatile 15-foot canoe, the Alumacraft 15-foot Quetico is hard to beat. And the price is right in line with others in its category.

Competing head to head with the Quetico 15 is the Navaho-15 from Browning Marine Division of Aero-Craft. While the Aero-Craft model lacks some of the sophistication that has made the Quetico popular with outfitters, the Navaho costs less and should be considered seriously. It has a practical configuration with low upsweeps at bow and stern; its three thwarts supply good rigidity; it has two web seats (which can be comparatively comfortable for paddling on hot days). The Navaho possesses what Aero-Craft calls Sta-Foil ribs along both sides. These are simple bulges in the sides just above the waterline that effectively widen the bottom, acting as sponsons to make the canoe more stable. A padded carrying yoke is optional, and pontoons are also available for added stability.

Another group of fine aluminum canoes is marketed by the Michi-Craft Corporation of Big Rapids, Michigan. Four models are offered; the T-15, S-15, FT-15 and FW-15. All but the S-15 are heat-treated, giving them extra puncture resistance and strength; all are available with smoothly rounded sides or with Michi-Craft's Safety-Foil design (bulges that run along both sides of the canoe at the waterline and which, like Aero-Craft's Sta-Foil ribs, act as sponsons, giving stability and added structural rigidity without added weight). Models with the "F" designation have flush rivets; that is, their rivets are flat-headed and countersunk so that they are even with the canoe's surface. Michi-Craft offers this design to boaters who are afraid of snagging their canoes in swift, rock-strewn waters. Both the FT-15 and the FW-15 are tempered. The difference between the two is that the latter has a whitewater keel, considerably more shallow than the one on the FT-15. Whereas all the other 15-foot canoes from Michi-Craft have four ribs, the FW-15 has five, giving it extra strength for its more rugged purpose.

Accessories for the Michi-Craft line include a side motor mount, a carrying yoke, a sailing kit, paddles of 4½- and 5-foot lengths, a folding anchor, safety pontoons, and more. As far as colors are concerned, natural-finish aluminum is standard, but a canoe painted dead grass green can be ordered for an extra cost or, for slightly more, other colors are available.

A relatively heavy aluminum 15-footer is Mirro-Craft's

F-3685-21 canoe. The extra weight, about 10 pounds over most canoes in the same category, is due to the slight extra thickness of the hull (.051 inch). This canoe is heat-treated for maximum strength and ruggedness. It features two seats, a painted non-skid interior, eyes at bow and stern for attaching painters, and carrying handles in the bulkheads. The guarantee for the Mirro-Craft canoes (which applies also to the 17-footer) is given for one year to *the original owner only* and covers the repair of defects in material and workmanship free of charge by the factory or an authorized dealer. The owner must bear freight charges to and from the factory, and any structural changes made to the canoe void the guarantee. This is a fairly typical guarantee, about par with Grumman's (which reads like a legal textbook). but it certainly does not compare with a guarantee such as Core-Craft's.

Another boat with a one-year guarantee to the original owner, similar to Mirro-Craft's, is the MonArk 4020. But this craft has a 20-year guarantee against bottom puncture in normal use. This aluminum canoe, with two seats, three thwarts, foam flotation under the decks, and flush-riveted construction, is suggested by its manufacturer for whitewater. It is available in olive green, red, blue, yellow, forest green, and olympic green, but all canoes have a gray interior.

Ouachita (pronounced Wash-a-taw), a firm from Little Rock, Arkansas, produces two fine 15-foot aluminum canoes, designated the Square-Stern and the Double End. The canoes are made of stretch-formed aluminum that is heat-treated to assure maximum toughness. The Square-Stern has two seats, three thwarts, five ribs, and spray rails that keep the water down when under power. The Double End model features two

*The Michi-Craft line features four models of 15-foot canoes. (Photo Michi-Craft)*

93

thwarts and four ribs and lacks the spray rails. Capacities are 630 pounds, for the double-ended model and 705 pounds for the squared-stern. These models are available in forest green, olive drab, turquoise, blue, white, red, yellow, gold, orange, and gray. The Ouachita canoes carry a conventional one-year guarantee under which the owner pays freight costs. Of course the boats are not covered for accidents that occur during improper trailering or because of misuse. Finally, when examining the Ouachita canoes, be sure your feet fit under the seats. They are placed low and a brace mounted beneath them may be an inconvenience when kneeling.

The Sea Nymph Division of Stanray Corporation produces a very accommodating double-end aluminum model with two seats, three thwarts, and a non-skid bottom. Flotation is provided by foam encased under the decks. The Sea Nymph's construction includes extended aluminum gunwales, an inner-outer interlocking keel, and heavy-duty bow and stern castings. The design of the Sea Nymph model should make it suitable for travel in the wind since both bow and stern have been kept low.

A fiberglass offering is Astra Boats' Scout. This canoe is boosted by its manufacturer for whitewater and for cruising. It is conducive to getting the most out of paddling and is exceptionally safe. But for the beginner it may be uncomfortable for its lack of seats. If he can live with paddling from the kneeling position all the time, he should like its oak thwarts and segmented gunwales.

### CANOES 15 FEET 7 INCHES TO 16 FEET 6 INCHES

Canoes from 15 feet 7 inches to 16 feet 6 inches (roughly classed as 16-footers) are good for two-man paddling and for extended trips because they carry hefty amounts of gear and, at the same time, provide reasonable comfort. They weigh less than the 17-footers, which helps on portages where a few pounds spell the difference between hard work and outright fatigue. Sixteen-footers should be considered seriously by novice paddlers who want a boat with adequate capacity for camping trips. They are superb for group travel and are highly satisfactory for teen-agers.

Among the canoes in this category is the attractive Papoose from Dolphin Products Incorporated (don't confuse this model with the Sportspal Papoose in the ultralight pack canoe category). This 16-footer has a lusty capacity, is made of fiberglass, and is finished in attractive colors: white, red, green, yellow, and harvest wheat. Dolphin claims that the Papoose is modeled after canoes used originally by the Royal Canadian Mounted Police. A flat bottom and full-length metal keel make it stable and give it good course-holding ability. Other features include foam-filled flotation compartments, hardwood thwarts, a non-slip interior, and vinyl seats. As with other Dolphin craft, the bow and stern feature a high upsweep, although it is slightly modified on the Papoose. The canoe provides good handling in all situations except moderate to strong wind.

The 16-foot Skimmar from Aero-Nautical Incorporated is another fiberglass model, this one having a more conservative

*The Dolphin Papoose. (Photo Dolphin Products)*

shape than the Dolphin. It has two flotation tanks and a flat, wide bottom. Its seats and end-caps are made of fiberglass, while the gunwales and center thwart are aluminum. Standard colors for the Skimmar are blue, yellow, green, and orange. The boat is guaranteed for one year on materials and workmanship.

Three 16-foot fiberglass models are available in Bemidji Boat Company's Core-Craft line: the CE-16, CS-16, and CSS-16. The last is a square-stern that accommodates 900 pounds. The other models are double-enders, and each accommodates 800 pounds. The CS-16 features two seats and a single thwart

## CANOES 15 FEET 7 INCHES TO 16 FEET 6 INCHES

| NAME<br>   *MANUFACTURER* | LENGTH | BEAM | DEPTH | WEIGHT<br>(LBS.) | PRICE | MATERIAL |
|---|---|---|---|---|---|---|
| Sport<br>  *Sawyer* | 15'9" | 36" | 12¼" | 63 | $230 | Fiberglass |
| Guide SS<br>  *Quapaw* | 16' | 35" | 12½" | 77 | INA | Fiberglass |
| Mohawk River Canoe<br>  *Mohawk Mfg. Co.* | 16' | 35½" | INA | 78 | $225 | Fiberglass |
| Papoose<br>  *Dolphin* | 16' | 35" | 12" | 73 | INA | Fiberglass |
| Skimmar<br>  *Aero-Nautical Inc.* | 16' | 36" | 12" | 79 | $245 | Fiberglass |
| Cherokee-16S<br>  *Browning (Aero-Craft)* | 16' | 37" | 13" | 75 | $240 | Aluminum (.050 ga.) |
| CS-16 (Core-Craft)<br>  *Bemidji Boat Co.* | 16' | 35½" | 13" | 70 | $269 | Fiberglass |
| CSS-16 (Core-Craft)<br>  *Bemidji Boat Co.* | 16' | 35½" | 13" | 75 | $269 | Fiberglass |
| CE-16 (Core-Craft)<br>  *Bemidji Boat Co.* | 16' | 35½" | 13" | 68 | $219 | Fiberglass |
| Whitewater (Oswego)<br>  *Fiberglas Engineering* | 16' | 34½" | 13" | 78 | $189 | Fiberglass |
| Osage (Oswego)<br>  *Fiberglas Engineering* | 16' | 35½" | 13" | 78 | $240 | Fiberglass |
| Carleton-16<br>  *Old Town* | 16' | 36" | 12" | 79 | $305 | Fiberglass/balsa sandwich |
| Chipewyan-16<br>  *Old Town* | 16' | 36" | 12" | 65 | $355 | Vinyl/ABS foam sandwich |
| F.G.-16<br>  *Old Town* | 16' | 36" | 12" | 79 | $385 | Fiberglass/balsa sandwich |
| Ojibway<br>  *Old Town* | 16' | 33½" | 13¼" | 59 | $465 | Fiberglass/balsa sandwich |

amidships; the CE-16 is constructed similarly but lacks the center thwart. Of the two, the CS-16 seems to be more practical, because gear can be lashed to the thwart. All three Core-Craft canoes feature moderate upsweeps on the bow and stern and very little thumblehome. All feature triple-keel bottoms (although they can be ordered without this feature), which make them good for holding course and also tend to reinforce the bottoms. A particularly helpful feature for paddling on rough water is the rolled gunwale that serves as a splash rail. Because of its tight inwale, it does not catch sand and water inside when tipped for cleaning or bailing.

(continued)

| NAME<br>*MANUFACTURER* | LENGTH | BEAM | DEPTH | WEIGHT<br>(LBS.) | PRICE | MATERIAL |
|---|---|---|---|---|---|---|
| Trailpacer<br>*Trailcraft* | 16′ | 36″ | 12″ | 75 | K $149 | Fiberglass |
| Trailfinder<br>*Trailcraft* | 16′ | 36″ | 12″ | 75 | K $149 | Fiberglass |
| Canadian<br>*Sawyer* | 16′ | 34″ | 12½″ | 67 | $250 | Fiberglass |
| Algonquin<br>*Vermont Tubbs* | 16′ | 34″ | 11″ | 70 | $380 | Fiberglass |
| Manitou<br>*Vermont Tubbs* | 16′ | 33″ | 13″ | 65 | $400 | Fiberglass |
| TS-16<br>*Michi-Craft* | 16′ | 37″ | 13″ | 76 | $235 | Aluminum |
| SS-16<br>*Michi-Craft* | 16′ | 37″ | 13″ | 76 | $220 | Aluminum |
| FS-16<br>*Michi-Craft* | 16′ | 37″ | 13″ | 76 | $250 | Aluminum |
| F-3688-21<br>*Mirro-Craft* | 16′ | 37″ | 13″ | 76 | $260 | Aluminum (.051 ga.) |
| 4024<br>*MonArk Boats* | 16′ | 36″ | INA | 80 | $260 | Aluminum (.050 ga.) |
| Guide<br>*Old Town* | 16′ | 35″ | 12″ | 70 | $700 | Wood/canvas |
| Octa<br>*Old Town* | 16′ | 36″ | 12″ | 70 | $695 | Wood/canvas |
| Explorer E16<br>*Trailcraft* | 16′ | 32″ | 13″ | 80 | K $79 | Wood/canvas |
| V-stern<br>*American Fiber-Lite* | 16′3″ | 36″ | 12″ | 75 | INA | Fiber-Lite |
| TSL II<br>*Easy Rider* | 16′6″ | 37″ | 13″ | 78 | $340 | Fiberglass |

Like the Core-Craft 15, the 16-foot canoes carry enough flotation to support three adults when full of water, and are backed by a one-year guarantee against defects in material and workmanship. They also have the same lifetime guarantee against puncture under the waterline as the 15-foot models.

Fiberglas Engineering Corporation of Wyoming, Minnesota, manufacturer of Oswego canoes, produces two fine fiberglass models 16 feet long: the double-ended Whitewater and the square-stern Osage. The Whitewater features expanded foam flotation in its bow and stern, two thwarts, and two seats. The Osage has one thwart and two seats; its sawed-off stern is shaped to a narrow "V" configuration. Capacity for the Whitewater is 800 pounds, while the Osage is rated at 900 pounds. The Osage accepts small outboards up to 3.5 horsepower. Both canoes are available in red, blue, green, gold, coral, and dead grass, the latter being used as camouflage when hunting. These canoes are average in size and weight, and they feature stylishly rounded ends with moderate upsweep. The Oswego warranty is for two years to the original owner, but cost of transportation to the factory must be borne by the owner.

Algonquin, a 16-foot touring canoe that also handles whitewater, is typical of the excellent specialty designs emanating from Vermont Tubbs. It features a low bow and stern for minimum wind sensitivity and better visibility when portaging. It has two woven seats and ash thwarts and rails, giving a handsome, traditional appearance. Large whitewater decks of ash keep out the spray. Its V-shaped hull is designed to hold course well yet provide good maneuverability. Overall, the canoe is constructed of an all-cloth layup similar to that of an Olympic-style kayak. There is no matt or roving to add weight. Although normally rigid, the hull flexes on impact without shattering. Urethane-filled tanks provide flotation. Despite its high price, the fast, comparatively narrow design of this canoe makes it worth considering. Here is a fine craft for people interested in entering marathons and in racing. But its design does not preclude touring and camping.

Another 16-footer from Vermont Tubbs is a closed-deck C-2, the Manitou, designed for slalom and whitewater but also suggested for family trips. It comes with built-in kneeling pads, adjustable leg straps and braces, and a deck-mounted holder that accommodates a square paddle. In design, the Manitou resembles Old Town's Ojibway.

Old Town produces no fewer than six canoes at this 16-foot length, representing fiberglass and wood-canvas construction and one model that exhibits partial decking. First is the Carleton-16, a fine canoe with moderate upsweep at the bow and stern, two seats, and a single thwart. This is a durable, sturdy, stable model fashioned of reinforced fiberglass-balsa-sandwich hull with natural interior. Rails are rigid vinyl, and seats and decks are molded acrylic-ABS plastic. Positive foam flotation under the decks provides good buoyancy in the event of a capsize. The Carleton is supplied without a keel (good for whitewater and other situations where lateral control is paramount) unless one is requested. If you plan to do much straightaway downriver canoeing for enjoyment in normal currents, you should ask for the keel. The Carleton's stock color is dark green, but other colors are available.

The second Old Town offering in this category is the Chipewyan-16, again a canoe with a single thwart, two seats, and expanded foam flotation in the bow and stern. The hull is formed of a tough vinyl-ABS-foam sandwich. The Chipewyan is recommended by Old Town for those who ply courses that normally abuse a canoe. Color scheme for the Chipewyan consists of green with a white interior.

The Old Town F.G. 16-footer boasts two seats but no thwarts. The F.G. is built of a fiberglass-balsa sandwich. Its decks, seats, and gunwales are molded in one piece and bonded to the hull. The major advantage of the F.G. is that, if capsized, it supports three times its own weight when full of water. Under pressure conditions, it could mean saving gear or even a life.

Old Town's Ojibway, while not considered by its manufacturer to be exactly a whitewater canoe, is at home in this element due to its considerable tumblehome, rocker, and lack

*Old Town's Ojibway-16 is excellent when conditions are demanding. (Photo Old Town)*

of keel. In its 16-foot version it features a molded-in rear-deck seat, a full seat in front, and a thwart amidships. Hull construction is of fiberglass-balsa sandwich. Positive foam flotation is tucked under the gunwales. For the novice paddler, Ojibway is rather expensive; it is more specialized than most canoe campers need. But for experienced canoeists who tackle demanding conditions, it has few peers.

Finally there are the two wood-canvas canoes from Old Town, the 16-foot Guide and Octa. These are offered for the purist who opts for tradition, good feel, and aesthetic beauty above other factors. But to get these characteristics he must be willing to sacrifice easy maintenance and a measure of permanence; he must be content to mend the canvas covering of the hull and revarnish the highly finished sheathing and ribs. The Guide and Octa both have two seats and three thwarts, and both are available with reinforced plastic coverings at $30 extra. Of the two canoes, the Guide is the more practical because it has a lower bow and stern, making it less wind-sensitive. These are excellent canoes if you confine your cruising to open lakes or unobstructed waters. Unfortunately, they cost more than most canoeists will care to invest.

If you want speed and if your inclinations run to competition, it is hard to beat the Sport and Canadian canoes from Sawyer in the 16-foot category. Sawyer canoes bear the mark of a heritage of racing—the parent company was formed under the supervision of Ralph W. Sawyer, eight-time winner of the World's Championship Canoe Race held in Michigan. Sawyer canoes do not have the curvaceous bow and stern that many romantic beginners demand. But the straight-up bow-stern configuration and the low upsweeps make them highly functional. The Sport provides a wide beam for extra stability, making it the better canoe for touring and camping, while the Canadian primarily meets the United States Canoe Association's specification for amateur racing in the 16-foot class.

A good example of Sawyer's racing design is the form-fitting molded fiberglass seats in all models, which are very comfortable when you first sit in them, but which, after a while, are likely to give saddle sores because you cannot move around or

*Sawyer's Sport.*

switch positions. Nonetheless, if speed is the goal, the seats readily transmit power from the stroke to the canoe, minimizing wasted effort. The Sawyers are beautiful in their simplicity —narrow and sleek as predatory gar fishes. Their gunwales are nicely finished in aluminum. Though somewhat unconventional, they are worth examining before making a final decision on purchasing a canoe.

Although expensive (it would appear that most paddlers could buy equally useful canoes for a lot less), Easy Rider's TSL II is a top-quality open canoe for family fun. Built-in bow and stern flotation, two aluminum thwarts, and wooden seats complement the fiberglass hull rimmed with wooden gunwales. The canoe is wide and stable and ranks among the best of its type. This is one of the largest craft covered in this category and in many ways could well be classified along with the 17-footers.

Quapaw's Guide SS, a fiberglass square-stern, boasts attractive and functional aluminum gunwales and two thwarts of the same material. It features ¾-inch-deep keel to help minimize wind drift and enhance structural strength. The major objection to most of the other Quapaw canoes is that the foam flotation is incorporated under the seats so that there is no room to extend the feet when kneeling. This may be no consideration at all in a square-stern propelled by a motor. But many paddlers buy square-sterns primarily for paddling, using motors only occasionally. It would seem that for them, more practical designs are available.

If you want a canoe for easing into paddling, but plan to use it later for running whitewater, the Mohawk River Canoe is a likely candidate. Its design includes a fine-pointed bow and stern to make paddling easy. It features sufficient rocker and no keel for maneuverability; the bottom is flat and wide, ostensibly for maximum stability. For the rough whitewater treatment the canoe may receive, the wide design minimizes draft. High seats make it comfortable to extend the feet under them when kneeling. The gunwales provide an attractive and functional finish to the fiberglass hull—they are made of heat-treated aluminum.

A handsome square-stern 16-footer is available from American Fiber-Lite, constructed, naturally, of Fiber-Lite. For a discussion of the merits and demerits of this material refer to the description of the American Fiber-Lite pack canoe under the section on ultralightweights. Like other offerings from this company, the square-stern, dubbed the "V"-stern for the shape of the transom, has a fine finish and a clean, attractive design. Its seats are wood, and it has two aluminum thwarts. Its gunwales and transom are attractively finished with aluminum, and eyes are designed on the transom so that safety chains can be attached to the motor—a nice touch not included on many canoes.

The configuration of the American Fiber-Lite 16-foot canoe shows a low bow and stern and its 36-inch beam makes for excellent stability. The major reservation about this model is that the hull material has about the same abrasion resistance as wood. This seems a detriment when running with a motor, for should the craft be driven hard on snags, the finish could be marred or damage to the hull could easily occur. This canoe must demonstrate its performance and durability in the hands of customers for several years before receiving an all-out recommendation.

The 16-foot category features a disproportionately high number of square-stern aluminum models—they are 17-foot models chopped off at the stern. For people who plan to use an outboard on their canoes from time to time, the Cherokee-16S from Browning Marine Division of Aero-Craft is worth serious consideration. This 16-foot square-stern has 845 pounds of carrying capacity, features three thwarts and two aluminum seats. It also boasts expanded foam flotation, non-skid bottom paint, and sponson-style shape along the waterline for added stability. It should be satisfactory for paddlers who indulge in serious fishing since it is roomy and stable and motors to your favorite fishing hole in minimum time.

Michi-Craft offers three square-stern models at 16 feet; actually, they are one model with three differing sets of characteristics. The standard model is the SS-16, which is alumi-

num, with two seats and three thwarts. It has foam flotation under the decks and is offered either with rounded, smooth sides or with sponsons stamped into the sides above the water-line to add strength to the construction and stability against tenderness or tipping. The TS-16 is the next step up in the line, and is a better buy than the SS-16, considering that there is only a $15 price differential. The difference between the two canoes is that the TS-16 is heat-treated when it is stretch-formed to give it up to two-and-one-half times more resistance to dents and punctures than the standard model. This seems a good investment for anyone who plans to do extensive canoe-ing where there might be snags, debris, or rapids.

The final 16-footer from Michi-Craft, the FS-16, is another square-stern that is essentially the same as the TS-16 (it is heat-treated) but features flush rivets—a decided plus. It costs only $15 more than the TS-16 (and $30 more than the Standard SS-16). If you can afford it, the FS-16 is the best Michi-Craft square-stern. It is well made, and its heat treatment and flush rivets are all the more valuable when you consider that it is often used at speeds many canoes never reach—with a small motor pushing at its squared-off stern.

Another square-stern 16-foot aluminum canoe is available from Mirro-Craft. This canoe, the F-3688-21, is constructed of .051-inch aluminum and accommodates a 5-horsepower motor. Its rated capacity is 770 pounds. It features expanded foam flotation in bow and stern, non-skid paint on its interior, and carrying handles in its bulkheads. It has two seats and two thwarts. Like the more expensive Michi-Craft models, the

*American Fiber-Lite's V-Stern. (Photo American Fiber-Lite)*

103

Mirro-Craft is heat-treated to provide extra dent and puncture resistance. It is guaranteed against defects in material and workmanship for one year, and against punctures occurring in normal recommended use while possessed by the original owner. Again this does not apply to damage suffered while trailering or transporting. Like other models, freight charges must be prepaid to the factory, and any structural changes nullify the guarantee.

Butting head to head with the other aluminum square-sterns is the MonArk 4024. This craft, from a company widely known for its well-constructed aluminum flat-bottom scows and fishing boats, has a capacity of 545 pounds, three thwarts and two seats, with the rear seat placed higher than the front one to aid the sternman's vision. The 4024 is constructed of .050-inch aluminum and features a one-year guarantee on materials and workmanship. Its 80-pound weight makes it less than suitable for one-man portages, but it is only about 4 pounds heavier than most other aluminum square-sterns. Theoretically, if waters are deep enough to require or accept a motor, you are not likely to encounter many portages.

Trailcraft, of Concordia, Kansas, a builder of canoe kits, offers three 16-footers; the Explorer E16 of wood and canvas, and the Trailpacer and Trailfinder of fiberglass. The main difference between the Trailfinder and the Trailpacer is that the former has fiberglass trim whereas the latter displays mahogany trim for a more traditional look. The wood-canvas E16 outweighs the Old Town offerings in this material by 10 pounds. This is just the tip of an iceberg, since wood-canvas canoes tend to soak up water, making them heavier as the

*Trailcraft's Explorer E16, a wood and canvas kit. (Photo Trailcraft)*

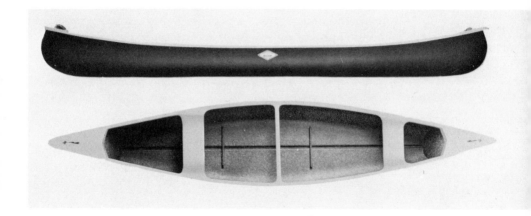

season progresses. But the price of the Trailcraft model is minuscule compared to those from Old Town. The E16 kit includes essentially the same materials as the Cub kit described under the 11-foot-1-inch-to-13-feet category, and the comments on building both wood-canvas and fiberglass kits stated there apply here too. When finished, the fiberglass Trailfinder and Trailpacer canoes have bonded foam flotation as do other fiberglass canoes. Colors for these canoes include white, or, for a premium, green, yellow, red, blue, dead grass, or gold.

*Trailcraft's Trailpacer fiberglass kit is a good buy if you are handy. (Photo Trailcraft)*

## CANOES 16 FEET 7 INCHES TO 17 FEET 6 INCHES

Canoes in the 17-foot category are the most practical choice for beginners who plan to use them for traveling and camping. A look at the chart accompanying this section and a comparison of typical 17-footers with the 16-footers discussed in the last section indicate that the weight differences between the two are not as great as might be imagined. But capacities are something else. Every foot of extra length in a canoe adds only about five pounds to the weight (subject to configuration, material, type of construction, etc.) but adds approximately 70 pounds carrying capacity.

Canoes in the 17-foot category normally hold their course well and are stable enough to accommodate two or three passengers in unquestionable safety. They are great for two paddlers, even with traditional heavy gear. Of course, every person discovers a critical weight and bulk that, if exceeded, prevents him from paddling for long periods. But the 17-footers seem to fall within the handling capabilities of **most** people, especially when they paddle with a partner.

The enormousness of the market for 17-footers is attested to by the fact that almost every one of the major canoe build-

105

ers offers a canoe in this size. Represented here are square-stern and double-ended models with an expansive price range from approximately $200 to $850. Canoes are available in all materials and types of construction. Here are offerings from no fewer than seventeen separate manufacturers and there are many others. Weights span the gamut from a highly por-

## CANOES 16 FEET 7 INCHES TO 17 FEET 6 INCHES

| NAME<br>*MANUFACTURER* | LENGTH | BEAM | DEPTH | WEIGHT<br>(LBS.) | PRICE | MATERIAL |
|---|---|---|---|---|---|---|
| Whitewater<br>*American Fiber-Lite* | 17′2″ | 37″ | 14½″ | 87 | INA | Fiber-Lite |
| Apache 17<br>*Browning (Aero-Craft)* | 17′ | 37″ | 13″ | 78 | $225 | Aluminum (.050 ga.) |
| CST-17 (Core-Craft)<br>*Bemidji Boat Co.* | 17′ | 36″ | 13″ | 78 | $299 | Fiberglass |
| C-17 (Core-Craft)<br>*Bemidji Boat Co.* | 17′ | 36″ | 13″ | 78 | $299 | Fiberglass |
| President-17<br>(Core-Craft)<br>*Bemidji Boat Co.* | 17′ | 36″ | 13″ | 78 | $399 | Fiberglass |
| Chief<br>*Dolphin* | 17′ | 37″ | 12″ | 77 | INA | Fiberglass |
| Brave<br>*Dolphin* | 17′6″ | 38″ | 12″ | 79 | INA | Fiberglass |
| Squaw<br>*Dolphin* | 17′ | 37″ | 12″ | 78 | INA | Fiberglass |
| Warrior Square-Stern<br>*Dolphin* | 17′ | 37″ | 12″ | 78 | INA | Fiberglass |
| Shagawa (Oswego)<br>*Fiberglass Engineering* | 17′ | 36″ | 13″ | 82 | $225 | Fiberglass |
| Namakan Square-<br>Stern (Oswego)<br>*Fiberglass Engineering* | 17′ | 36″ | 13″ | 85 | $255 | Fiberglass |
| Carleton Voyageur<br>*Old Town* | 17′2″ | 37″ | 15″ | 88 | $335 | Fiberglass/balsa<br>sandwich |
| Carleton Square-End<br>*Old Town* | 17′ | 37½″ | 12″ | 92 | $345 | Fiberglass/balsa<br>sandwich |
| Chipewyan Tripper<br>*Old Town* | 17′2″ | 37″ | 15″ | 74 | $385 | Vinyl/ABS foam<br>sandwich |
| Peter Pond Std. Wt.<br>*Moore Canoes* | 17′ | 34″ | 12½″ | 67 | $279 | Fiberglass |
| Peter Pond Lt. Wt.<br>Wilderness<br>*Moore Canoes* | 17′ | 34″ | 12½″ | 57 | $279 | Fiberglass |

tageable 57 pounds for the fiberglass Peter Pond Lightweight to the heavy Carleton Sponson Square-Stern at 115 pounds.

Since canoes in the 17-foot category are tops in sales, their manufacturers usually offer a good selection of accessories for them. The buyer can purchase motor bars, sailing rigs, and outrigger sets, as well as a number of other options. If the

(continued)

| NAME<br>*MANUFACTURER* | LENGTH | BEAM | DEPTH | WEIGHT<br>(LBS.) | PRICE | MATERIAL |
|---|---|---|---|---|---|---|
| Varmint (SS)<br>*Moore Canoes* | 17'2" | 34" | 13" | 69 | $285 | Fiberglass |
| Carleton Sponson SS<br>*Old Town* | 17' | 42" | 13" | 115 | $425 | Fiberglass/balsa<br>sandwich |
| Pioneer<br>*Quapaw Canoe* | 17' | 35" | 13" | 80 | INA | Fiberglass |
| Challenger<br>*Quapaw Canoe* | 17' | 35" | 13" | 94 | INA | Fiberglass |
| Drake<br>*Quapaw Canoe* | 17' | 35½" | 13" | 96 | INA | Fiberglass |
| Mohawk Guide<br>*Mohawk Manufacturing* | 17'6" | 36" | INA | 90 | $170 | Fiberglass |
| Royale II<br>*Smoker Craft* | 17' | 39" | 12¼" | 94 | INA | ABS |
| Otter<br>*Vermont Tubbs* | 17' | 30¼" | 12¼" | 70 | $400 | Fiberglass |
| Whitewater<br>*Malbar Plastics* | 17' | 36" | 14" | 75 | $279-<br>$299 | ABS |
| Quetico Cruising<br>*Alumacraft Boat Co.* | 17' | 36" | 23½" | 74 | $255 | Aluminum (.050 ga.) |
| Quetico Cruising<br>Lightweight<br>*Alumacraft Boat Co.* | 17' | 36" | 23½" | 69 | $255 | Aluminum (.040 ga.) |
| Quetico Wilderness<br>*Alumacraft Boat Co.* | 17' | 36" | 23½" | 69 | $255 | Aluminum (.040 ga.) |
| Camper-17<br>*Alumacraft Boat Co.* | 17' | 37¼" | 22" | 85 | $270 | Aluminum (.050 ga.) |
| Camper-Outboard-17<br>*Alumacraft Boat Co.* | 17' | 37½" | 32" | 92 | $285 | Aluminum (.050 ga.) |
| 17-Foot Lightweight<br>*Grumman* | 17' | 36 1/8" | 13 1/8" | 60 | $269 | Aluminum (.032 ga.) |
| 17-Foot Standard<br>*Grumman* | 17' | 36 1/8" | 13 1/8" | 75 | $255 | Aluminum (.050 ga.) |
| 17-Foot Whitewater<br>*Grumman* | 17' | INA | INA | 81 | $280 | Aluminum (.050 ga.) |

(CONTINUED ON NEXT PAGE)

manufacturer of the boat selected does not have a catalogue listing accessories, do not hesitate to contact him and ask where to get the items wanted. Canoe catalogues often omit mention of important pieces of auxilliary gear available from the company itself. Usually it is left to the company representative at the point of sale to explain the accessories and their functions to the buyer. Above all, do not be afraid to ask penetrating questions of clerks, sales representatives, company officials, or fellow canoeists.

## CANOES 16 FEET 7 INCHES TO 17 FEET 6 INCHES (continued)

| NAME<br>  *MANUFACTURER* | LENGTH | BEAM | DEPTH | WEIGHT<br>(LBS.) | PRICE | MATERIAL |
|---|---|---|---|---|---|---|
| 17-Foot Square-<br>  Stern<br>  *Grumman* | 17' | 36 5/8" | 13 1/8" | 85 | $285 | Aluminum (.050 ga.) |
| T-17<br>  *Michi-Craft* | 17' | 37" | 13" | 78 | $230 | Aluminum |
| FT-17<br>  *Michi-Craft* | 17' | 37" | 13" | 78 | $245 | Aluminum |
| FW-17<br>  *Michi-Craft* | 17' | 37" | 13" | 78 | $265 | Aluminum |
| S-17<br>  *Michi-Craft* | 17' | 37" | 13" | 78 | $214 | Aluminum |
| F-3687-21<br>  *Mirro-Craft* | 17' | 35" | 13" | 87 | $254 | Aluminum (.051 ga.) |
| 4026<br>  *MonArk Boats* | 17' | 36" | INA | 75 | $260 | Aluminum (.050 ga.) |
| Sea Nymph-17C<br>  *Sea Nymph Division—Stanray Corp.* | 17' | 38" | 12" | 85 | INA | Aluminum |
| Deluxe Chippewa<br>  *Smoker-Craft* | 17' | 39" | INA | 86 | INA | Aluminum (.051 ga.) |
| Standard<br>  *Smoker-Craft* | 17' | 37½" | INA | 89 | INA | Aluminum (.051 ga.) |
| Octa<br>  *Old Town* | 17' | 35" | 12" | 75 | $655 | Wood/canvas |
| Molitor<br>  *Old Town* | 17' | 35" | 12" | 80 | $845 | Wood/canvas |
| 17-foot Double End<br>  *Ouachita* | 17' | 33" | 13" | 73 | $274 | Aluminum (.051 ga.) |
| 17-foot Double End<br>  Whitewater<br>  *Ouachita* | 17' | 33" | 13" | INA | INA | Aluminum (.051 ga.) |
| Pelican EPP-17<br>  *Eskay Plastics* | 17' | 39" | 15" | 78 | INA | HMW polyethylene |

Typical of a manufacturer who targets more than one canoe at the 17-foot category is Alumacraft, which produces no fewer than five outstanding aluminum canoes 17 feet long: the Quetico Cruising canoe, the Quetico Cruising Lightweight, the Quetico Wilderness, the Camper-17, and the Camper-Outboard-17 (square-stern).

The Quetico Cruising and Cruising Lightweight differ primarily in the gauge of aluminum used in their hulls. The Cruising canoe uses .050-inch aluminum while the Cruising Lightweight uses .040-inch material. Both are stretch-formed and heat-treated for maximum strength. The Lightweight is beefed up with two extra ribs, to make it suitable for whitewater and to add overall extra rigidity (giving it five ribs instead of three). Both canoes feature two aluminum seats and three thwarts, and both have expanded foam flotation in the bow and stern. Both feature Alumacraft's cruising keel, which is shallower than the standard keel used on the Camper, Camper-Outboard, and Wilderness. The cruising keel makes them slightly more maneuverable in fast water, although the boats are said to feature sufficiently good course-holding ability for use on open rivers and lakes. The Cruising canoe has countersunk, flush-mounted rivets so that it is excellent for paddling over rocks and through snags. Both models feature an attractive Indian geometric design running under and along their gunwales. While the Cruising and the Cruising Lightweight should be sufficiently durable no matter how rough the going gets, the Lightweight is more susceptible to dents than its counterpart. This means that after several years of good use a

*The Quetico Cruising (top) and the Quetico Lightweight differ primarily in the gauge of aluminum used in their hulls. (Photo Alumacraft)*

Lightweight may not be as cosmetically attractive as the standard-weight. If aesthetics do not bother you, the Lightweight model is probably a better investment because it shaves five pounds off the total weight—not a lot, but less to bear when lifting onto a car or portaging. The Lightweight definitely would not be the better investment if you plan to navigate snag-ridden streams where the boat will run over rocks and stumps slightly below the water level.

The Quetico Wilderness is similar in configuration to the Cruising canoes. It is essentially the same canoe as the Cruising Lightweight but with the deeper standard keel. This canoe should be considered in place of the Lightweight for straight-line cruising where little need exists for swift pivotal movement, and where you may have to hold course against side winds.

The Cruising, Cruising Lightweight, and Wilderness all rate between 735 and 1075 pounds capacity, depending on the formula used in calculation. A larger capacity (980 to 1110 pounds) characterizes the Alumacraft Camper-17, which offers 1¼ inches greater beam than the Quetico models. This canoe is fashioned of heavier-gauge aluminum and features a full complement of five ribs for durability. It is rugged and is intended for use by campers who take more than an overnight trip. Its relatively heavy 85 pounds make it difficult to portage, so it is recommended for two-man paddling in order that more than one person can share the carrying duties. General construction and configuration are similar to those of the Quetico models.

Still heavier, at 92 pounds, is the hefty Alumacraft Camper-Outboard 17. This durable aluminum model has five ribs and a wishbone-shaped transom that rides completely above the waterline, not altering the shape of the stern at water level. The Camper-Outboard accepts motors up to 3.5 horsepower. Its weight makes it more suitable as a full-time motorboat than a cruising paddlecraft, and if you prefer a motor to a paddle, it should certainly be considered. The square-

*The Alumacraft Camper. (Photo Alumacraft)*

stern is based on the Camper and shares its rated carrying capacity.

The 17-foot Aero-Craft Apache 17, from Browning Marine Division, features three thwarts and two webbed seats inside its aluminum hull. It has foam flotation in both the bow and stern and incorporates the Aero-Craft sponson-type design, with bulges running immediately above the waterline. These sponsons provide added stability and increase the carrying capacity. Apache is rated to carry 820 pounds and handles up to a 4-horsepower outboard on a side motor mount (optional). An optional padded carrying yoke is a good investment, since the 78 pounds, although about average for a canoe of this length, is nonetheless tough for one man to tote. Non-skid bottom paint is also a worthwhile feature—it could keep you from slipping in the canoe or tumbling into the water.

Grumman offers four models in the 17-foot category; the Standard, the Lightweight, the Standard with a shallow-draft keel beefed up with extra ribs for whitewater and the square stern. All are stretch-formed of heat-treated aluminum, .050 inch thick for the Standard models and .032 inch thick for

*The Alumacraft Camper-Outboard 17 is more suitable as a full-time motorboat than a cruising paddlecraft. (Photo Alumacraft)*

*Grumman's 17-foot Standard. (Photo Grumman)*

the Lightweight. The latter, according to Grumman, is durable enough for just about any kind of service, and is easier to portage than the Standard models. But, as in the case of the Quetico Cruising Lightweight, it dents more easily. Overall, it seems to be the better model for the person who will give it only moderate use. The 17-foot Grumman Square-Stern features the same fine construction as the other Grumman canoes. It has two seats, three thwarts, and accepts up to a 5-horsepower motor. Splashguards are standard on this model. The Whitewater model features seven ribs as opposed to five in both the Standard and the Lightweight and costs more than the other two. For most occasional paddlers, either of the two less expensive canoes are a more logical choice; but if you intend to rough it, the Whitewater should take just about anything the stream can offer.

Grumman's standard keel is about one inch deep. A shallow-draft ⅜-inch keel is also available on standard-weight models and provides better maneuverability. All Grumman canoes feature foam flotation bow and stern.

*The Grumman 17-foot Square-Stern features fine construction as does the entire Grumman line. (Photo Grumman)*

Respective capacities for the Grumman models are 805 pounds for the double-enders and 860 for the square-stern. For an extra charge your Grumman can be painted red, yellow, blue, or green. For slightly less you can get the dead grass color. Just about all the accessories it is possible to offer for canoes are available from Grumman, including paddles, vinyl gunwale covers, floorboards, rowing attachments, carrying yoke, outrigger pontoons of styrofoam, outboard motor

bracket, seat cushions, and a seat for an extra passenger. The firm also sells a sailing kit that greatly extends the pleasurable possibilities of its canoes.

Michi-Craft's 17-footers can be purchased with standard "smooth-side" configuration, or sponson-type construction with a bulge along the waterline for added strength as well as added carrying capacity. The double-end canoes have two seats, three thwarts, and ribs of extruded aluminum. Four models are available: the T-17, S-17, FT-17, and FW-17. All of these canoes are rated to carry 780 pounds, and are constructed of stretch-formed aluminum. The standard S-17 is not heat-treated, while the T-17 undergoes heat treatment said to give the hull two and a half times the strength of the former. The FT-17 and FW-17 models are both heat-treated, and the F in their designations indicates that they have flush-mounted rivets. The FW-17 is for whitewater; its keel is inverted to limit depth, which allows greater lateral maneuverability. Also, the FW-17 has been beefed up with a sixth rib, one more than the other Michi-Craft models have. The canoes are natural in finish, but colors are available at extra cost. On the basis of extra durability, the FT-17, when compared to the S-17, is well worth the additional money.

Competing with the Michi-Craft canoes is Mirro-Craft's 17-footer, the F-3687-21. This aluminum model features two seats, three thwarts, and sizable compartments filled with foam for flotation. Its hull is fashioned of .051-inch-thick heat-treated aluminum, making it rugged and durable. It is rated

*Michi-Craft's 17-foot model F-3687-21, a rugged and durable canoe. (Photo Michi-Craft)*

at 800 pounds capacity and comes standard with a non-skid bottom. At 87 pounds, it is comparatively heavy and is best for the paddler who does not portage often.

Another aluminum canoe competitive in price with those mentioned is the MonArk 17-footer designated 4026. This craft has three thwarts and two seats and is rated at 565 pounds carrying capacity. It is 12 pounds lighter than the Mirro-Craft, so if you do not have enormous gear requirements, it may be a better choice—especially if you intend to sling it on top of a car or portage it. The MonArk has countersunk flush rivets and is available in olive, red, green, blue, yellow, and forest green. Interiors are gray.

*Ouachita's 17-foot double-ended canoe. (Photo Ouachita)*

Ouachita produces an excellent 17-foot double-ended aluminum canoe. It is offered with a standard keel, three thwarts, and two seats. The standard model features five ribs. The

whitewater model is the standard 17-footer beefed up with two extra ribs for added strength, and a shallow-draft keel for maximum maneuverability when running among rocks and obstructions. The Ouachita 17-footer falls toward the medium to upper end of its category in price, but is well made. It is available in several colors as well as a natural finish. However, paint does scratch off aluminum rather easily and a lot of touching up must be done to maintain the good look of any painted aluminum canoe.

Sea Nymph, by Stanray, comes from a company with long experience in building aluminum fishing boats, as do the Ouachitas. In most ways, the Sea Nymph is a good, conventional canoe, featuring two seats and three thwarts, all of aluminum. The bottom is reinforced by six ribs and is painted inside with non-skid paint. A standard keel is featured. Bow and stern bulkheads are sealed to enclose expanded foam; and a sponson design is featured to provide greater initial stability and interior capacity. This canoe totes a lot of gear. Its bow and stern have been kept low, resulting in minimum wind sensitivity.

Among the more popular aluminum canoes are Smoker

*Stanray's Sea Nymph, a good, conventional canoe. (Photo Sea Nymph Division, Stanray Corp.)*

115

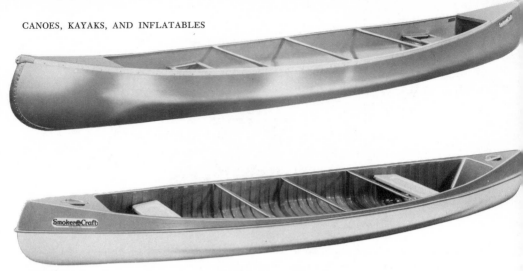

*Smoker-Craft's Deluxe Chippewa (top) features unispon design, which increases initial stability and interior space. The Royale II is made of rugged ABS plastic. (Photo Smoker-Craft)*

Craft's Deluxe Chippewa and Standard. The Deluxe Chippewa features three thwarts and what Smoker Craft calls its "unispon" design, which simply consists of sponsons just above the water level that assure greater initial stability and increase the interior space. The Chippewa is made of heat-treated aluminum. The Standard, on the other hand, lacks sponsons and is not heat-treated. Both canoes feature a keel, a benefit for holding the course. Both canoes are rated to carry 760 pounds.

Smoker Craft also offers the Royale II, an ABS high-impact-resistant plastic canoe of double-hull construction and molded ribs for extra strength. It has sponson design and built-in grab handles flush with the deck. Three thwarts are positioned conveniently for lashing gear. It is highly floatable, with styrofoam in the bow and stern. Its rated capacity is 800 pounds. Seats feature a slight contour, making them more comfortable initially, but, as has been mentioned, this is not always good for long trips. One of the best things about all the canoes from Smoker Craft is their lifetime guarantee against skin puncture under normal recommended use.

The three 17-footers listed from Bemidji Boat Company are the Core-Craft C-17, CST-17, and President-17. These fiberglass models are all basically the same in configuration and materials, featuring triple-keel bottoms wherein the keel strengthens the bottom as well as provides better course-holding ability. Like the smaller Core-Craft models, they are designed with rolled gunwales that serve as splashrails, which not only keep you dry but help you rock out water when righting the canoe after a capsize. Non-skid seats and enough flotation to carry three adults in a canoe full of water are other Core-Craft claims. The bows and sterns of these canoes are upswept somewhat more than is ideal for use on open water, but the upsweeps are not too extreme. The principal difference between the C-17 and the CST-17 is that the latter features a thwart shaped to accommodate shoulder pads, which provides, in effect, a carrying yoke. This is the Core-Craft canoe to select if portaging is in the future. Since both the C-17 and CST-17 carry the same price tag, you are wise to opt for the latter.

The flagship of the Core-Craft line is the President. Structurally, it is identical to the C-17 and CST-17, but its trim is truly striking; it features a white hull with wood-grain trim along the top half of the exterior and throughout the interior. This is the best to buy if you want to be seen and complimented. On the negative side, it costs $100 more and for that $100 you do not get a whit more performance or longevity than from the other Core-Craft canoes.

Dolphin, of Wabasha, Minnesota, offers four 17-footers, one of which is a square-stern (the Warrior). Dolphin's Chief, Brave, and Squaw all have the same rated carrying capacity of 950 pounds, all are 17 feet long except the Brave at 17 feet 6 inches, all feature metal keels, and all have foam-filled flo-

*The Core-Craft President, flagship of the Core-Craft line. (Photo Core-Craft Division, Bemidji Boat Co.)*

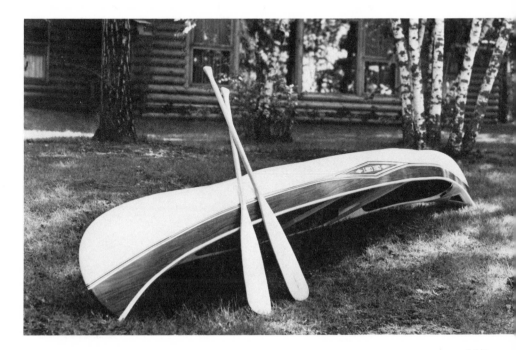

tation compartments, hardwood thwarts, non-slip interiors, and vinyl seats. But in looks the three canoes differ vastly.

Dolphin makes attractive canoes—there is no question about that—with design based on historic precedents. However, for open water or river touring under varying conditions, Dolphin's upswept bows and sterns are a little impractical. It is true that the early canoes of the fur traders featured prominently upswept ends, but there were reasons for this. First, the fur-trading canoes had a sufficient number of strong and well-conditioned paddlers to propel and control them at most times. And second the high bow and stern were executed to allow the paddlers to stand their canoes on edge at night in order to sleep under them. Few of today's paddlers will want to sleep on the ground under their canoes: so the advantages of high bows and sterns such as Dolphin's are more or less negated.

Dolphin's Chief is a two-thwart, two-seat fiberglass canoe. Aesthetically it is magnificent, resplendent in white, red, lime-kist green, yellow, or harvest wheat (camouflage). Optional metalflake colors are available at an extra cost: red, gold, blue, turquoise, and violet. This is a well-made canoe, but, because of its bow and stern upsweeps, it is best for calm conditions and should be handled by two paddlers when touring.

Dolphin's Brave features another beautiful design, with the stem pieces of the bow and stern turning back upon themselves and meeting gunwales that exhibit a more or less con-

*The Brave.*

*The Brave (opposite page), the Chief (top), and the Squaw from Dolphin—three attractive canoes. (Photos Dolphin Products)*

stant curve along the length of the craft. This canoe has two thwarts and three seats. Its bow and stern are not as high as those of the Chief, although the general design provides a lot of side exposure to the wind.

The Squaw, a low-profile model, has the most efficient design of the three. It features two thwarts and two seats, and its low bow and stern enhance its handling as well as making it easy to portage. The Warrior Square-Stern also features a high bow, but this should not be detrimental to performance when using a motor. A hardwood mount in the stern accommodates motors up to 3½ horsepower. Accessories from Dolphin include a carrying yoke, stabilizer floats, a motor bracket, and a sailing kit.

From Wyoming Minnesota's Fiberglass Engineering come

119

*Old Town's Voyageur (above) and the Carleton Square-End (opposite page) are steady canoes, good for family sport. (Photo Old Town)*

two Oswego 17-footers: the Shagawa double-ender and the Namakan Square-Stern that accommodates motors up to 3.5 horsepower. Both models have two seats, but the Shagawa has three thwarts while the Namakan has two. Both are rated for 1100 pounds capacity. They are well-designed, fast canoes with low upsweep at the bow and stern. Their prices are comparable with those of canoes from rival manufacturers. Oswego 17-footers are available in red, blue, green, gold, coral, or dead grass.

Prolific Old Town offers no fewer than five outstanding fiberglass and wood-and-canvas canoes in the 17-foot category. First there are two under the Carleton designation: the Carleton Voyageur and the Carleton Square-End. The Voyageur measures 17 feet 2 inches in length. It has two seats and a single thwart amidships for lashing down gear. Its price is relatively high, and at 88 pounds, its weight can be a lot to portage. The Square-End adds an extra thwart, but also tags an additional four pounds onto an already heavy canoe, mak-

120

ing it one of the heaviest 17-footers listed. These are steady canoes, good for family sport. But they are at home in white-water as well. Their hulls are fashioned of fiberglass-balsa sandwich with a natural interior; rails are rigid vinyl, while seats and decks are molded of acrylic-ABS plastic. There is foam under the decks for flotation. The Voyageur model comes without a keel, and one cannot be ordered specially. The square-stern also comes from the factory without a keel, but on this model one can be ordered if desired. The keel is a good investment if a motor is to be used frequently.

New to the Old Town line for 1974 is the Carleton Square-End Sponson. This is, essentially, the Carleton Square-End, and, like that model, it is built to accept a motor. The dif-ference between the two is that the Sponson comes with built-in Ethafoam flotation under the gunwales that lets you carry heavier loads onto big lakes with rough water. The spon-sons give the craft extra flotation and reportedly make it harder to tip.

*The Carleton.*

*Old Town's Chipewyan Tripper can take a pounding over rocks and other obstructions. (Photo Old Town)*

Very much like the Carleton double-ender in design is Old Town's Chipewyan Tripper with two seats and a single thwart amidships. But the Chipewyan is made of a different material—a vinyl-ABS-foam sandwich—that lets it take a pounding over rocks and obstructions. Old Town claims that the hull material furnishes its own flotation. Lack of a keel indicates Chipewyan's use in whitewater. The stock color is green with a white interior.

For those who want the ultimate in aesthetics and "feel" and who are willing to pay for it, Old Town offers two fine wood-and-canvas models at 17-feet: the Octa and the Molitor. The graceful Octa comes equipped with a canvas exterior, but for an extra $30 it can be purchased with reinforced plastic on the hull. Aside from the fact that this covering prevents a certain amount of maintenance, it also prevents water absorption during normal paddling. This, in turn, keeps the canoe's weight more constant throughout the season—making the plastic covering worth the extra cost. The Octa is a flat-bottomed, stable canoe with a good carrying capacity and, at 75 pounds, is lighter (at least at the time of purchase) than many of the aluminum and fiberglass canoes with which it competes.

The Molitor has the same general configuration as the fiberglass Brave from Dolphin, with the stem pieces in the bow and stern bending back over themselves to create a "torpedo" design. It features two seats but lacks thwarts—an unfortunate omission. If you want a boat of real beauty to paddle in situations where the thwart is not needed, it's the Molitor. The Molitor, like the Octa, can be obtained with a plastic covering; and it is a good idea to invest in the superior hull. Neither of the Old Town wood-and-canvas 17-footers is especially suited for a beginner, and it is best to learn to paddle elsewhere befor captaining one of these canoes. You would not want Junior to take his first driving lesson in the family Rolls Royce if there were a Volkswagen available.

Among the Peter Pond models offered by Moore Canoes Incorporated (formerly Vega Integral Products) are three 17-footers: the Standard Weight, the Lightweight Wilderness Tripper, and the Y-stern Varmint that is built to take a motor. These canoes are well designed with low upsweeps. They are not perfectly symmetrical, and their design at the waterline reflects an attempt to give them outstanding hydrodynamic

*The Peter Pond Standard Weight. (Photo Moore)*

*Moore's Y-Stern Varmint. (Photo Moore)*

properties. They feature four aluminum thwarts in a fiberglass shell and gunwales of aluminum. The seats of all three models are sufficiently high so that feet fit under them when paddling from a kneeling position. Foam flotation is molded into bow and stern. A feature the Peter Pond canoes share with those from Sawyer is their molded contour seats. Like the Sawyer seats, these are comfortable when you first sit in them, and they impart maximum power through your body to the canoe on each stroke of the paddle—especially good when racing. Capacities of 830 pounds for the Standard Weight and Lightweight Wilderness Tripper and 845 pounds for the Varmint accept all the gear needed for two paddlers on extended trips, and you will appreciate the light weight of these canoes when the time comes to portage or load them on a car.

Three different 17-footers are offered by Quapaw Canoe Company: the Pioneer, the Challenger, and the Drake square-stern. Pioneer and Challenger are both rated to carry 890 pounds while the Drake is rated for 1,000 pounds. These craft have three aluminum thwarts and aluminum gunwales. Aside from the extra 14 pounds of weight of the Challenger, the major difference between it and the Pioneer is that the latter has a standard ¾-inch-deep keel, while the Challenger's keel is only ¼ inch high for whitewater use. The Drake and Pioneer share the objection that has been raised about Quapaw canoes in other categories—their flotation is encased under the seats, making it difficult to assume a kneeling position. The Challenger has flotation in its bow and stern, but its seats are slung low, and you should test it before buying; be sure your feet fit comfortably. The seats in all the Quapaw canoes are slightly contoured, sharing a disadvantage with Sawyer and Peter Pond canoes (although not in the same degree): they limit the paddler from moving around.

A likely fiberglass offering is the Mohawk Guide's model, a 17-foot-6-inch offering with extruded aluminum gunwales and decks. The seats are high enough to permit extension of the feet under them when kneeling. The flat bottom lends good initial stability. Added bottom rigidity is furnished by fiberglass-covered aluminum ribs.

*The Quapaw canoe line showing (left to right): the Drake, the 16-foot Guide, the Pioneer, the Challenger (three models), and the 15-foot Scout. (Photo Quapaw)*

The Otter is a top-quality (and expensive) canoe from Vermont Tubbs. It is suitable for touring, is fast, and is suggested for serious whitewater paddling. Its "V"-shaped hull and sharp bow are conducive to holding a straight course. As with all Vermont Tubbs canoes, the Otter shows excellent craftsmanship and design. It is constructed of flexible fiberglass with internal ribs and ash rails. There is a single center thwart. Seats are woven, and expanded polyurethane is incorporated for flotation. Large whitewater decks deflect spray and signal the canoe's intended purpose.

The Whitewater canoe, from Malbar Plastics Incorporated,

is a striking design, with hull fabricated from extruded ABS thermoplastic, an extremely tough dent-and-puncture-resistant material. The basic canoe comes in red, yellow or green, or, for an extra $10, it can be purchased in hunter's camouflage. And for a $20 premium, it can be emblazoned from stem to stern with Budweiser beer labels in three colors. Or you can buy the Spirit of '76, which consists of a patriotic design of red, white, and blue stars and stripes—a floating flag.

Modern construction methods are used to build this canoe. Its hull is fashioned in two halves that are bonded together with a combination of adhesives and ultrasonic bonding. Capacity is 940 pounds. The canoe has contoured foam liners in the bow and stern to absorb impact as well as to provide flotation. The flotation chambers contain compartments that can also be used as cooler and storage boxes to keep beverages, food, meat, and fish, or they can be used for dry storage.

*The flamboyant Budweiser canoe (left) and the Spirit of '76 canoe (above) from Malbar Plastics Inc. (Photo Malbar)*

*Some canoes have modern, built-in cooler and storage compartments (below). The foam interiors of these compartments keep food, beverages, and fish cool for hours and are ideal for storing cameras and other equipment. (Photo Malbar Plastics)*

*American Fiber-Lite's Standard, the flagship of its line. (Photo American Fiber-Lite)*

The flagship of the American Fiber-Lite line is the 17 foot 2 inch Whitewater Canoe, and the comments on its hull material are the same as those expressed for the company's Ultra-lightweight Pack-Canoes. Essentially, the hull material should prove very satisfactory, except that the problem of abrasion resistance, which it shares with wood, must be considered a limiting factor. Fiber-Lite does have about the same specific gravity as wood and thus floats well; more flotation is provided in the form of expanded foam. This appears to be a fine canoe for family outings and for lake paddling; its lack of a keel suggests it might also be used for whitewater. Its wooden seats are set high so that your feet can fit under them comfortably when you assume the kneeling position. Its aluminum gunwales and two aluminum thwarts provide suitable rigidity. The bow and stern are moderately low and should limit wind sensitivity. All told, more information is needed on Fiber-Lite in actual use before a final judgment can be made on its durability. At a glance, it would seem that the Fiber-Lite canoe's good design offsets, if not outweighs, any possible problems with its construction material. And the company reports that its canoes have been tested successfully in rugged whitewater runs.

Like the Fiber-Lites, the hull of the Pelican EPP-17 from Eskay Plastics Limited, is constructed from a material that floats. The Pelican's high-molecular-weight polyethylene hull is fashioned with low bow and stern, and is rated to carry over 800 pounds. In the area of flotation, the Pelican excels, having two hefty Ethafoam sponsons along the sides and an interior lining of Ethafoam supported handsomely by aluminum ribs. Grab handles are molded into bow and stern decks to facilitate easy two-man portaging. Two wood thwarts are a plus for lashing gear. The seats are padded. This, in short, is a luxury canoe.

On the whole, the Pelican is designed to catch your fancy at the point of purchase. While my own preference runs more to traditional designs, this canoe should provide extra comfort and stability that many paddling families will like. On the negative side, however, it is possible that the Ethafoam sponsons might catch in tight quarters when brushed against branches and other snags protruding from the water. And the padded seats might crack or produce other problems after several years of service.

## CANOES OVER 17 FEET 7 INCHES

There is a point after which canoes become difficult to portage, a point where the addition of five or ten pounds adds true hardship to the work of moving the canoe when it is out of the water. Of course that point varies with the strength of the individuals concerned. For some people, as little as 50 pounds may create logistical problems. Though the breaking point is usually around 75 pounds for a healthy adult male, even boats of this weight are better handled by two men.

But what if you want to transport heavy loads over shallow water with uncertain bottoms? Or what if you have a family and want a stable canoe into which they can fit? Or what if you run a summer camp or canoe livery where troops of Boy Scouts or children soak up the fun by paddling in group fashion? The answer is the 17-foot-7-inch (or over) canoe. Listed here are 24 canoes over 17 feet 6 inches. In weight they range from 59 pounds, for the Sawyer Saber, to 117 pounds for the big 20-foot Grumman Peace canoe. Every major type of construction material is included: aluminum, fiberglass, and wood-canvas. Most of these canoes have counterparts of lesser length listed in other categories, and share construction and configuration with the smaller models. If you are in the market for a big canoe, you should find one here that satisfies your needs.

Grumman features no fewer than six canoes in this category, all excellent aluminum craft with either 18- or 20-foot lengths, except for the square-stern model, which is 19 feet long. The 18-footers include a canoe fabricated from .050-inch stretch-formed, heat-treated aluminum that is designated as "Standard-Weight." It has two seats and three thwarts, five ribs, foam-flotation cavities under the decks, weighs 85 pounds, and carries 850 pounds capacity. The Standard-Weight 18-footer has the normal 1-inch-deep Grumman keel to make it hold course well.

Similar in configuration to the Standard-Weight is the Light-weight, which is the same size and shape but uses .032-inch stretch-formed, heat-treated aluminum to shave off no fewer than 18 pounds, resulting in an excellent canoe that can be portaged even more easily than most 17-footers. This canoe also features the standard keel. Grumman suggests the Light-weight for canoeists who do not expect to punish their craft, although, according to the manufacturer, there is no danger of puncture, due to the heat treatment. But dents are taken more easily by this boat than by the Standard-Weight canoe. What it comes down to, finally, is that the Lightweight's easy portageability may be a sufficient advantage to recommend it over almost any other competitor.

The third 18-footer from Grumman is similar to the Standard-Weight in gauge, but has four extra ribs for reinforcement (as does the Lightweight). It features the Grumman Bulb "T" keel which is deep and capped by an aluminum bead (a thick-

## CANOES OVER 17 FEET 7 INCHES

| NAME MANUFACTURER | LENGTH | BEAM | DEPTH | WEIGHT (LBS.) | PRICE | MATERIAL |
|---|---|---|---|---|---|---|
| Cruiser *Sawyer* | 17'9" | 33" | 12½" | 68 | $275 | Fiberglass |
| 18-Foot Ltwt. *Grumman* | 18' | 36 5/8" | 13 1/8" | 67 | $285 | Aluminum (.032 ga.) |
| 18-Foot Std. *Grumman* | 18' | 36 5/8" | 13 1/8" | 85 | $269 | Aluminum (.050 ga.) |

(continued)

| NAME<br>   *MANUFACTURER* | LENGTH | BEAM | DEPTH | WEIGHT<br>(LBS.) | PRICE | MATERIAL |
|---|---|---|---|---|---|---|
| 18-Foot (White-<br>water)<br>*Grumman* | 18' | INA | INA | 91 | $294 | Aluminum (.050 ga.) |
| Voyageur<br>*Dolphin* | 18' | 38" | 14" | 107 | INA | Fiberglass |
| Carleton-18<br>*Old Town* | 18' | 37½" | 12" | 89 | $320 | Fiberglass/balsa<br>sandwich |
| Chipewyan-18<br>*Old Town* | 18' | 37½" | 12½" | 75 | $375 | Vinyl/ABS/foam<br>sandwich |
| F. G.-18<br>*Old Town* | 18' | 37" | 12" | 89 | $400 | Fiberglass/balsa<br>sandwich |
| Guide Special<br>*Sawyer* | 18' | 36" | 12" | 78 | $275 | Fiberglass |
| Safari<br>*Sawyer* | 18' | 36" | 12¾" | 80 | $295 | Fiberglass |
| Timagimi<br>*Vermont Tubbs* | 18' | 35" | 11¾" | 78 | $415 | Fiberglass |
| Guide<br>*Old Town* | 18' | 37" | 12" | 85 | $740 | Wood/canvas |
| Octa<br>*Old Town* | 18' | 37" | 12" | 80 | $735 | Wood/canvas |
| Champion<br>*Sawyer* | 18'6" | 33" | 11½" | 65 | $285 | Fiberglass |
| Super<br>*Sawyer* | 18'6" | 33" | 11¾" | 62 | $275 | Fiberglass |
| Viper<br>*Moore Canoes* | 18'6" | 34" | 12" | 65 | INA | Fiberglass |
| Venom<br>*Moore Canoes* | 18'6" | 34" | 11½" | 61 | INA | Fiberglass |
| Voyageur<br>*Moore Canoes* | 18'6" | 36" | 14" | 85 | INA | Fiberglass |
| Canadien<br>*Moore Canoes* | 18'6" | 36" | 13¼" | 76 | INA | Fiberglass |
| 19-Foot Sq.-Stern<br>*Grumman* | 19' | 40 1/8" | 15" | 116 | $369 | Aluminum (.050 ga.) |
| Guide<br>*Old Town* | 20' | 39" | 13¼" | 100 | $820 | Wood/canvas |
| Peace Canoe<br>*Grumman* | 20' | INA | INA | 117 | $389 | Aluminum (.050 ga.) |
| Guide<br>*Grumman* | 20' | 40 1/8" | 14" | 115 | $350 | Aluminum (.050 ga.) |
| Saber<br>*Sawyer* | 24' | 26" | 11½" | 59 | $350 | Fiberglass |

ening at the bottom of the keel running its entire length) to provide extra course holding and strength to the bottom. This model, known as the Whitewater model, is six pounds heavier than the Standard and costs $25 more. If your needs call for a big, rugged canoe, this is it.

The 19-foot Square-Stern from Grumman shares an exceptionally wide beam with the Grumman 20-foot double-enders —40⅛ inches. This means the craft has tremendous stability and is, therefore, ideal for fishing when coupled with a motor up to 7.5 horsepower. The Square-Stern is formidably reinforced with no fewer than 12 ribs, and has two seats and three thwarts, with foam flotation in the bow and stern. This is a heavy canoe, far more adaptable to motoring than to paddling for any extended distance. But it is versatile, and must be seen as a very good investment for the family that likes to paddle together but uses a motor for getting to their favorite fishing areas fast.

The 20-foot offerings from Grumman include the Guide and the Peace Canoe. The latter is especially adaptable to the needs of summer camps where children can be loaded in, side by side, and given instructions and practice in paddling together. The Guide, $39 less than the Peace Canoe, represents a better investment for families. Both canoes are rated for 1210 pounds capacity and both have the Bulb "T" keel to provide good course holding. The bottom construction of these models utilizes .050-inch-thick heat-treated, stretch-formed aluminum, and they both boast 12 ribs that provide a maximum strength. As always, Grumman seems to offer quality products at a moderately high, but realistic, price.

Since the canoes in this category are used primarily for family enjoyment, a certain amount of aesthetic and nostalgic license may be tolerated. With this in mind, many people seek canoes with classic lines—embellished dramatically with strikingly high bows and sterns.

Such a canoe is the Dolphin entry, the Voyageur. Here is a canoe with a healthy 1150-pound cargo capacity. Styled after the canoes of fur traders, the Voyageur's bow and stern are high enough to support the canoe if the family wants to sleep under it or use it for protection from the rain. There are three seats and two thwarts. The depth of the fiberglass hull is 14 inches at the center—2 to 3 inches more than the average canoe. Kids will be proud to be seen in this canoe, and it is superb for families that want to use it on Saturday afternoons to skirt lakes or do some fishing. The colors available enhance its appeal: white, red, limekist green, sun yellow, and harvest wheat.

Old Town builds six canoes that can be classified in the over-17-foot category. They appear in the Carleton, Chipewyan, and F.G. series as fiberglass 18-footers; in the Guide and Octa series as wood-canvas 18-footers. In the Guide series is a 20-foot wood-canvas model. The Carleton uses a fiberglass-balsa-sandwich hull. Rails are of rigid vinyl, while seats and decks are molded of acrylic-ABS plastic with positive foam flotation under the decks. The Carleton comes without a keel, but one may be ordered if you plan to use it on open water or on downstream expeditions. The standard color for the model is dark green. The bow and stern are moderate in upsweep, and there are two seats and two thwarts to which to lash gear. Old Town's Chipewyan has about the same general shape and thwart-seat layout as the Carleton, but is made of vinyl-ABS-foam sandwich for an exceptionally tough hull that makes it a good craft for whitewater. This model is offered without a keel. The 18-foot F.G. features a fiberglass-balsa hull; its seats and gunwales are molded in one piece and bonded to the hull. There are no thwarts, which must be seen as an inconvenience by the camper, despite the company's claim that the absence of these reinforcing members contributes to greater gear and passenger space. Positive foam flotation under the gunwales and in the bow and stern are said to enable the F.G. to support up to three times its hull weight when full of water, a handy advantage in event of a capsize.

The Old Town wood-and-canvas models in the over-17-foot category exhibit the usual beauty and solid feel of canoes made by traditional construction. They also have all the disadvantages.

Eighteen- and 20-foot models are available in the Guide series. This series, in the 18-foot models, has slightly less upsweep at the bow and stern than the Octa canoe, making it more controllable in crosswinds. Both have two seats and three thwarts. You pay considerably more for the 20-foot Guide than for the 18-footer. Since the price of these craft is already high, question whether you really need the extra room or cargo capacity afforded by the 20-footer.

At first glance, many people will find the Sawyer canoes in this category singularly unattractive. They invariably feature almost perfectly vertical bow and stern. The upsweep of their bows and sterns is negligible. But these characteristics make them practical when portaging and when paddling in windy conditions. In fact, the Sawyer canoes bear a heritage of racing design, and on some the best aspects of that racing design are well integrated with the design necessities of cruising and family canoes. All of these craft are made of fiberglass; most feature comparatively narrow beams, meaning that they tend to be a little less stable than the Grummans, Old Towns, Dolphins, and other canoes in their class. The Sawyers also feature contour-molded seats with all the attendant benefits and problems. Furthermore, the seats are mounted too low to accommodate the feet of most kneeling paddlers. But for fast, swift, lightweight canoes—boats that win marathons and races—Sawyer definitely merits serious consideration.

The Cruiser is Sawyer's all-purpose model that can be used for camping, cruising, and amateur racing. Its hull complies with the United States Canoe Association (USCA) requirements for amateur racing in the cruising class. Load capacity, with six inches freeboard (distance from the lowest point on the gunwale to the waterline), is 649 pounds. This canoe features two seats and three thwarts. Three inches wider, with a flat bottom, is the 18-foot-long Sawyer Guide Special, also suggested by its manufacturer for cruising enthusiasts. Light enough for children to use, its wide, flat bottom makes it as stable as a small fishing boat. It is rated for 813 pounds capacity with 6 inches of freeboard, and, like the Cruiser, it features two seats and three thwarts.

Fast—that's the word for the Sawyer Champion, which has won the USCA National Championship four times. This is a narrow craft with only 33 inches width at the bilge and 30 at the gunwales. Upsweep at bow and stern is almost nonexistent. There are three thwarts and two seats, and the weight is 65 pounds. The Champion is an excellent craft for the experienced canoeist who has good balance and needs raw speed. *The Sawyer* Even though it is 18 feet 6 inches long, other brands surpass *Champion, an* it in cargo-carrying capacity because it is narrow. Still, Sawyer *extremely fast* rates it highly for cruising as well as for amateur racing. *canoe. (Photo* The Sawyer Safari is the square-stern version of the standard *Sawyer)* fiberglass Sawyer canoes. It is recommended for use with mo-

tors up to 5 horsepower and features the usual two seats and three thwarts. Like the other Sawyer models, its bow and stern feature little upsweep, making it comparatively maneuverable in the wind. With 6 inches of freeboard, it handles 968 pounds. Its 36-inch beam puts it in a category with most other popular canoes as far as stability is concerned. For those who want to try canoe racing with a capital "R," there is the Sawyer Super, an 18-foot-6-inch canoe with three thwarts. When paddling this boat, you are expected to assume the kneeling position in order to get maximum power. With a 6-inch freeboard showing, the Super carries 757 pounds. Its bow and stern are typical of canoes in the Sawyer line—low and insensitive to wind. Finally there is the 24-foot Saber, a long, narrow canoe with no upsweep and only a ½-inch rocker. It has four thwarts, no seats, and long spray decks. Paddlers kneel and can propel the needle-like hull to incredible speeds. The Super and Saber are best left to experienced canoeists, and have little attraction for most beginners.

*Sawyer's Safari, a square-stern recommended for use with motors. (Photo Sawyer)*

*The Super and Saber from Sawyer are for experienced canoeists. (Photo Sawyer)*

Vermont Tubbs Timagimi is best for longer trips and occasions on which a large capacity is needed. It is rated at 975 pounds. In construction it is similar to the 16-foot Algonquin—flexible fiberglass with traditional-looking ash gunwales, thwarts (two) and decks. Seats are made of beautifully woven rawhide. This canoe rates high in quality and construction.

Another excellent source of racing canoes is Moore Canoes Incorporated. Fine fiberglass canoes from this manufacturer feature much the same configuration as the Sawyer canoes. The two specifically designed for racing are the Viper and the Venom, both championship-winning designs that feature the same racing seats used in the Sawyers. Viper is considered a deep-water hull, whereas Venom is best for shallow water. Both are quality craft, worth looking into if racing is on your mind.

Of more interest to paddlers who do not care to race are two other canoes from Moore measuring 18 feet 6 inches: the Voyageur and the Canadien. These fiberglass canoes have sizable spray decks, three thwarts, and two bench seats. The Voyageur is designed for expedition cruising, the Canadien for whitewater. Moore boasts that a boat using the *hull* of the *The Canadien from* Canadien won the 1973 National Wildwater Championships in *Moore Canoes.* Maine. The canoe should, however, also function well for *(Photo Moore)* wilderness expeditions and general cruising.

# Manufacturers'-Distributors' Directory

The foregoing sections covered only representative canoes, kayaks, and inflatables. Just about everywhere you look are others that have not been described. Nonetheless, an attempt has been made to cover the models made by the largest manufacturers as well as some of the smaller and little-known companies producing fine paddlecraft.

Before you purchase your boat, examine it in the showroom. If possible try out a similar craft owned by a friend, or even persuade the salesman to let you take a model out for a trial. If you cannot arrange an on-the-water trial, carefully apply the knowledge you have gained from this book. Check workmanship, straightness of keel, and symmetry. Be sure the craft has thwarts to which to tie your gear. If you are serious about traveling or camping with your canoe, forego the romance of high upsweep to the bow and stern and prefer a conservative profile. Compare models and prices. Remember that the prices given here are suggested retail prices in some instances, factory-direct prices in others. They are useful for making a general comparison but are not always the lowest prices available. Also they are the prices operative at the time this research was completed. Expect them to rise—they may even rise by the time you read this—but they should rise proportionately.

Get the best price you can. But remember that your boat is *the* fundamental piece of equipment for paddling. Do not compromise on it any more than absolutely necessary. Be prepared to spend a little extra to get what you want. After all, you may live with the boat the rest of your life, so a few extra dollars represent only cents per month over the years.

In some cases, there may be canoes listed that have special characteristics that appeal to you, but you may not be able to find a dealer who carries that particular model. When this happens, find out more about the craft involved by writing directly to the manufacturer, whose address may be listed below. Study carefully the brochures you receive. If satisfied, send for the craft sight unseen. Remember, however, that shipping costs will add an extra $20 or $30 to the factory-listed price.

As soon as you receive the new boat, unpack it and examine it thoroughly for defects. If any are found, send it back and make use of the warranty. You may even get a new boat if you act quickly enough, provided the craft has never been used. Fortunately, problems do not happen often with craft from reputable manufacturers; and when they do, amends are made quickly.

The following firms will provide information to help in your selection of an inflatable, kayak, or canoe:

## INFLATABLES

American Safety Equipment Corp.
7652 Burnet
Van Nuys, California 91405

Gladding Corporation
P.O. Box 586
Back Bay Annex
Boston, Massachusetts 02117

Gloy's Division of Amdis Corporation
12 East 22nd Street
New York, New York 10010

Leisure Imports, Inc.
104 Arlington Ave.
St. James, New York 10780

Recreational Equipment Corp.
1525 11th Avenue
Seattle, Washington 98122

Sevylor U.S.A. Inc.
4476 E. Washington Blvd.
Los Angeles, California 90023

Stebco Industries Inc.
1020 W. 40th Street
Chicago, Illinois 60609

## KAYAKS

Astra
910 West Balboa Blvd.
Newport Beach, California 92662

Baldwin Boat Company
Hoxie Hill Road
Orrington, Maine 04474

Easy Rider Fiberglass Boat Company
8822 S. E. 39th Street
Mercer Island, Washington 98040

Folbot Corporation
Stark Industrial Park, F72
Charleston, South Carolina 29405

Bart Hauthaway
640 Boston Post Road
Weston, Massachusetts 02193

Hollowform, Inc.
6345 Variel Avenue
Woodland Hills, California 91364

Kayak Specialties, Inc.
R.R. 1, Box 83
Buchanan, Michigan 49107

Hans Klepper Corporation
35 Union Square West
New York, New York 10003

Moor & Mountain
Main Street
Concord, Massachusetts 01742

Old Town Canoe Company
Box 548
Old Town, Maine 04468

Vermont Tubbs Incorporated
18 Elm Street
Wallingford, Vermont 05773

## CANOES

Aero-Nautical Incorporated
154 Prospect Street
Greenwich, Connecticut 06830

Alumacraft Boat Company
315 West St. Julien
St. Peter, Minnesota 56082

## CANOES CONTINUED

American Fiber-Lite
Box 67
Marion, Illinois 62959

Astra
910 West Balboa Blvd.
Newport Beach, California 92661

Baldwin Boat Company
Hoxie Hill Road
Orrington, Maine 04474

Bemidji Boat Co., Inc. (Core-Craft)
Box 249
Highway 2 West
Bemidji, Minnesota 56601

Browning Marine Division
Aero-Craft
St. Charles, Michigan 48655

Dolphin Products Incorporated
Wabasha, Minnesota 55981

Easy Rider Fiberglass Boat Company
8822 S. E. 39th St.
Mercer Island, Washington, 98040

Eskay Plastics Limited
2565, boul LeCorbusier
Chomedey, Laval, Quebec H7S 1Z4

Fiberglas Engineering
Box 3
Wyoming, Minnesota 55092

Grumman Allied Industries Inc.
Grumman Boats
Marathon, New York 13803

Bart Hauthaway
640 Boston Post Road
Weston, Massachusetts 02193

Malbar Plastics Inc.
Whitewater Canoe Division
401 East Iowa Street
P. O. Box 278
Indianola, Iowa 50125

Michi-Craft
19995 19 Mile Road
Big Rapids, Michigan 49307

Mirro Aluminum Company
Manitowoc, Wisconsin 54220

Mohawk Manufacturing Company
Box 668, Highway 427
Longwood, Florida 32750

MonArk Boats
Monticello, Arkansas 71655

Moore Canoes Inc.
Box 55342
Indianapolis, Indiana 46205

Old Town Canoe Company
Box 548
Old Town, Maine 04468

Ouachita Marine and Industrial Corp.
721 Main Street
Little Rock, Arkansas 72201

Quapaw Canoe Company
600 Newman Road
Miami, Oklahoma 74354

Sawyer Canoe Company
234 South State Street
Oscoda, Michigan 48750

Smoker Craft Division
Smoker Lumber Company Inc.
New Paris, Indiana 46553

Sportspal Incorporated
Drawer T
Emlenton, Pennsylvania 16373

Sea Nymph Division
Stanray Corporation
P. O. Box 298
Syracuse, Indiana 46567

Trailcraft Incorporated
Box 60638
Concordia, Kansas 66901

Vermont Tubbs Incorporated
18 Elm Street
Wallingford, Vermont 05773

# 8

## Paddles: Their Selection and Use

Selecting a canoe paddle is a relatively simple task. There are several common configurations for kayak and canoe paddles, each with its own properties for meeting hand and water. Paddles can be bought from all inflatable, kayak, and canoe manufacturers, as well as from some firms specializing in high-quality paddles for racing. Among these firms specializing in paddles are the following:

Carlisle Au Sable Paddle Co.
110 State Street
Box 150
Grayling, Michigan 49738

Elray, Inc.
Route 1, Box 27 N
Beaumont, Texas 77708

Kayak Specialties
R. R. 1, Box 83
Buchanan, Michigan 49107

Swanson Boat Oar Company, Inc.
Walnut and Bradish Avenues
Albion, Pennsylvania 16401

Sports Equipment Inc.
Box T, Dept. C
Mantua, Ohio 44255

Plasticrafts Inc.
2800 Speer Blvd.
Denver, Colorado 80211

J & B Products Co.
P.O. Box 958
West Point, Mississippi 39773

Iliad Inc.
170 Circuit St.
Norwell, Massachusetts 02061

Raymond A. Dodge
1025 Broadway
Niles, Michigan 49120

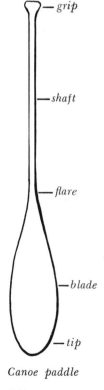

*Canoe paddle*

For the beginner, the best suggestion about paddles is to stick with those recommended by an experienced paddler, or those recommended by the manufacturer of your boat, who usually buys his paddles directly from paddle companies. Stay away from paddles having exaggerated width—they are hard for a novice to control and can cause fatigue if he is not in good physical shape. The other extreme is also undesirable—a paddle that does not have enough width will not push the boat through the water swiftly. Choice, however, is not much of a problem today, for paddles come with more or less standard blade areas. When you become more experienced, and especially if you should ever want to try racing, blade area and other factors such as flexibility of shaft, shape of blade, quality of lamination, and handle comfort take on more importance.

Paddles traditionally have been made from spruce (preferably laminated) or from hardwoods. Today there are many paddles made in aluminum, fiberglass, and various space-age plastics. You may feel the latter paddles lack the aesthetic appeal of traditional types, but in many instances they are lighter, more controllable, and better-shaped for maximum propulsion. Also, they do not splinter, can be designed scientifically for specific paddling properties, and never require maintenance.

If you use wood paddles, it might be a good idea to purchase two paddles for each paddler—one of softwood, one of hardwood. (You will want to have at least one extra paddle in the canoe at all times anyway.) In this way you can enjoy the lightness and flexibility of spruce under normal conditions, but can switch to maple or ash when going over gravel or rocks, or between snags, since less damage is likely to occur to the hardwood paddle than to the softwood.

Fitting a canoe paddle to individual size is not difficult. Al-

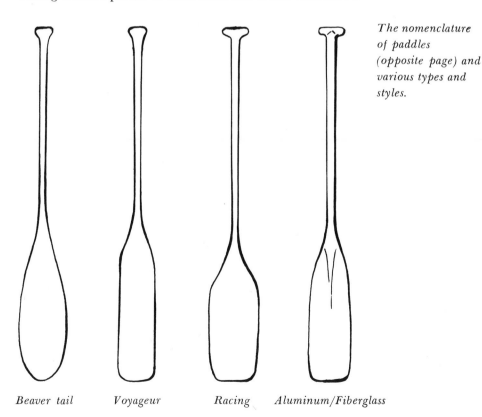

*The nomenclature of paddles (opposite page) and various types and styles.*

*Beaver tail*    *Voyageur*    *Racing*    *Aluminum/Fiberglass*

*An age-old invention with a new catch: Elray's floating molded fiberglass paddle is also a boat hook. It is highly desirable for docking, retrieving fishing lines, or hooking lost gear. (Photo Elray)*

though many experienced paddlers are finnicky about the paddles they choose and demand the utmost flexibility, hand feel, and balance, the beginner needs only to select a paddle of the right length. Once he learns what to do with it, there will be ample time to select one exactly right for his personal preference.

To select a canoe paddle of the right length, follow a simple rule of thumb: if you plan to paddle in the bow, select a paddle that, when standing on the ground, comes up to your chin. The sternman should select a paddle that reaches his eyes. Of course, rules of thumb admit to exceptions. Some people do prefer paddles that extend slightly beyond the tops of their heads. And it is important to note that different people have

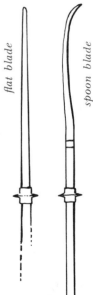

*Notice the ferrules on this kayak paddle. (Photo Sevylor)*

*Be sure kayak paddles are
the proper length for the boat you will use them with.*

different physiques, so that the length of one's arms and one's torso measurement have much to do with fitting the paddle. Nevertheless, if you stick by the rule of thumb when buying your first paddle, you cannot go too far wrong. When you purchase another, you can make adjustments in length.

A tip when considering kayak paddles: many popular touring kayaks, particularly the folding models, come equipped with two-part paddles joined with center ferrules that tend to loosen with use, allowing wiggling in the center of the shaft and twisting of the blades. Most experienced kayakists refuse to put up with this nuisance and select paddles constructed with one-piece shafts. If you are buying a kayak for camping and touring, the ferrules should not create serious enough problems to send you scurrying to an independent paddle-maker for a single-shaft paddle; those with ferrules do a thoroughly adequate job on the water, and are easier to carry in the trunk of a car.

Another tip: if you ever replace kayak paddles, be sure to take their measurement before purchasing another set. Paddles come in various lengths that depend on your size. But perhaps even more important, the proper size of a paddle depends upon the width of the kayak, for it must clear the side decks.

*Kayak paddles*

143

## BASIC CANOE STROKES

Canoeing manuals usually spend an inordinate amount of time detailing the various strokes for paddling a canoe. Presenting theory is fine, but it seems that people who might take up canoeing are often frightened away by the apparent complexity of the strokes, not realizing that the strokes are, in practice, not at all difficult. Because this guide is written to help beginning paddlers take up an exciting, relaxing, challenging, and just-plain-fun hobby, a brief description of a few basic canoeing strokes follows. But one point should be made strongly before you examine the strokes: they are usually dictated by common sense. Most people can canoe successfully on calm water without ever reading a book telling them how to paddle correctly. And a small amount of practice gives them sufficient technique to handle their boats safely in all but difficult situations.

Of course it may take a little time and practice to coordinate your strokes with a partner, and you might not keep the canoe perfectly on course at first. But these problems are to be expected. The best way to learn paddling is to get started and then let nature take its course. Once you have tried your hand on gentle water, that is the time to read in more detail about various paddle strokes. You will then have a feel for how a canoe behaves in the water and how it will respond to the motions indicated by the diagrams used in the book being read.

One other precaution: read the canoe manuals and practice thoroughly (especially those strokes that must be made in concert with a partner) before you try whitewater or difficult passages. On an easy river or quiet lake there is plenty of room to make a turn, even if you have not mastered fully the appropriate stroke. But whitewater can force you to execute sudden and precise pivots that require agile and well-timed action. Failure to use the right stroke at the right time may result in an upset. Beginning paddlers, or those with little time on the water, should limit themselves mostly to quiet water, perhaps taking occasional short stretches of fast water. For calm conditions the following basic strokes should suffice:

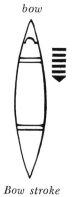

*bow*

*Bow stroke*

## BOW STROKE

The basic stroke of the bowman is the bow stroke. It provides a forward motion to the canoe and is not primarily used for steering. Common sense dictates its fundamentals—it consists simply of drawing the paddle straight back along the side of the canoe, close to the gunwale and parallel to the keel. At the end of the stroke the paddle is lifted from the water and returned to the starting position for the commencement of another stroke.

Basic as the bow stroke is, several tips can save work and help achieve maximum power. First grab the paddle grip tightly with one hand and grasp the shaft, just above the blade, with the other. The stroke proves easiest when using both arms equally in performing it. At the start of the stroke, extend the lower arm. As it draws the paddle back from its forward position, thrust the upper arm forward, boosting the power imparted to the paddle and helping to guide it.

Do not try to take too long or deep a stroke, for this is tiring and causes the canoe to yaw. Start the stroke at the normal extent of the lower arm, and end it shortly after the paddle passes behind the hip. If you draw the paddle back any farther, you simply lift water as the blade swings in its arc; this expends considerable energy but does not impart the desired forward action.

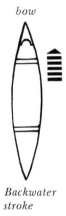

*bow*

*Backwater stroke*

## BACKWATER STROKE

Stopping a canoe's forward movement, or paddling it backward, are easily achieved by the backwater stroke. Essentially the reverse of the bow stroke, it can be used by both bowman and sternman. It consists of putting the paddle in the water behind the hip and forcing it forward until the lower arm is extended. The upper arm meanwhile proceeds from a fully extended position to a pulled-back position. When the blade reaches its farthest comfortable point forward, it is lifted from the water and returned to the starting position for another stroke.

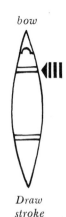

*bow*

*Draw stroke*

## DRAW STROKE

Another common-sense stroke is the draw stroke. Assume that you want to bring a canoe close to a dock. The simplest way, obviously, is to reach out with the paddle and, keeping the width of its blade parallel to the keel, draw the paddle toward you. This moves the canoe sideways. Both paddlers can perform the draw stroke on the same side of the canoe, but it also is possible to use this stroke to effect a pivot turn. This is done by two paddlers executing the draw stroke on opposite sides. The sternman effectively pushes the stern away while the bowman pulls in the direction desired. Naturally you would not extend the limits of the draw stroke beyond comfortable reach, for if you lean over too far in executing it, stability is jeopardized.

145

*bow*

*Pushover &*
*Pry strokes*

*bow*

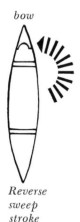

*Sweep*
*stroke*

*bow*

*Reverse*
*sweep*
*stroke*

## PUSHOVER AND PRY STROKES

Opposite to the draw stroke, is the pushover stroke, in which the paddle's blade enters the water parallel to the keel and is pushed away from it. This pushes the canoe away from the direction of the stroke. Like the draw stroke, it can be executed by two paddlers on the same side of the canoe to move the craft sideways, or it can be used to effect a pivot turn when the paddlers employ it on opposite sides.

The pry stroke is a variation of the pushover stroke and comes to the rescue when you need an extremely fast turn. It involves bracing the shaft of the paddle on the gunwale and using the shaft as a lever to pry the blade away from the canoe. This gives extra power to the pushover stroke, but it could damage both the boat's gunwale and the paddle. Therefore, use it sparingly, mostly for emergencies.

## SWEEP AND REVERSE SWEEP STROKES

In all the strokes we have discussed there is a high arm and a low arm, the high arm performing its function at about shoulder or chest height, while the lower arm directs the paddle with the hand at, or below, the gunwales. There are two strokes that do not share this characteristic, however, and they too are useful when making swift turns. These are the sweep and the reverse sweep strokes. If paddling alone, you can execute the sweep stroke to turn a canoe away from the paddling side. Holding the paddle with one hand at the waist and the other extended low outside the canoe over the water, enter the blade (turned parallel to the keel) far forward toward the bow, and sweep it back in a 180° arc until it again extends parallel to the keel. The result is that the bow is pushed away from the stroke and the stern drawn toward the paddle, providing a pivotal effect.

The reverse sweep is exactly opposite, starting with the paddle at the stern and winding up with it parallel to the keel at the bow. This turns the canoe toward the side on which you are paddling. The key to the effectiveness of these strokes lies in the low hand position and wide arc of the sweep.

## J STROKE

From whichever side a canoe is paddled, the force generated turns it in the opposite direction. The reason is that paddling causes a faster flow of water on one side of the canoe—the side being paddled. In other words, the canoe is moving faster on the one side than on the other. If paddling is compared to two wheels mounted on the end of an axle, one can easily visualize the physical principle involved. If one of the wheels is held stationary while the other rotates, the wheel that turns proceeds in a circle around the inert one. This is the same principle that accounts for a canoe's tendency to turn—all the power is applied to one side of the boat, reducing the other side to a pivot point.

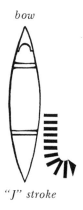

*bow*

*"J" stroke*

Given this factor, if two paddlers use the bow stroke on the same side of a canoe, the craft turns away from that side. Sufficient correction does not always come from simply paddling on opposite sides. If the bow swings away from the side of its paddler and the stern swings away from the side of its paddler, then both the canoe's ends travel in opposite directions. That is, the canoe pivots. In order to keep the canoe on course, yet maintain full power forward, a stroke is needed that provides steerage. That stroke is the J stroke.

Beginning sternmen have a natural and universal tendency to guide the canoe from the stern by trailing a paddle like a rudder. This results in adequate steerage in most instances, but fails to provide forward motion. Not only does the sternman fail to provide his share of locomotion, but the bowman has to overcome the additional drag caused by the trailing paddle. The J stroke eliminates most of the problems associated with "the rudder technique."

To learn the J stroke, assume the same position as for the bow stroke. When you finish this stroke, however, turn the paddle slightly so that its blade ends up parallel to the keel, and push the paddle away almost as if making the pushover stroke. This gives the stroke the "J" configuration. When this stroke is applied on the same side as the bowman is paddling, it helps the canoe proceed in a straight line.

At first the J stroke may be difficult to master, and you may be tempted time and again to return to the rudder method. But the J stroke is worth practicing: it is a fundamental in making canoeing well-controlled and easy. Spend time on it and make it habitual. The stroke will be useful whether you paddle alone, or as sternman with another.

## KAYAK STROKES

Although there are as many distinct strokes used in kayaking as in canoeing, few manuals dwell on them. Let it suffice to say that voyageuring kayaks are extremely easy to paddle even if you have never done so before. The strokes are alternating, right to left; keeping on course is a simple matter of applying equal force to both sides.

Of course, many basic canoe strokes apply to the kayak too—

147

the bow stroke, the backwater stroke, the draw and pushover strokes, the sweep and reverse sweep. Missing from the arsenal is the J stroke. Also, when paddling a kayak, the bowman, unlike paddling a canoe, participates more in steering, often initiating it. Furthermore the sternman must "dance in tune" with his bowman; one cannot choose to paddle to starboard while the other paddles to port.

Personal Flotation Devices

In addition to a boat and paddles, there is one more basic requirement for taking up the sport of paddling—the personal flotation device (PFD). Unlike the other two basic pieces of equipment, PFDs are not essential to getting on the water; instead they are required when actually on the water by federal law as part of the Boat Safety Act of 1971. According to the act, all recreational boats not carrying passengers for hire must carry various types of PFDs according to the size of the boat. The requirements for canoes and kayaks, regardless of length, are that they must carry one PFD of Type I, Type II, Type III, or Type IV for each paddler. Ski belts may appear to be an alternative to this requirement, but they are not approved by the Coast Guard nor do they satisfy the requirements of the law.

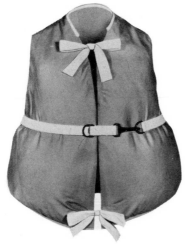

*Type I PFD (Photo RedHead Corp.)*

What are the various types of PFDs and which is best for you? PFDs are grouped in types according to their configurations, the way they cause the human body to float, and the amount of flotation (in pounds) they produce.

Type I PFDs have the configuration of jackets and are designed to turn an unconscious person from a face-down position in the water to a vertical or slightly backward position.

149

They must have more than 20 pounds of buoyancy. Generally they are recommended for offshore cruising and deep-water use, and are therefore unpopular with canoeists, who seldom ply that kind of water. Nonetheless, if you carry them, they provide an extra measure of safety.

Type II PFDs, the typical "life preservers" you may have been acquainted with as a child at summer camp, are designed to turn an *unconscious* person from a face-down position to a face-up vertical, or slightly backward position and to have at least 15.5 pounds of buoyancy. They are excellent for paddlers, and especially for children.

Highly popular are the array of colorful vests that are widely available. These are Type III PFDs. They are the most wearable type for active paddlers, designed to keep a *conscious* person in a vertical or slightly backward position and to have a minimum of 15.5 pounds of buoyancy. Since a conscious person normally helps to right himself, a lesser requirement for turning is necessary. This makes it possible to design more comfortable and wearable devices for active water sports. These are the most suitable PFDs for adults.

The last type of PFD, Type IV, is represented by life cushions and life rings. These are not worn, but are carried in the boat and provide sufficient buoyancy to support a swimmer after capsizing. They are designed to be thrown to a person in the water and provide at least 16.5 pounds of buoyancy. The disadvantages of Type IV PFDs for the canoeist are obvious. Should he capsize, it is likely that his PFD will float away with the current. For this reason, Type IVs are unsuitable for children and those who cannot swim. In whitewater, where there

*Type II PFD's
(Photo RedHead
Corp.)*

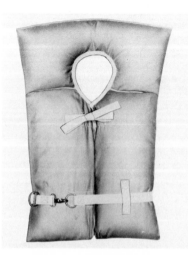 

*Type III PFDs are extremely popular with paddlers. These devices are available in all sizes and in form-fitting models for women. (Photo Texas Water Crafters)*

151

are rocks close to the surface that could knock the paddler unconscious, it is impractical to have a life preserver that is not worn.

A good recommendation is to prefer Type II or III devices and wear them constantly, taking along Type IV cushions to sit or kneel on and to use as seats for reclining around the campfire or as pillows for nighttime sleeping.

*PFDs are even made for dogs. (Photo Texas Water Crafters)*

# PART THREE

# GEAR FOR PADDLE CAMPING

Once you own a canoe and the necessary accessories, and after you have practiced enough to know your boat and develop physical endurance, you will probably want to undertake voyages lasting more than one day. No longer will leisurely outings on Sunday afternoons be entirely satisfying. If you are like thousands of other paddlers across the United States, you will take overnights, tackling, first, nearby rivers that pass through the countryside and link small towns. At this point you must become interested in camping gear.

As a paddler, you share with the backpacker a desire to pare all possible weight so you do not have to tote more gear than is necessary. But you need not push weight-saving to the same extreme as the hiker. Because you do not have to carry all your gear on your back at any single time except possibly during portages (and portages can be made in several trips), you can take along a little heavier gear or a little more gear to make yourself comfortable. For example, while backpackers must use the smallest, lightest stoves they can find, the paddler can afford the luxury of a heavier model, perhaps even a two-burner; or he can carry a larger cooking kit for added convenience.

Do not compromise on the weight of all your gear. Extra ounces quickly turn into extra pounds, causing paddling to become a chore and camping to result in physical fatigue. The art of purchasing gear for paddle camping exists in knowing on which items to compromise and on which not to.

As emphasized in the Introduction, one of the best features of paddle camping is that you can start by using camping equipment already owned. But as time goes on, you will want to replace old gear—the heavy canvas umbrella tent or the weighty army duck tarp, for example. And when you do, that is the time to pare weight, streamlining your impedimenta.

In the following pages, some of the most modern equipment on the market is described. The coverage is not meant to be all-inclusive. Rather, it shows some equipment that typifies the latest trends. All the equipment specifically mentioned is of excellent quality and, if properly cared for, should provide years of good service. But there are many other products on the market equal in quality, and you should not shy from a product merely because it does not happen to be mentioned here.

There are times when it is expedient to order camping equipment through the mail, and in these cases you should contact various mail-order houses. But where possible, visit an outfitter or sporting goods store yourself to examine the equipment. In this way flaws can be spotted right on the showroom floor, and the inconvenience of receiving faulty merchandise through the mail and then having to return it is eliminated.

One worthwhile tip on buying camping equipment: most often you get what you pay for. When you add all your equipment costs together, they should not total more than several hundred dollars, even if you spend well over $100 on a very good lightweight tent. With this in mind, purchase the best equipment you can afford. You pay premiums for light weight and quality, but these attributes save bulk in packing, make portages easier, and render camping more efficient and enjoyable. It is better to invest in quality basic equipment and delay purchases of less important gear than it is to purchase all your gear at once and compromise on all of it.

Tents and Tarps

$S$ome backpacking *aficionados* scorn the use of tents, preferring instead to sleep directly on the ground so they can gaze at the stars deep into the night. When the rains come, these campers wrap themselves in a sheet of plastic, with little more than a foot-long stick propping one end around their heads to keep a breathing hole open. Those who are experienced campers and like to rough it attest to the comfort of sleeping behind hedges and in hollow logs, beneath rock outcroppings, or on the open faces of mountains. They rhapsodize the feeling of waking up wet from light rain or in a moist sleeping bag. The most shelter they are willing to tolerate is often a polyethylene "tarp" with a few visklamps (lightweight clamps used for clamping a tarpaulin to its guy lines) and some string.

Longtime paddlers may or may not want to camp under such primitive conditions, but average campers definitely should depend on tents, especially when just beginning. The reason is that sleep is critical for those who paddle vigorously when unaccustomed to it. Sleep is the only balm for fatigue and sore muscles, and paddlers cannot afford to sacrifice it. It is not true that you can sleep through anything simply because you are exhausted. Sleep is a function of habit as much as of necessity. People used to retiring to a soft bed with a high pillow and reading for a half hour until they drop off to sleep have a hard enough time accommodating themselves to sleeping on the ground with a rolled-up sweatshirt under their heads—especially when no reading material is at hand or when there is insufficient light to enjoy it if it is available.

Add to these novel conditions a swarm of mosquitoes buzzing in the ears, eyes, or nose or the stipple of drizzle on the face, and you have the makings of a thoroughly sleepless night. No matter how you lather your exposed skin with insect repellent, the incessant buzzing of mosquitoes—coupled with certain knowledge that, at some time during the night, at least one insect will try to penetrate your defensive barrier—must necessarily induce insomnia. If they don't, the first raindrop certainly will. Where will the next drop spatter? You will find yourself counting raindrops rather than slumbering. To assure sleep on a camping trip there is no substitute for a tent—or, in relatively bug-free climes, at least a tarp.

There are thousands of tents available, all differing in materials, design, quality, and other facets. As a paddler, you must answer certain questions to determine which type is best for you.

Will you paddle areas that require frequent portages, areas where extremely light weight is needed to enable long hauls overland? Or do you foresee stationary camping on islands or in remote areas, where a heavier tent will be no hindrance? If you plan family trips, do you prefer one large tent for the whole group or would it be better to pack several smaller models? Will most campsites be on grass, or do you plan to paddle sand-bottomed rivers where sand-bar camping is a way of life? Will your tent be simply an overnight shelter to ward off the elements, or must it also function as an area in which to move around and even cook on inclement days?

The answers to these questions are certain to be reflected in the type of tent you choose. Since camping conditions cannot be predicted in all circumstances, compromise is probably necessary. The tent should be ideal for conditions encountered most often, but it must be versatile enough to function in all other *likely* situations.

If numerous portages are expected, take a tip from the backpackers and limit the weight of your tent to no more than three to five pounds per man (and this brings up the question of how many people will normally be involved in your paddle trips and, consequently, how large the tent must be). The tents that fit this category are constructed of nylon and range from low-profile models to versions that let you stand up inside. On the other hand, where little portaging is done or where stationary camping is the order of the day, heavier tents made of drill (a heavy cotton fabric) or poplin—such as the smaller wall tents, umbrella tents, or the popular compression-rib tents—offer comfort and dependability.

When families or groups travel together, a choice must be made as to whether each subgroup of paddlers will carry its own small tent or whether the group will carry one large tent of the wall or cabin variety. There are advantages and disadvantages to each choice. Sometimes a number of small tents can outweigh one big one; they certainly take up more space and, therefore, cause more complications in packing. Extra man-hours will probably be spent pitching and taking them down. Finally, using many small tents does not provide a central place in which all members of the expedition can stand up and stretch when pinned down by stormy weather. On the other hand, a number of small tents may be easier to pitch than a single large one, because it may be difficult to find a suitable level spot large enough to accommodate a big shelter.

The question of whether you will most often camp on grass or sand should determine whether you choose a tent with a sewn-in floor or a tent with no floor, substituting instead a ground cloth. On grass it is hard to beat tents with sewn-in floors. They are bug-free and dry. But on sand, problems crop up. It is impossible to enter a tent with a sewn-in floor without tracking in sand, which is abrasive and, if it remains in the tent, can cause untold damage to the floor. Furthermore, sand is uncomfortable to sleep on and is incredibly difficult to get out with a simple sweeping. In fact, it is virtually impossible to remove the sand without turning the tent inside out. If you try to vacuum a tent floor, the vacuum cleaner sucks the floor into its nozzle, adding further difficulty. Thus, for staking out on sand bars, the best tent is probably one with-

*Camp Trails' Chevelon is a "baker's" tent in configuration. It is ideal for camping on sand where insects are scarce. It is designed so that campers are kept warm when a fire is burning in front of the tent. (Photo Camp Trails)*

out a floor. By combining a bottomless tent with a ground cloth, you need only shake the ground cloth to get rid of most unwanted sand.

If you feel that camping is only a necessary chore that sustains you while plying the water for several days, you may be satisfied with a small, low-profile tent of the backpacker type, and you may even be able to live with a small plastic tent of the tube or InflataTent variety. Such tents may be adequate if you travel alone or with a single companion, but they are not meant for stationary camping by groups unless a large fly (or tarp) is used to protect a central area where the group may gather.

Two types of tents seem especially appropriate for the majority of paddlers—campers that rate as "normal" on the canoe-kayak bell curve: the compression-rib tents of the Pop-Tent or Draw-Tite variety, and breathable nylon tents covered by waterproof flies.

Three materials are commonly used in today's tents: cotton,

*Coleman's Family Umbrella Tent shows the external framework that eliminates the traditional center pole. (Photo Coleman)*

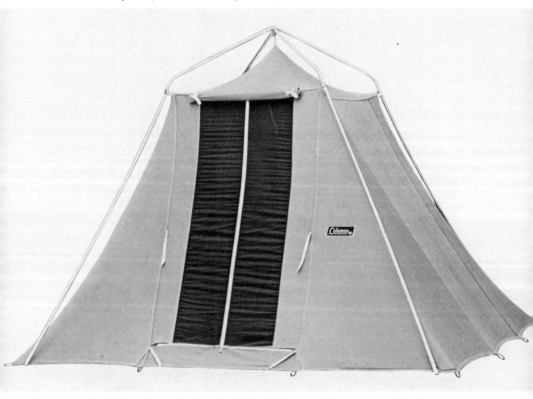

*Palco's InflataTent.
(Photo Palco
Products)*

nylon, and plastic. Cotton (canvas) offers durability, breathability combined with good water repellency, but considerable weight. Nylon is extremely light, but often fails to combine breathability with water repellency; it is also more expensive than cotton. Plastic is the lightest material of the three and the least expensive. It is completely waterproof but unfortunately is lowest in durability.

Cotton or canvas is available in three fabrics—duck, drill, and poplin. Duck is heaviest, with drill being a lighter material, and poplin the lightest of the three. Whichever cotton material is chosen, the most important factor is thread count (or the number of threads per square inch). This is usually stated for each tent on the shelf, and you owe it to yourself to get the highest thread count possible for the type of tent you want.

Canvas is usually treated to enhance its water repellency (most cotton tents are almost waterproof following this treat-

159

ment). Two types of coating processes may be used. The less expensive method uses a wax-type substance that coats the threads, adding considerable weight and tending to stiffen the material. When the tent is folded, the wax coating thins at the folds, meaning that leaks occasionally spring up where the fabric has been bent. A tent with this preparation can be spotted by noting its sticky or waxy texture. If the fabric is rubbed between the fingertips, a residue remains on the fingers.

The second type of treatment uses a chemical processing that is hardly noticeable to glance or touch. It is the preferable treatment, and be sure the tent you are considering has it. Like most good systems, it does add slightly to the cost of the tent.

Cotton tents are not usually considered waterproof because the basic fiber is porous. Porosity is good, however, because it lets the tent breathe and limits the amount of condensation that accumulates on the walls while you sleep, exhaling carbon dioxide that combines with the air's oxygen in the form of water. The fact that the word "waterproof" is not used to describe cotton tents does not mean they leak. When treated, most will not allow water to penetrate the outer surface unless you touch their inner walls, initiating a capillary action that results in a steady drip. It is a property of cotton to swell when it gets wet, and as the threads enlarge and are forced closer to one another, the tent becomes less pervious to water. (For this reason many campers hose down their cotton tents at home before taking them into the field. Even when the tents are packed dry, enough moisture remains trapped in the fabric to seal it.)

Nylon, in contrast to canvas, is extremely light and can eliminate up to half the weight of an equivalent cotton tent design. But nylon does not have the same water resistance as cotton because the individual threads in the weave do not swell. For this reason, untreated nylon tents will stand nothing more than a light mist. Most nylon packing tents are fabricated from flat-weave nylon taffeta weighing from 1.8 to 2.5 ounces per square yard. The heavier the material, the greater the durability, but also the greater the weight. Another type of nylon material—ripstop—also is commonly used in tent construction. Ripstop features up to about four heavy threads per inch woven into the material. This stops rips from running the length of the fabric and enhances strength. Nylon tents with breathable walls and separate flies often feature taffeta for the walls and coated ripstop for the flies. Heavier-weight nylon with a double coating often is used for the floors. Most nylon tents are waterproofed with materials such as polyurethane, rubber, and vinyl. This makes them totally waterproof and highly wind-resistant, but it precludes their ability to breathe. If you purchase a tent of waterproof nylon, be sure that it has plenty of vents to admit air and prevent sweating. Since the average sleeper exhales about a pint of water during the night, it is all too possible to wake up in the morning under clammy, dripping walls.

Many solutions are being tried to solve the condensation problem. One method combines canvas and nylon, with canvas being used for the roof where the greatest abuse from water is likely, and nylon being used for the tent sidewalls. This provides a lightweight but breathable tent that sheds water. Another solution incorporates a layer of polyurethane foam, bonded inside the waterproof nylon tent to act as an insulator. This design is used in Camp Trails' Chapparal. Still another design, by Warmlite, puts an air space inside a double wall of nonbreathing materials, with the enclosed air space acting as an insulator to offset the effect of temperature differences that cause condensation. Perhaps the most popular solution to the condensation problem, though, is found in a tent made from breathable nylon taffeta that is covered by an exterior nylon

*Camp Trails' Chapparal uses a design incorporating a layer of polyurethane foam bonded inside a waterproof nylon tent. (Photo Camp Trails)*

fly. Tents of this type are comfortable because they eliminate condensation. They seem to have the best of both worlds, the total waterproofing of coated nylon and much more breathability than most canvas tents.

Finally there are plastic tents for use either as a principal sleeping quarter or as an emergency shelter that can be carried in a pocket. Plastic is not the best material for tents of this type, although it is totally waterproof. The problem with pastic is that it tears easily. Before pitching one of these shelters it is a good policy to scour the ground and remove anything abrasive. The most common type of plastic shelter is a simple tube of polyethylene, about 12 feet in circumference. A shelter of this type can be erected by passing a rope through the material and anchoring the rope to a tree at each end. Or the ends can be supported by short poles or sticks. No flaps or netting are provided for this kind of shelter—the ends remain open.

All told, plastic is a marginal material for tents. Perhaps its most exciting quality is that it is inexpensive, so the tents can be thrown away when rips get started.

Large polyethylene sheets are often used as dining flies (awnings), and for this purpose they are most useful. Grommets can be installed with tape reinforcement, and the result is a large, ultralight rain shelter. Given the low cost of a large sheet of plastic, it seems a good investment, perhaps better than a weighty canvas tarp or an expensive coated nylon model.

One factor too seldom discussed in regard to plastic tents and shelters is safety. Most of these tents are very small and windproof. If they should collapse during the night they could cause suffocation by creating the effect of putting yourself inside an oversized baggie and sealing it. The same thing might be said of waterproof nylon tents, but most of these have sufficient volume to enable the occupant to notice the collapse long before the air inside is consumed. In short, it seems best to use plastic only for tarps—not tents—except in emergencies.

When shopping for a tent, there are certain construction features to watch for, features that ensure a quality product that will not let you down when you are camped on the banks of a remote backwater, far from the nearest town.

Generally, two types of seams are used in tent construction: the taped seam and the double lap-fell seam. The tape seam is the weaker of the two, and tents using it should be avoided. In seams of this type the edges of the material are butted and tape is placed over them both—outside and inside. A row of stitching on each side of the seam attaches the material to the tape and holds the seam together. Better is the double lap-fell seam, in which the edges of the fabric are rolled over and interlocked. Two rows of stitching, with each stitch penetrating four layers of material, create a strong seam that will not separate.

Also, when investigating a tent in a dealer's showroom, be sure the seams are straight and there are no loose threads hanging out. Another point to examine in tent construction is the reinforcement of stress areas. Be sure ample reinforcement is provided at points of strain and stress such as roof peaks and ridges, points where tent poles are to be inserted, and where grommets or loops are set to hold tent pegs or stakes.

Ridgelines and roof sleeves usually are reinforced with a double layer of fabric. In canvas tents, rope reinforcement is often used where the walls join the floor at ground level. If this is the case, then grommets should be inserted well away from the edge in a double fold of fabric. Lightweight nylon tents often use nylon webbing for reinforcing all stress points, including side pull-outs. Here, look for double stitching at critical areas such as those in which stake loops are sewn into the material.

Also examine floors. Be sure the floor of any tent you purchase is sufficiently treated to avoid water soaking through. The floor should be durable enough to withstand stones and little sticks that might puncture it. And it should be mildew-proof. The best floors extend a few inches up the sides of the tent to keep splatter from soaking through the fabric in hard rains. Such floors are designated "bathtub floors" because of their shape, even though they are meant to keep water out, not in.

Check flap and window construction carefully. Some tents have outside flaps that must be tied down from the outside. This has disadvantages and advantages. The obvious disadvantage is that you must go out in the rain to adjust the flaps or tie them shut. But the advantage is that the flaps can be utilized as awnings, so they need not necessarily be shut except in the case of driving rains. This is a real help to ventilation. Other tents have flaps that shut from the inside. The best design for this type probably is an inverted "V" with zippers at both sides. This lets you adjust the width of the opening and enables you to close the flap without running out in the rain.

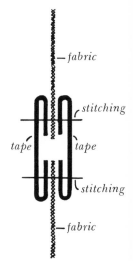

*Taped seam*

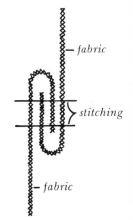

*Double-lap felled seam*

*The two most common types of seams used in tent construction.*

163

Be sure the tent you purchase has sufficient window and door space to provide adequate ventilation; few things are more miserable than a tent with insufficient airflow. The windows and doors should close with zippers made of either metal or self-repairing nylon. Choose zipper configurations you like. Many tents of the separate-fly construction and low-profile versions utilize three zippers on the door, one opening vertically and two joining horizontally at the bottom center. This is a good configuration, for it lets you open only half the door at a time. Other tents utilize a single zipper, running around the ark of a "D" configuration. This too is an excellent type of opening because the single zipper minimizes trouble and provides a simpler design.

Check the type of mosquito netting used—the best is self-repairing, either of nylon or dacron. Often the netting in the door opens in a different way from the flap. For example, the outside flap of a tent may have zippers running down the sides in an inverted "V" while the netting inside utilizes the three-zipper system. This is not a major factor in determining whether or not to buy a tent, but if you foresee difficulty in getting out of layers of material, avoid the tent.

Look over the various types of tent frames available too. Most modern tents utilize exterior framing, so that you need not curl around poles when trying to sleep. Most lightweight tents employ segmented aluminum poles that fit through sleeves sewn into the outside of the tents. Many other tents are suspended from exterior frames by elastic shock cord. This is an excellent design for canvas tents, since they expand and shrink depending on the weather, and the shock cord both gives and takes up slack. In the case of nylon, the shock cord allows flexibility of the material in winds.

Which type of tents are best for canoeing? Many paddlers still prefer the traditional umbrella tent, and professional outfitters in some parts of the country remain wedded to the old-fashioned canvas wall tents. For most paddlers, however, there appear to be two types of tent that are outstanding. They are the compression-rib tents and the breathable nylon tents with separate flies.

Compression-rib tents are available in several configurations in both canvas and nylon. From Thermos comes the world-famous Pop-Tent, typifying the igloo type. These tents are constructed of 8.16-ounce drill with vinyl-nylon floors. Their flaps zip from the inside, and they have a screen door with an awning that also functions as a storm flap. Fiberglass ribs link together to provide an outside framework, and run

through channels sewn to the outside of the tent.

Three models are available. The Giant Pop-Tent is 72 inches high and 100 inches wall to wall. It sleeps four and comes complete with stakes, ropes, and awning poles, and fits a 32-inch carrying case. Shipping weight is 32 pounds. Smaller, but perhaps more appropriate for paddle camping because of its lesser weight, is the two-man version—the camper model. This tent is but 56 inches high and 81 inches wall to wall. It sleeps two and also fits a 32-inch carrying case. Shipping weight is 16 pounds, just half that of the larger version. Also available from Thermos is the pocket camper, a tiny pop-tent 44½ by 80 inches by 42 inches high. This little tent weighs just 9 pounds, and Thermos suggests it for youth outings and father-and-son trips. It appears, however, that the tent is best for paddlers who travel alone.

Another interesting series of compression-rib tents comes from Eureka and consists of the Alpine line of Draw-Tite tents. These tents are high quality, 6.5-ounce combed poplin with floors of vinyl-coated nylon that extend up the sides.

*The Thermos Pop-Tent. (Photo Thermos Products)*

165

The Draw-Tites are suspended from their frames by shock cords, unlike the Thermos models.

What are the advantages of compression-rib tents for paddlers? First, most are rapidly pitched and disassembled, permitting the paddler to make and break camp fast so as to have more time on the water. More important, they do not need staking except in very high winds—an outstanding advantage for paddlers who often must camp where stakes cannot be driven—on sand bars or on rock slabs. Finally, they can be moved after they have been erected. If a person wants to change the direction of the tent in response to changing wind and rain directions, he can simply pick it up and rotate it.

Nylon tents with separate flies also offer several advantages for paddlers. First, they are extremely light. Second, the flies can be erected separately when rain mars the day and an instant shelter is sought. Then there is the comfort afforded by the tent's lack of sweating. These tents are available both in low-profile models and in those models that are high enough to allow the paddler to stand in the center. One of the better-designed of these nylon tents is the Timberline from Eureka. This tent is suspended by shock cords from an exterior aluminum frame; the fly fits over the frame; the floor extends up the sides of the tent and is made of urethane-coated ripstop nylon; the upper side walls are breathable ripstop; the door is the "A" type with nylon zippers and mosquito net; triangular rear windows give sufficient ventilation. The fly is hooded in both the front and rear, which is important because the door is made of breathable fabric that would not withstand a driving rain if exposed to it directly. The total weight of the tent with fly, frame, and stakes is 7 pounds 14 ounces.

Another good design of this type is available from Laacke & Joys. This tent has a less-complicated frame, consisting of an exterior flat-topped "A" frame at mid-tent. "I" poles support the front and rear. The mosquito netting is polyester, and utilizes three zippers. The door employs an "A" configuration, while the back of the tent provides a flap that opens from the inside to provide flow-through ventilation. The highest point of this tent is at the center and measures about five feet, meaning that the occupant can nearly stand in it.

Nylon tents with separate flies are available from most major tentmakers, and should be considered when buying a tent for paddle camping. Even though they weigh slightly more than nylon tents with coated walls, their extra flexibility and comfort are merits no paddler should overlook.

One type of shelter particularly adaptable to paddle camping is the jungle hammock. You may remember that when you were a child, jungle hammocks were advertised in comic books and army surplus catalogues for as little as $6. As the years went by, the price rose to around $13. Thousands of these military hammocks were sold as surplus at prices that belied their utility. Then the jungle hammock disappeared, having been apparently, sold out. To my knowledge, no one today is producing the design.

Nevertheless, it is conceivable that many people still have these hammocks packed away in their attics, and they are unsurpassed in practicality for the paddler. The jungle hammock consisted of a canvas hammock with a waterproof roof and mosquito netting sewn in between forming an enclosure. It proved itself perfect for rugged military use in the insect-infested jungles of Borneo and the South Pacific. It was airy, comfortable, and kept a person off the ground and away from snakes and other crawling creatures. These hammocks are not big enough to accommodate gear, but they are very light. By combining a hammock for each camper with a plastic or coated nylon tarp under which gear can be stowed, a very comfortable campsite can be arranged.

What are the advantages of jungle hammocks for paddlers? First of all, they can be hung rapidly, just by tying ropes to two trees. Second, a paddler does not need to level the ground or pick up debris. Third, the hammocks do not need staking, unless they are to be pitched on the ground. For paddlers who want to keep on the move, there are few better pieces of equipment. If you still have one of these hammocks, it is worth its weight in gold. Don't throw it away—take it out and use it. It is a shame that some tentmaker does not return to this design and reissue it. It is perfect for modern styles of camping.

# 12

## Sleeping Bags and Mattresses

Hitting the hay at the end of a day of heavy exercise is one of the most pleasant experiences a person can have . . . or it can be the most exasperating. When a camper nestles down into a warm, soft cocoon, his worries terminate for about eight hours. At the end of that time he wakes up refreshed and recharged, ready to paddle on, to find new trails, and to explore another length of river. But should his bed be lumpy, or fail to supply enough warmth, he tosses and turns through the hours of darkness, never more than half asleep, mostly wide awake and acutely aware of his discomfort. The next day he emerges stiff and tired, hardly enthusiastic about breaking camp and meeting the challenges and adventures ahead.

The entire mood, of a camping trip can depend on the quality of the camper's bedding. Of all the places not to skimp, this is perhaps the foremost. You can purchase sleeping bags from as little as $6 to well over $400. Most paddlers need spend nowhere near the top of the range, for the most expensive bags are comfort-tested to extremes of 70 or more degrees below zero and are intended for conditions canoeists and kayakists should never encounter. A bag in the $50 to $75 range is probably worth investing in for comfort and durability. And if you do not plan to stretch your camping trips into the chilly nights of fall, you can probably get by spending less.

The first thing prospective buyers should realize about a sleeping bag is that it does not impart warmth. Rather, it holds body heat by trapping dead air in its insulation to form a buffer between the warmth inside and the cold outside. Whatever type of insulation the bag uses, it is composed of fibers that interlock, leaving thousands of little air spaces between them. The thicker the insulation, the more air pockets, hence the more heat-holding power.

Two kinds of insulation are common in today's sleeping bags: natural down or synthetic fibers. Down has long proven superior for keeping campers warm, just as it does the waterfowl from which it is taken. Thus it is the standard by which synthetic fibers are evaluated. To date, no synthetic has been developed that can boast the same insulating power as down on a pound-for-pound basis. But some of the better synthetics come close and have other advantages.

When shopping for a sleeping bag, you will find that two types of down are available—duck down and goose down. The latter is generally considered better, but the former is somewhat less expensive and does a perfectly satisfactory job. In other words, you are not likely to feel a difference in warmth between a bag with three pounds of duck down and a bag with three pounds of goose down, providing the bags are of the same size and construction. Bags from reputable manufacturers with two or three pounds of down should serve paddlers well for summer camping. Warmth is really a question of loft, and such bags have sufficient loft if fluffed before you sleep in them.

The advantage of down for the canoe or kayak camper is that it compresses into a very small volume, so that a large sleeping bag can be crammed into a small stuffbag. This minimizes the room taken up in the boat. The disadvantage of down is that it loses its loft and its ability to hold warmth when it gets wet. And it takes an extremely long time to dry out a wet down sleeping bag. Once it gets wet, the paddler is virtually without a place to sleep. Therefore, if choosing a down bag, pack it tightly in a waterproof plastic bag and stow it where it will not take splash. Do not pack it in the bottom of the boat where it can be soaked if water is shipped over the gunwales.

Synthetic fibers are composed of such well-known materials as polyester, acrylic, and dacron. They have the fibrous characteristic of down and operate in the same way, by providing pockets of dead air for insulation. Bags containing synthetics are bulky to pack and often must be rolled, rather than stuffed into small sacks.

Why, then, are synthetic bags gaining steadily in popularity? Principally because they cost less than down bags. Where weight and bulk are not critical, synthetic bags may represent a better investment. But there is another feature of synthetic insulation that is especially appreciated by paddle campers and others whose camping brings them around water. Some of the better synthetics, such as DuPont's Dacron II or Celanese's Fortrel PolarGuard, do not lose their loft when wet, and hence can hold some warmth. Moreover, they are fast-drying and take only a fraction as long on the clothesline as down bags. These are real advantages, and considering that it takes only about 1.4 pounds of a synthetic fiber to equal the heat-holding ability of a pound of down, you are picking up only a few pounds and a small amount of bulk for some very real advantages.

After deciding upon the type of insulation, the next decision to be made in selecting a bag for paddle camping is the type of cover the bag should have. Most ultralightweight bags feature nylon taffeta or ripstop covers and linings. These are smooth and easy to slide in and out of. The only problem with nylon linings is that they are not as absorbent of perspiration as is, say, flannel. For this reason, people who are normally irritated by the synthetic fabrics in clothes may prefer bags with other types of linings. Cotton sheeting is used as both a cover and a lining in some of the least expensive bags. It is not especially durable, but it is comfortably breathable. Cotton duck and denim are used in bags slightly higher on the price scale, adding extra durability. Poplin and duck cover fabrics are used in rugged bags where weight is not a prime factor.

Beware bags with waterproof bottoms. Sleeping bags must let moisture escape freely in order to keep the person inside warm and dry. Rather than relying on a waterproof sleeping bag bottom, carry a ground cloth.

Other factors to be aware of in selecting sleeping bags are zippers, stitching, and the type of construction used to hold the insulation in place. Zippers should be rugged, whether of metal or nylon. You must choose between a zipper that runs halfway down the side of the bag or a full-length zipper. The former should be preferred where maximum warmth is sought, while the latter is designed to provide more comfort for warm-weather sleeping. Some bags provide maximum flexibility by using zippers that open from either end, allowing you to adjust the bag for your comfort. Some bags can be zipped together to form double bags, ideal for couples who canoe together. In any case, an insulation-filled baffle should be positioned inside the bag behind the zipper to prevent the escape of heat.

In many synthetic bags, there will be stitching in the body of the bag. Essentially, the insulation is formed into battens that are bonded together to keep insulation from shifting.

Stitching, penetrating through the bag and battens, holds the insulation in place but creates spots where there is insufficient loft to hold heat. In down bags you may or may not be able to observe stitching. It is wise to check the construction, whatever the bag may look like. Most down bags make use of one or another type of baffle system to keep the insulation from shifting, yet eliminate spots where loft is destroyed and cold can creep in (or heat can creep out). In baffle construction, strips of fabric are sewn between inner and outer covers to form compartments for the down. Popular are such constructions as the box baffle, slant-box baffle and overlapping "V" tube.

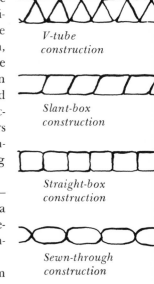

*V-tube construction*

*Slant-box construction*

*Straight-box construction*

*Sewn-through construction*

By shape, sleeping bags fall roughly into three categories— rectangular, tapered, and mummy. Each is designed for a different type of sleeper, and if you do not fit any of the categories exactly, some shopping may turn up a bag that combines these shapes in a way that suits you.

Rectangular bags are squared off at the ends, making them the best type for sleepers who toss and turn or roll over in their sleep. There is plenty of room in these bags to stretch your legs and to roll without binding. The disadvantages of rectangular bags are their relatively large interiors which the body must heat and their requirement for extra fabric that adds weight and makes them bulky to pack.

*Coleman's Dacron II sleeping bag exemplifies the rectangular configuration. (Photo Coleman)*

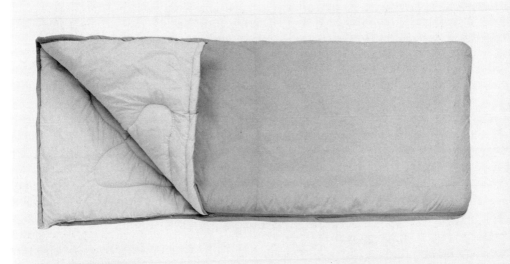

At the other extreme is the mummy bag, designed to be as form-fitting as possible. It tapers toward the feet and provides a hood that can be drawn around the face by a draw string. The advantages of the mummy bag are that a minimum of fabric is used (meaning that it can be packed in a small stuffbag) and there is virtually no extra volume for the body to heat. The problem is that the sleeper is confined pretty much to lying in one position.

*Sierra Designs'
Superlight
illustrates the
mummy
configuration.
(Drawings from
Sierra Designs)*

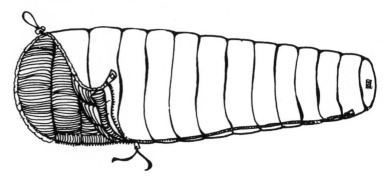

In between the rectangular and mummy bags is the tapered bag, an effort to provide some room for movement (although not a lot) and at the same time cut down on fabric. No hood is featured on most bags of this type, and various degrees of taper at the foot are available.

An observation on sleeping bags is in order, since there are so many factors involved in selecting the one that will be most comfortable and suitable. Most paddlers who ply the streams primarily on weekends do so between the latter part of March and mid-October (assuming a temperate climate). If you plan to stretch your paddling into the extremes of this period, you may encounter chilly nights, even frost. A good bag for this

*Coleman's Dacron
II bag with a
tapered design.
(Photo Coleman)*

type of paddle camping would be either a down or synthetic bag comfort-tested to about 20 degrees Fahrenheit. If, however, you restrict camping only to the hot months of summer, you can probably get by with a bag comfort-tested down to only 40 or 50 degrees. In choosing a bag it is a good idea to go about ten degrees lower than the coldest weather expected. The reason for this is that you cannot altogether trust comfort ratings. Many reputable firms rate conservatively, but others exaggerate. Also, the bottom range of comfort depends in large part on you—whether you are a "hot" or "cold" sleeper.

When buying sleeping bags, you get just about what you pay for; you will not go wrong by investing money in this area. On the other hand, for warm-weather camping only, not much may be needed in the way of warmth or, assuming you have a good tent, durability. For several years I used a $6 sleeping bag in Wisconsin, and it always proved adequate from about the middle of June to the middle of August. A $30 bag with a 30-to-40-degree comfort rating should extend that season from May through September.

All the warmth in the world will not make you comfortable enough to sleep if you are used to sleeping on a soft mattress at home and then must settle for sleeping on hard clay or rock in the wilds. You will wake up with aching ribs and a stiff back and neck—if you manage to sleep at all. For this reason, all but the most experienced outdoor enthusiasts carry mattresses with them.

Traditionally popular has been the air mattress, an extremely lightweight adjunct to comfortable slumber. Air mattresses are constructed from all sorts of plastic, but the better ones are fabricated of impregnated canvas for extra durability. Air mattresses feature two inherent disadvantages. First, you have to blow them up and this takes considerable lung power. Even worse is their propensity—almost a perversion —to puncture. The problem is minimized in the more expensive and durable mattresses, but it never seems to be eliminated. If you do not suffer a tear that renders the device totally unusable, you may suffer a worse fate—the slow leak. This means you go to sleep on a plump mattress, ensconced in comfort, only to awake lying on hard ground.

There is, however, one substantial advantage to the air mattress. It packs extremely compactly, leaving room for other things. If you prefer an air mattress, buy one with "I"-beam construction, preferably a rubberized fabric model for about

$25. Be prepared to tote a few extra pounds compared to a less expensive model. A plausible alternative to the traditional air mattress in which there is only one air compartment, and one that seems infinitely preferable, is the new Air Lift mattress, composed of lightweight ripstop nylon sewn into chambers. Into the chambers are inserted individually inflated vinyl tubes. If one should deflate, there is still plenty of mattress inflated—a clever twist on the "divide and conquer" concept.

If there is space to pack them, foam pads are a better choice than air mattresses. Pads made of Ensolite closed-cell foam or polyurethane foam are available full length or three-quarter length to support the torso. They are about $1\frac{1}{2}$ to 2 inches thick, and the more expensive ones are covered with breathable fabric. Although bulky when rolled up, the pads are very light, often lighter than folded air mattresses. They provide sufficient comfort to help the weary get to sleep. Prices for these pads range from about $5 to $17.

With tent, sleeping bag, and mattress, your essential shelter needs are met. Overall, the best advice is to get the lightest-weight gear you can in all categories, but be sure that the lightweight equipment is substantial enough to keep you comfortable in the circumstances under which you anticipate camping.

Heat and light are crucial on almost all camping trips. Man, having long domesticated fire, depends on its attributes and is hard-pressed to survive without them. In many areas it is still possible to roast or fry meals over the embers of a wood fire, which also provides light for enjoyable evening activities after supper. But there are an increasing number of areas where fires are allowed only by permit, if at all. And when it rains, building an open fire can be a painstaking process of splitting wet wood to expose dry surfaces.

Because the wood supply is sometimes unpredictable and making open fires involves time-consuming labor, many canoe and kayak campers prefer to carry their fire supply along in metal cases. This enables them to leave the environment without a scar of ashes, and it provides a reliable source of heat for cooking no matter what the weather. In fact, even campers who rely primarily on wood fires find camp stoves a valuable aid when the going gets rough.

It is appropriate to discuss stoves and lanterns together because both must operate from a source of fuel. It is also a decided benefit to make sure when purchasing both pieces of equipment that they use the same fuel.

What type of stove is best for the canoeist or kayakist? Obviously, he needs the lightest one possible that provides a sufficiently hot flame for his cooking purposes. He does not want any extra weight to carry on portages, or any extra bulk to pack; he does want to be able to make dinner as quickly as possible after putting in a hard day's paddling. Moreover, if his stove is convenient enough, he may not mind using it during brief stops for the noon meal. An array of stoves is available, ranging from compact units weighing only a few ounces to three-burner models designed to cook full meals for a campful of people. In price, they range from about $17 to $25 for single-burner models to $20 to $40 for two-burner stoves, depending on the quality of the model sought.

For paddlers who travel alone or with only one other person, there seems to be little reason to use more than a single-burner stove. However, do not rush out and buy the lightest single-burner stove until you ascertain that it can perform all the functions you are going to demand of it. A two-burner model might be heavy and a little hard to pack, especially in a kayak, but it provides the convenience of heating a meal and warming water for washing dishes at the same time, or of preparing separate courses simultaneously. This frees you to custom-make your meals, and it means you will be less reliant on hashes, stews, and other dishes that blend the ingredients of the meal together. Moreover, most two-burner models have windscreens built into their lids, a decided advantage for cooking in the open. Finally, two-burner models provide stability. They will not tip over easily, and there is room on the grill to set pans without fear that they will fall off the stove.

Contrast these advantages to the single-burner models that force you to prepare dinner courses one at a time, compelling you to rely on one-pot casseroles as much as possible. Few one-burner models provide windscreens, so their flames are subject to the whims of the wind. Many of them are comparatively unstable; and their grills are usually much smaller than the pans to be set on them. You will recognize this drawback for what it is when you pour water into a kettle or try to stir your meal, only to have the pan tip off the burner and spill its contents upon the ground.

This is not to say the single-burners do not have their place. They do. But you have to get used to cooking on them. Their major advantage is that they reduce weight to a minimum and can be packed right in your packsack along with the food.

Much of the single-burner versus double-burner decision depends on your attitude toward the camping aspects of your trip and on the general bulk you have to pack. If camping is to be a last-minute condescension to the necessity of sleep and you are satisfied to keep it spartan, prefer the single-burner. Also, if you intend to rely primarily on wood fires, there is seldom need for more than a single burner. On the other hand, if you can make room for it, if you do not care to spend the time building wood fires, and if you want the luxury of eating meals whose courses are ready at the same time the way they are at home, opt for an extra burner.

Whatever the general configuration of the stove you prefer,

it is important to know that both single- and double-burner versions are available in models using a number of different kinds of fuel. Stoves can burn white gas or lantern fuel, propane, butane, kerosene, or alcohol. Each fuel has its positive and negative points and you should be aware of them in making your final selection.

Long the most popular type of fuel has been lantern fuel or white gas—the fuel used in the famous and dependable Coleman camp stoves. Stoves using this fuel provide an intense flame that is easily controllable, and they make cooking easy. There are, however, two drawbacks to white gas. First, the fuel tanks on many gas stoves require pumping to establish pressure. Second, there is the problem of carrying extra liquid fuel in a boat, with the attendant possibilities of spills, leaks, and fire. For the most part, the first difficulty seems to be a minor price to pay for the dependability and excellent heat provided by this system. The second problem, carrying extra fuel, can be solved by using a tightly closed aluminum cylinder that can be purchased from most mail-order outfitters.

Propane provides a relatively hot flame and is preferred by many go-light campers for its cleanliness. Sealed cylinders are used that do not need pumping because they are already pressurized. The problem with propane is that you are forced to carry at least two cylinders, because there is no meter to point out when one cylinder is running low. If you happen to start with a half-empty cylinder from a previous trip, you may have to make a fast switch to the new one right in the middle of frying the morning omelette. In the case of the white-gas stoves, the amount of fuel needed for short trips can be estimated and you may not have to carry extra fuel at all. To do this with propane, you must start with a full cylinder, wasting a partially used one that must be left at home.

Butane offers the same conveniences as propane, but has one shortcoming: it does not vaporize below 32 degrees. This should be no problem to most paddlers, but those who want to do some camping at colder times of the year would do well to choose another source of fuel.

Kerosene and alcohol offer the same spillage and fire problems as white gas, but many stoves that employ the two fuels are extremely lightweight. Also, they burn with sufficient heat to make them very attractive to paddlers who wish to shave pounds off their gear.

For all-around use there is no better stove than the Coleman two-burner #413G499. Here are the hot flame and stable configuration that are hard to beat, all wrapped up in a durable steel case. If you prefer propane, likely alternatives are available from Primus, Zebco, Trailblazer, and others.

Touring paddlers who do not want to carry the weight of a two-burner stove, for all its advantages, should consider the single-burner lightweights. The disadvantages of having only one burner can be offset easily by canoeing parties that travel in more than one canoe and pack more than one stove. Or you can simply stick to the one-pot freeze-dried meals. First among the white-gas models is the Coleman Sportster, comparatively heavy and large for a one-burner stove, but hot-burning and rugged. This stove, like the two-burner model, requires pumping to establish pressure. Other white-gas stoves are, however, lighter than the Coleman. Among them are the 80, 8R, 99, and 111B from Optimus and the SVEA 123. Except for the 80, the Optimus offerings boast a flat, low construction that makes them stable. The Optimus 80 and SVEA 123 are upright cylinders and cannot be judged quite as stable.

Optimus also offers three kerosene stoves—96L, 00L, and 48 —ascending in size. Generally these stoves don't burn as hot as the white-gas stoves, but they do collapse into boxes and are equally as portable. Moreover, they offer longer burning times.

Propane and butane models are available from Primus, Optimus, GAZ, Browning, and others. Many of them feature what is known as the "grasshopper" configuration. This means that they consist of a burner supported by two slim but sturdy legs, with the propane or butane cylinder functioning as the third leg. Not only do they physically resemble grasshoppers, but they are excellent for use where the grass is fairly high because their burners stand above, straddling or "hopping" the grass. The disadvantage of these stoves is that they are

*Left to right: Coleman Sportster, SVEA 123, Optimus 80. (Photos Coleman, SVEA, and Optimus)*

difficult to use on sand or soft earth. When weight is placed on them, the slender legs sink into the ground, tilting the burner and tipping the contents of your dinner. On firm ground, however, they are at their best, for the three-legged configuration gives them the widest base of all the single-burners.

STOVE COMPARISON TABLE*

| Stove Model | Capacity Pints | Burning Time Minutes (1) | Boiling Time—Minutes | |
| --- | --- | --- | --- | --- |
| | | | Sea Level (2) | 14,000 Ft. (3) |
| SVEA 123 | .35 | 60 | 6-8 | 8-11 |
| Optimus 80 | .45 | 75 | 6-8 | 8-11 |
| Optimus 8R & 99 | .30 | 45 | 7-9 | 8-11 |
| Optimus 96L | .50 | 120 | 7-9 | 11-12 |
| Optimus 00L | 1.00 | 150 | 4-6 | 8-9 |
| Optimus 48 | 1.75 | 240 | 5-7 | 7-12 |
| Optimus 111B | 1.00 | 150 | 3-5 | 4-6 |
| Bleuet S 200 | Cartridge | 180 | 10-12 | 12-15 |

(1) Burning time is at continuous full flame. In actual use, burning time could be extended considerably.
(2) Time required to bring 1 qt. water at $70°F$ to boil $212°F$ in uncovered pot.
(3) Time required to bring 1 qt. water at $35°F$ to boil $187°F$ in covered pot.
* (*Table prepared by Recreational Equipment Incorporated*)

Recreation Equipment Incorporated, an outfitter that supplies many of the lightweight single-burner stoves, has published in its catalogue a table comparing the fuel capacity,

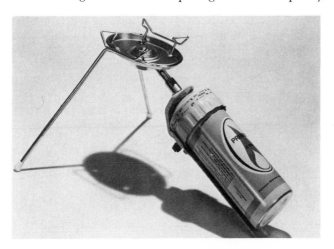

*Primus "grasshopper" design. (Photo Primus)*

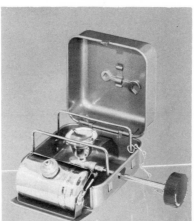

*Optimus 111B and Optimus 8R folding stoves. (Photos Optimus)*

179

burning times, and heat (measured in boiling time at constant sea level) for the stoves it markets. This information should be helpful in assisting you to choose a model suitable for your needs.

When it comes to lighting your camp, the most popular lanterns, like the most popular stoves, burn white gas, propane, or butane. Kerosene lanterns also are available, but they are odorous, and are therefore less attractive. The relative strong and weak points of the various fuel sources are much the same as for the corresponding stoves. The white-gas lanterns are extremely bright but require pumping and must be filled with messy liquid fuel. As in the case of stoves, these disadvantages can be overcome. If you are careful to fill your tank in the open (*not in your tent*) and *not to smoke* while you do it, or not to refill it while it is still burning, you should have little trouble. And the pumping is not really difficult. Propane and butane lanterns are cleaner than white-gas or kerosene lanterns: their fuel is in cylinders and they need no pumping. Generally they do not supply the candlepower gasoline lanterns do, but they are entirely sufficient. Again, stay away from butane if you plan to camp in sub-freezing temperatures, since it does not vaporize below freezing.

Most of the stove manufacturers—Coleman, Primus, Optimus, Garcia, Trailblazer, and others—supply lanterns to complete their heat-light systems. A review of the various models is not provided here because most of the lanterns from the various sources are closely competitive. One thing to watch for when buying a lantern, however, is that the base be sufficiently stable to support it without tipping, even when the lantern is placed on uneven ground or when it must stand in a wind.

Both gasoline and propane lanterns are available in either single- or double-mantle versions. Generally the single-mantle variety should do the job, although double mantles are unsurpassed for lighting large areas with a bright white light. The most popular butane lanterns are single-mantle models from Garcia and Primus—the L200 and the Explorer 2220 respectively. They provide the same light output in terms of candlepower, but the Primus model is almost a pound lighter.

Lanterns are not as popular with touring paddlers as they are with some other campers. One of the reasons is that a lantern takes up a considerable amount of space in the boat. The hollow glass globe usurps room in a pack that might better be used for other things. Also, lanterns take a banging in the bottom of the pack or in the canoe, and their globes are easily broken or their mantles dislodged. To date only two manufacturers provide carrying cases for their lanterns, Coleman (whose case is an optional feature) and Garcia for its L400 lantern in which the lantern body itself acts as the carrying case. The Coleman carrying cases are steel, with a baked-enamel finish, and require considerable packing space.

For these reasons, most paddlers prefer flashlights powered by dry cells rather than lanterns. Flashlights are compact, easy to pack in packsacks, rugged, and reasonably dependable. Moreover, models are available that are watertight and float. And if you want a mellow light for your campsite rather than a focused beam, there is even the Ray-O-Vac Nite Owl 90S, with a non-glare globe that diffuses light over 360 degrees.

*Left: The Coleman double-mantle lantern, a white gas lantern with extreme candlepower. Center: the Primus 2220 butane lantern. Right: the Primus 2183 propane lantern. (Photos Coleman and Primus)*

# 14

## Packs

With backpacking mushrooming as a major sport, hundreds of different packs are offered by a host of manufacturers. Essentially the backpacker makes use of four different types of packs: the fanny pack, the day pack, the rucksack, and the full pack and frame.

The fanny pack is a small bag that suspends from a belt tied around the hiker's waist. The day pack is larger and is strapped to the shoulders. The most popular design currently used on day packs is the teardrop shape, desirable because it rides well on the back. The rucksack is a medium-sized pack usually having two, but possibly more, outer pockets. It is sometimes divided within. Many rucksacks have integral frames, but some mount on external frames. Finally, the full-sized pack may be constructed either in a two-thirds length or full length. The two-thirds length pack is designed so that a sleeping bag or tent can be slung underneath on the frame, while the full-length type accommodates this gear inside.

It is not our purpose to discuss the pros and cons of the multitude of designs available in packs, but rather to point out a few special requirements that paddlers have, and that should be kept in mind when choosing a pack for paddling. Whenever possible, it is best to choose a boat before buying a pack. Different boats require packs with different shapes. For example, if you paddle a kayak, you probably will not want a full-length pack with a frame—it just won't fit into the boat. You are better off with either day packs, or small square packs with no frames at all—for example, the Boy Scout haversack. Sport-type kayaks of rigid fiberglass, with sharply defined space under the decks, require small packs, and it is wise to match pack to boat with a measuring stick. Larger kayaks such as Folbots and Kleppers can accommodate small, two-thirds type packs without frames if they are lashed upright to the center braces. These packs should not stand so high that they interfere with placement of spray covers.

Canoes can handle larger packs than kayaks: packs that are

*Camp Trails'
Vagabond fanny
pack. (Photo Camp
Trails)*

*Camp Trails'
ALPAK day pack.
(Photo Camp
Trails)*

183

deeper, and packs with frames. This gives them an advantage when it comes to portaging, for the more gear you can carry on your back in a single trip, the faster the portage. New from Camp Trails in 1974 was the Kenora, a packsack designed especially for canoeing. It exemplifies the large, deep pack that can be borne by a canoe. It is a straight-through bag that extends to the bottom of its frame. It is designed so that the canoe can rest atop it when portaging, removing some of the weight from your shoulders. The Kenora is made from urethane-coated nylon, with Cordura on the storm flap and the bottom for durability. Four large outside pockets feature desirable covered zippers. Lash rings are also featured so the pack can be tied to the canoe. The medium width of the pack is designed to fit between the canvas gunwales. The overall dimensions of the Kenora are 31 inches x 14½ inches x 8½ inches and its weight is only 26 ounces.

Whatever type of pack is chosen, it should be made from canvas or nylon in one of various weaves and weights. The best nylon is 11-ounce Cordura, the most serviceable and durable of the materials used for packs. Water-repellent, urethane-coated nylon also is extremely light. Since weight is not the problem for the paddler that it is for the backpaper, waterproof or water-repellent duck may be perfectly satisfactory, and it is less expensive than nylon.

In choosing a pack for paddling, remember that there are many times when you will want to dig into the pack for small miscellaneous items of gear while you are on the water. The pack will either be flat in the bottom of the boat or propped on a thwart and lashed in. Either way, it is inconvenient to have to open the pack and rummage through it. The problem is compounded when you find what you are looking for and extract it, only to have other gear fall into the cavity and become scrambled. Much of this problem can be eliminated by choosing a pack with as many outside pockets as possible. With advance planning these pockets can be used to keep small, much-used items of gear readily at hand—items such as ponchos, pliers, and nylon jackets.

Another factor to consider is compartmentalization within the pack. Arguments may be made for packs with a single large cavity as well as for those with at least two major cavities. The single large cavity is easier to pack in some instances, depending on the type of gear you have. But the double-cavity model helps organize gear so that it is easier to find, and you need not disorganize the entire pack every time you retrieve something from it.

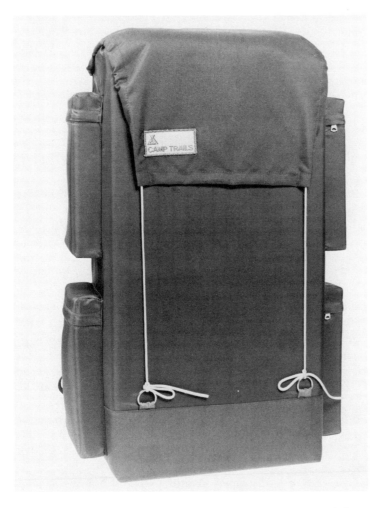

*Camp Trails'
Kenora pack,
designed especially
for canoeing.
(Photo Camp
Trails)*

The question of how to carry your sleeping bag and foam pad should be considered when you purchase a pack. Need these items fit into the pack itself? If you own a canoe that can hold a large full-length pack and frame, you may prefer a full-length pack that will hold your sleeping bag and foam pad inside, since it provides a convenient, water-repellent cover for items that must necessarily be kept dry. If you own a kayak, it may be to your advantage to pack the pads and sleeping bags separately and to stuff them under the decks so as to achieve maximum utilization of space.

If you plan to pack separately items that must be kept dry, there are polyethylene bags available in which to put them. Waterproof nylon stuffsacks for this purpose are available at most outfitters, although a simple plastic garbage bag pilfered

185

from the kitchen cupboard does a commendable job for less money. A step above the garbage bag are the waterproof canoe and kayak gear bags from Great World, 250 Farm's Village Road, West Simsbury, Connecticut 06092, a mail-order house specializing in equipment for canoeing and kayaking. These gear bags are yellow, heavy-duty polyethylene and polypropylene with sure-seal tops. They feature double walls for protecting not only sleeping gear, but items such as cameras, film, underwear, binoculars, radios, etc. They are airtight and are said to float in the event of a capsize. Their price is about $9 per bag.

Basically the paddler need not concern himself with the fine points of pack design the way many backpackers do, for the paddler's maximum stint with the pack on his back will probably be only a few hundred yards. The important questions to ask yourself when examining packs are: Does the pack fit the boat? Is it sufficiently waterproof to protect gear in the event of heavy rain? Does it have enough exterior pockets so important items are readily at hand? Is a frame for the pack needed and, if so, can the boat accommodate it? Is the pack large enough to hold sufficient supplies for the kind of trips taken most frequently, or is more than one pack needed? Is a single-cavity or multiple-compartment design preferred? Is the construction of the pack in question strong enough so that the pack will bear up under the type of camping planned?

When you find the pack that provides the best answers to these questions, examine it carefully for quality. There should be no crooked seams. Reinforcements should be provided where the straps meet the bag and at any other places where there will be stress. Zippers should preferably be nylon, and should be covered so that sand and water will not get into them. The pack that meets these criteria will be satisfactory for your paddle needs.

# The Inexpense of Equipping Yourself

M any hobbies consume an inordinate percentage of their devotee's income. Thousands of dollars, for instance, can be invested in antique cars, racehorses, guns, speedboats, and even bicycles. Camping trailers can run into several thousand dollars and motor homes even more. In many of these diversions, fuel and maintenance costs absorb extra money every year. By comparison, the paddler, who has only three essential pieces of equipment to buy, can afford his hobby and enjoy it to the fullest while remaining a comparative piker. Most people will at most find cost a temporary barrier to buying the right kind of equipment.

Having examined canoes, kayaks, inflatables, and appropriate camping gear, let's discuss what this equipment will cost altogether.

The first—and usually the single most expensive piece of equipment you need—is your boat. Prices for new boats range from under $100 for small, single-man craft to over $800 for outfits complete with accessories such as sail and splash covers. You should be able to buy a suitable craft from a reputable firm for around $250. If you are handy, kits can reduce this cost to about half the price of factory-finished units (see Part II for specifics).

In addition to a boat, you will need paddles. Three canoe paddles (always carry an extra) or two double-bladed kayak paddles should cost about $25.

The last item that is an absolute must is a life preserver. Legally, in almost every state, one safety device is required for each person in the boat. A pair of safety cushions can cost as little as $10. Vests that fit over the torso like jackets (Type III) cost anywhere from $14 to $20 apiece—but they offer style and comfort.

Total the expenditures for your boat and related equipment. Assuming $250 for a craft, $25 for paddles, and $15 for life preservers, we get a total cost of about $290. If your needs dictate only a small craft, or if you can build your own boat from a kit, you can probably cut this initial investment to around $200. Either way, when comparing this expenditure to the money needed to equip a runabout with a high-powered motor, you are probably spending only about one-tenth of the runabout's purchase price. If you put your canoe or kayak to good use, you can have a lot of fun for a very minimal investment. In fact, the investment is so small that you may want to add other miscellany as time goes by: a spray cover, sailing equipment, a motor bar and small outboard, etc. In any case, considering the virtual indestructibility of most of today's paddlecraft, the money spent is incredibly small when amortized over the boat's life. Even if it lasts only ten years, the yearly investment should not be much over $30.

One thing the budget-minded paddler will appreciate is that he can use old-style camping equipment if he has any. There is no need to invest immediately in a lightweight tent if an old canvas wall tent is languishing in the garage. A large Coleman stove and lantern will serve well on overnight trips, and you may even be able to tote a cooler along, depending on the nature of the trip. Of course, paddling is easier and pitching camp is quicker and less work with many of the modern lightweight equivalents of older gear. But the carrying capacity of a canoe or kayak makes it possible to stretch your expenditure for camping equipment over a period of months or even years. You can purchase a new piece of equipment whenever enough money is saved up and still enjoy excellent paddling in the meantime.

Extended trips require camping gear, and you should not skimp when it comes to paying for that of the best quality. Once you start buying lightweight equipment, you will take extra pride in your gear and in its proper use, and constantly try to improve it.

Having acquired the three essentials for paddle adventure—boat, paddles, and safety devices—approximately what should you expect to spend on basic camping gear? The cost of a tent can vary greatly, depending on the style, size, material, and quality of the model you select. Costs range from less than $50 for two-man backpacker-style tents of nylon to well over $400 for lightweight tents designed for use in any weather—including high altitudes in sub-zero temperature. When all is said and done, you should certainly be able to purchase a highly satisfactory tent for less than $150, perhaps considerably less.

After your tent, the next most important items for camping are your sleeping bag and mattress. Again, prices vary. Of course, there are inexpensive bags available for approximately

$10 but these are suspect. If you are out for summer paddle camping only, a good lightweight backpacker's sleeping bag can be purchased for around $50. If you plan to make your bag do double duty for winter camping, you can easily spend over $200.

Mattresses should not cost over $10 apiece whether foam or air.

Once you are settled on shelter and sleeping gear, you must consider your stove and lantern. Whatever your choice, you are ill-advised to spend over $40 (total) for a good, long-lasting stove and lantern.

With shelter, sleeping gear, cooking facility, and light you have accumulated the most fundamental and most indispensable equipment. You will still want a good canteen, cooking kit, ax, saw, shovel, perhaps a tarp, a folding bucket, and other miscellaneous small items. All told, these items need not cost more than another $50.

We have been tossing out round figures—figures that are averages extrapolated after a thorough investigation of what is available from outfitters. On some gear you will want to spend more than has been suggested, but on most equipment there is plenty of room for cost-cutting. The figures we have discussed are deliberately on the high side. In this way, when expenditures are added together they provide a generous assessment of what it costs to outfit yourself for canoe or kayak camping.

Considering $150 for a tent, a generous $100 for two sleeping bags, $20 for mattresses, $40 for a stove and lantern, and another $50 for miscellaneous, you can outfit yourself and a partner with very adequate basic gear for around $360. Be assured, however, that you can equip yourself for comfortable camping of considerable duration for about half the price by buying the lowest-cost gear for situations that give it little use or stress.

Even if you opt for top quality and spend the $360, your investment can be made over a period of years. And when you add the cost of camping gear to the cost of your boat, your total output is still about $660 (or as little as $350 if you can be satisfied with inexpensive equipment). For this price, you are basically equipped to undertake a satisfying hobby, to explore areas that few people reach, to discover excellent fishing spots, and to participate as a full-fledged enthusiast in one of America's fastest-growing outdoor sports. The arbitrary figure of $660 may represent a significant chunk of the family budget, but spread over a number of years it becomes minimal.

189

Perhaps it is not altogether fair to compare the cost of outfitting for paddle adventure to the price of purchasing equipment for other water hobbies, but it is interesting and provocative nevertheless. Buying a runabout fiberglass boat, for instance, can cost anywhere from about $1500 to $5000. Then you need a trailer to pull the boat behind your car—another $150 to $400. In addition you need the same safety devices that are needed for a canoe or kayak. If you plan to leave the runabout docked in a slip at a marina, you must buy a canvas cover for it. And you pay several hundred dollars a year for slip rental. Neither outboards nor inboards are notably economical on gas, and premixed gas, if you can still get it, costs upward of 70 cents a gallon in many areas. In addition, there are continuing expenses for engine maintenance and occasional hull repair.

When all is said and done, the cost of purchasing a small fiberglass runabout, at the very least, is approximately triple the cost of completely outfitting yourself for paddling.

# PART FOUR

# HOW TO PLAN AHEAD

## Mapping Your Trip and Scouting the Area

You have just bought a graceful canoe or kayak. All the accessories needed to launch it to adventure are at hand. The boat is full of camping gear, bundled and lashed. You cast off the lines and dip your paddle, easing away from the shore. An unspoiled green world awaits, stretching to the limit of your vision—and imagination.

Up to now, this book has helped you select equipment that is comfortable, practical, and sturdy; and it has illustrated the elementary paddle strokes. What other knowledge should you have in order to use that equipment on safe, enjoyable trips? The beginner usually knows little about watercourses before traveling them. But he can muster sufficient knowledge to keep himself safe and to know the distances he must cover.

Many short trips on popular paddle trails require a minimum of advance planning. But extended trips and journeys in remote areas make it critical to know the direction, length, and difficulty beforehand. The best way to learn about a paddle trail is from a map. And the best maps are produced by canoeing clubs, the American Canoeing Association, state departments of recreation, occasionally state departments of fish and game, local writers on the subject of canoeing, and others. There is no central source that provides all these maps, but rather a conglomeration of sources from which the information can be extrapolated.

For navigable rivers, charts are available from the United States Army Corps of Engineers—and these are indispensable. Extremely detailed, they point out marinas, dams, locks, bridges, cables, mile markers, and countless other physical characteristics. Utilizing these charts, you should have no trouble tracing a trip mile by mile when on the water.

Another source of information about rivers and their sur-

*Charts from the Army Corps of Engineers are indispensable for navigable rivers such as the Mississippi. (Map from Army Corps of Engineers)*

rounding environs is the topographic map. "Topo" maps show detailed sections of the area through which you intend to paddle. They are more useful to backpackers, however, since they cover a wide area that often dwarfs a river itself and makes it hard to spot water features. But topo maps do show swampy areas and areas that can be expected to flood. Also, these maps are marked with contour lines that indicate visible land elevations that can be used to mark the progress of a trip. Streams, lakes, springs, and other water features appear in blue; woodland features in green; and principal works of man such as roads, buildings, railroads, power lines, and dams in black. (Be careful not to rely on topo maps to identify dams, however. Sometimes they miss marking low ones. And where they do mark them, the dams sometimes appear so small that it is easy to miss them.) Also shown are trails, campsites, springs, scenic overlooks, and other features worth knowing about. Historical points of interest are marked to help you plan brief, but fascinating, breaks in the stroke-after-stroke routine. By watching the topography of the surrounding landscape, you generally can anticipate areas suitable for camping.

*See pages 194 and 195 for an example of a topographic map.*

Topographic maps are available for the continental United States as well as Alaska, Hawaii, and Puerto Rico. Each of these areas has been marked off in sections. For a layout of each section write to the Map Information Office, United States Geological Survey, Washington, D.C. 20240, and ask for a map of the state and area you have in mind. Or write to the Washington Distribution Section, United States Geological Survey, 1200 South Ends Street, Arlington, Virginia 22202, or the United States Geological Survey, Denver, Colorado 80255. Once you have these maps, you can use them to identify individual sections from which to order detailed maps. These maps cost 75¢ apiece from the government. (They can be purchased for $1.00 from many sporting-goods stores or outfitters.)

Topographic maps come in two scales. It is to your benefit to purchase the map scaled to the fewest possible square miles. This type of map is more detailed and easier to read because it covers less territory in greater size and detail. Therefore, when ordering topographic maps, be sure to specify 7½-minute maps. These feature a scale of 1:24,000; that is, one inch on the map equals 24,000 inches on the ground. A 7½-minute map covers about 49 to 70 square miles and measures about 22 x 27 inches. On the second type of topographic map one inch equals one mile on the ground. Such a map covers an area of 207 to 281 square miles, and is called a 15-minute map. Generally speaking, the scale of a 15-minute map permits coverage of an

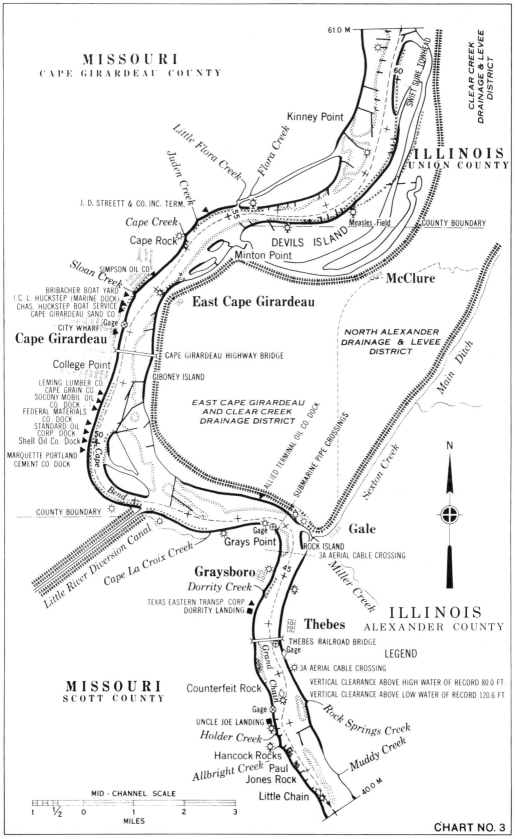

MISSOURI
CAPE GIRARDEAU COUNTY

61.0 M

CLEAR CREEK DRAINAGE & LEVEE DISTRICT

SWIFT SURE TOWHEAD

60

Kinney Point

ILLINOIS
UNION COUNTY

Little Flora Creek

Flora Creek

Juden Creek

J. D. STREETT & CO. INC. TERM.

55

Measles Field

COUNTY BOUNDARY

Cape Creek

DEVILS ISLAND

Cape Rock

Minton Point

McClure

Sloan Creek

SIMPSON OIL CO.

BRIBACHER BOAT YARD
( C. L. HUCKSTEP (MARINE DOCK)
CHAS. HUCKSTEP BOAT SERVICE
CAPE GIRARDEAU SAND CO.
CITY WHARF

Gage

East Cape Girardeau

Cape Girardeau

CAPE GIRARDEAU HIGHWAY BRIDGE

NORTH ALEXANDER
DRAINAGE & LEVEE
DISTRICT

Main Ditch

College Point

GIBONEY ISLAND

LEMING LUMBER CO.
CAPE GRAIN CO.
SOCONY MOBIL OIL
CO. DOCK
FEDERAL MATERIALS
CO. DOCK
STANDARD OIL
CORP. DOCK
Shell Oil Co. Dock

EAST CAPE GIRARDEAU
AND CLEAR CREEK
DRAINAGE DISTRICT

Sexton Creek

MARQUETTE PORTLAND
CEMENT CO. DOCK

50

Cape Bend

ALLIED TERMINAL OIL CO. DOCK

SUBMARINE PIPE CROSSINGS

N

COUNTY BOUNDARY

Little River Diversion Canal

Cape La Croix Creek

Gage

Grays Point

Gale

ROCK ISLAND

3A AERIAL CABLE CROSSING

Graysboro

45

Miller Creek

Dorrity Creek

TEXAS EASTERN TRANSP. CORP.
DORRITY LANDING

Thebes

ILLINOIS
ALEXANDER COUNTY

THEBES RAILROAD BRIDGE
Gage

LEGEND

☼ 3A AERIAL CABLE CROSSING

MISSOURI
SCOTT COUNTY

Counterfeit Rock

VERTICAL CLEARANCE ABOVE HIGH WATER OF RECORD 80.0 FT.
VERTICAL CLEARANCE ABOVE LOW WATER OF RECORD 120.6 FT.

Grand Chain

Gage

Rock Springs Creek

UNCLE JOE LANDING

Holder Creek

Hancock Rocks

Muddy Creek

Allbright Creek  Paul
Jones Rock

Little Chain

40.0 M

MID - CHANNEL SCALE

1   ½   0        1        2        3
MILES

(BLACK RIVER FALLS)

194

Mapped, edited, and published by the Geological Survey

Control by USGS, USC&GS, and USED

Topography from aerial photographs by multiplex methods
Aerial photographs taken 1946.  Field check 1947

Transverse Mercator projection.  1927 North American datum
10000-foot grids based on Wisconsin coordinate system south
and central zones.

TRUE NORTH
MAGNETIC NORTH

APPROXIMATE MEAN
DECLINATION, 1947

UNITED STATES
PARTMENT OF THE ARMY
CORPS OF ENGINEERS
(BLACK RIVER FALLS)

MELROSE QUADRANGLE
WISCONSIN
15 MINUTE SERIES (TOPOGRAPHIC)

*Left: a full-size detail of a 15 x 22 inch, 15 minute series U.S. Geological Survey map, showing a section of the Black River in Wisconsin. Scale 1" equals 1 mile.*

*Above: the top edge of the same map, reduced, showing the information that identifies the area covered.*

area so large that important points cannot be included, or, if included, are practically too small to notice.

When ordering maps directly from the United States Geological Survey, be sure to ask for two pamphlets available at no extra charge: *Silent Guides for Outdoorsmen* and *Topographic Maps.* These publications explain the symbols used on the maps and tell how to mount them permanently for use in the field. While it is a good idea to mount maps, they are of sufficient quality and durability that they can be folded and packed right in your packsack. One final word of caution: when ordering maps, do so far in advance of your trip. A good practice is to order them six weeks to two months before they will be needed. When you need them fast, purchase them from an outfitter.

No matter how much preplanning you do for a paddle-camping trip, certain aspects of every river and its surrounding territory cannot be known ahead of time. Travel brochures can tell you where to rent boats and equipment and sometimes indicate whether a stream is generally recommended for paddle adventure. But there is much more knowledge available, and you should take advantage of as much of it as possible.

If your job restricts you to weekend paddling with two

*Below: the bottom edge of the same map, reduced to about 75% of the original size. The date of the survey, indicated at left, is an indication of the limitations, as well as the detailed completeness of these maps.*

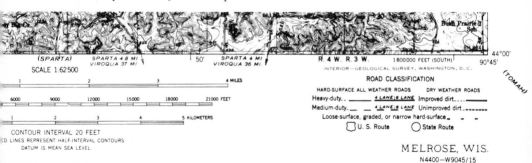

weeks' vacation every year, then your time may be limited for searching areas for information about rivers. But it does not take much time to scout an area when you arrive at the take-off point for the trip.

Many paddlers like to drive on Friday night to the town from which they will later embark. When they arrive late in the evening, they either rent a motel room, sleep in their cars, or pitch tents in nearby campgrounds. Upon arrival, there may not be much more than an hour or two left before they must hit the hay. But in that brief interlude they can glean a lot of information.

I have always found motel owners especially helpful sources. Because paddling is so rapidly growing as a sport, many inn-keepers have had canoeists stay in their motels, and they have learned from them. When you approach the desk, do not hesitate to tell the motel owner you plan to paddle down such and such a river. More often than not his interest picks up. Ask him what he knows about the river. Hit him with a few general questions: What's the river like in this area? How far is it from here to my destination? Has anybody taken this trip before?

Once you find that the motel owner is willing to talk, make the questions more specific: Are there any dams between my put-in and take-out points? Do you know of places I will have to portage? Are there any rapids? Is there anyplace between here and there where I can put ashore to camp? Where can I get drinking water? Are there many boats—canoes, kayaks, or otherwise—on this part of the river?

Do not forget to ask about side trips if you have time for them. Ask about points of historical interest—they are all that many small towns have left to offer as attractions and they never cease to be interesting.

Another excellent source of information consists of local taverns. People in bars like to talk, and if they find that you are taking a paddle trip, they will volunteer just about all the information they can muster. The same questions should be asked here that you ask the motel owner. The price of a couple of beers can lead to discussions that will make the trip smoother and safer. The "boys at the bar" in a small-town saloon usually are chock-full of tales about their fishing exploits, about the times they have been out on the river, and about all sorts of topics that may or may not be germane. Discount the Paul Bunyan tales and the myths about the ones that got away, but listen closely for information about the physical course of the river. More than one paddler has found it ex-

pedient to alter his trip plans entirely rather than face an obstruction or portage that is too difficult.

A third source of information is found in local filling stations. Albeit the owners of small-town gas stations are in business to sell fuel and provide service for motor vehicles, many
pump jockeys are authorities on their localities. A gas station
is one of the best places for directions about landings. But its
proprietor may also be able to tell you whether a given river
has unpassable snags, how long your trip is in miles, whether
others are taking the same trip, and so forth.

Other good sources include local chambers of commerce (if
they are open when you arrive in town), tourist bureaus, store-
keepers, and attendants at campgrounds. Some of these sources
may be better than the first three that have been discussed, but
when trying to save time, it is not always practical to seek
information from people or bureaus who have to be contacted
at "regular" hours. Sometimes, you are better off to seek knowledge in the most common places.

The point of scouting an area is this: keep talking. Never
stop telling people about what you are going to do and asking
them every imaginable question about the area in general and
the river in particular. And when you get an answer from one
person, do not let it keep you from attempting to get the same
answer restated from someone else. Even the local experts dis-
agree about many things. It is always a good idea to get all
their thoughts and then make a judgment of your own based
on what you have heard.

# 17

## What to Pack for Paddle Camping

Once you decide on camping, it is important to know what gear to take along. Of course, the gear must be appropriate for the kind of camping you will be doing. There are two ways to camp from a boat and the one you choose determines the type and amount of equipment you need. First, you can paddle to a spot and pitch a permanent camp. From this base you can strike out on day trips, exploring the waters and adjacent forest land. Your camp is the sanctuary to which you retire in the evening to build a fire and fry the fish you have caught. This manner of camping matches in every way the comfort and satisfaction found in renting a cabin at a woodland resort and is highly recommended for families that like to take very in-expensive vacations with their children. It is also an ideal vaca-tion for two or more couples to take together, since two boats can carry more than enough gear for total comfort.

For stationary camping, heavy gear is quite satisfactory. The only time you must paddle the full weight is when you are go-ing to, and returning from, your campsite. At all other times the gear stays out of the craft and does not interfere with the use of the boat for fishing or exploring. But even for this type of camping, you are well advised to undertake a multi-year program of replacing old-fashioned, heavy camping gear with new, lightweight equipment. Working with lightweight mate-rials makes most aspects of camping easier.

The second method of canoe and kayak camping is highly mobile. The purpose of a mobile trip is to explore the channels that connect points of interest, to pit physical strength and endurance against a predetermined length of water, to main-tain a pace that you set for yourself. The right kind of camp-ing gear for this type of travel is lightweight and easy to use. Also it must be organized for efficiency and put back as it was packed originally every time you use it.

Whichever type of paddling you prefer, the following check-list can help you pack what you need to be comfortable on the water. There are many lists available for campers, lists that are

## PERSONAL GEAR

*Clothes*
—sweatshirt or jacket
—swimming trunks
—long trousers
—belt
—T shirt
—underwear
—2 pr. socks
—extra shoes
—pajamas
—hat
—bandannas
—poncho

*Toilet Gear*
—towel
—washcloth
—toothbrush
—toothpaste
—razor
—shaving cream
—after shave
—soap
—toilet paper
—sunburn lotion
—insect repellent

## SHELTER AND SLEEP

*Shelter*
—tent
—tarpaulin
—extra rope
—extra tent pegs
*Sleeping gear*
—sleeping bag
—mattress

*There are two extra
copies of this checklist
at the end of the book
that can be torn out
and used or duplicated.*

## BOATING EQUIPMENT

—boat
—extra paddles
—life preservers
—repair kit
—spray cover or
—extra poncho(s)
—sponge
—kneeling pads
—padded yoke

## COOKING GEAR

*Gear to cook with*
—cook kit
—knives, forks, spoons
—tongs
—can and bottle opener
—canteen
—plastic or flexible
   water jugs
—stove and fuel
—matches
—candles
—grate
—large spoon or ladle
—fileting knife
—paper plates
*Gear to clean with*
—liquid dishwashing soap
—scouring pads
—dish cloth
—dish towel
—paper towels
—tinfoil

## TOOLS

—flashlight or lantern
—hatchet
—campsaw
—trenching tool
—bilge pump
—folding bucket
—oil stone
—file
—saw
—pliers

## FISHING GEAR

—rod
—reel
—line
—sinkers, bobbers
—stringer
—lures
—hooks and leaders

## FOOD

—water
—cheese
—sausage
—dark bread
—wine
—flour
—powdered milk
—powdered fruit drink
—margarine or lard
—salt and pepper
—cereal
—coffee
—dried foods
   as on planned menu

## MISCELLANEOUS

—jackknife
—Boy Scout field book
—log book and pencil
—camera
—binoculars
—radio
—first-aid kit
—twine
—extra rope
—compass
—wash basin
—extra matches
—sewing kit
—stop-ravel
—litter bag and
   garbage bags
—money box
—. . . . . . . . . . . . . . . .
—. . . . . . . . . . . . . . . .
—. . . . . . . . . . . . . . . .

199

designed so that you can check off each item as you pack it. This one evolved from the personal camping experiences of a number of paddle enthusiasts. If you follow it, you will never find yourself stranded without vital accessories.

At first glance a list of equipment as long as the one suggested distresses the prospective canoe camper. "How can I ever afford so much equipment?" he asks himself. "How can I fit so much gear into a small boat? How can I keep track of so many things?"

A closer analysis reveals why there should be little difficulty either in assembling, packing, or maintaining this gear. To begin with, you probably already own just about every piece of equipment listed. The only things you probably will not find around the house are a poncho and a money box. You can substitute a raincoat for the poncho, or if worse comes to worst, you can make a temporary poncho out of a plastic refuse bag. While it is true that you may want to add lightweight and water-repellent clothes to your gear as time goes on, there is no reason to rush out and spend a lot of money on clothes; what you already have should do fine.

Another category in which you should be able to fulfill most of your needs from items around the house is cooking gear. Your kitchen surely will yield a pair of tongs (you can accomplish the function of tongs with sticks picked up enroute if you do not have a pair), spoons, knives and forks, a can and bottle opener, matches, ladle, soap, scouring pads, a dish towel and cloth, paper towels, and tinfoil.

One of the most important pieces of gear needed for camping is a cooking kit. Many people still have their old Boy Scout cook kits; these last virtually forever. They are perfectly satisfactory, but have the capacity to serve only a single person. More practical cooking kits are available in combinations of aluminum pots, pans, cups, and dishes that will cook for as many as twenty people at one time.

Most canoeists consider kits of this size an extravagance; usually the only time such a cooking kit is of service is when you are paddling with a flotilla of ten canoes carrying two paddlers each. Then, one large cooking kit would prevent needless duplication of gear. A good cooking kit for most paddle camping is one designed around eleven or twelve aluminum pieces that include four plates, four cups, a coffeepot, a frying pan, and one or two buckets of eight-quart and four-quart capacities. Sets of this type cost from $5 to $12 depending on their quality and where you buy them. Even if you plan to camp with two persons most of the time, the extra plates

and cups that come with these kits are a real advantage when preparing multiple-course dinners. One of the extra cups can be used for measurement, eliminating the need to carry a separate measuring cup along. Of course, you can throw some plastic dishes and cups together, along with a frying pan and some pots, to make your own cooking outfit. This is an acceptable, inexpensive way to get started but sacrifices valuable storage space in the boat. The available cooking kits are designed so the pieces fit within each other to be as compact as possible. They constitute a wise investment for utility and convenience.

*Palco 415 Cooking Kit. This is a highly desirable cooking unit for paddle campers. (Photo Palco Products)*

In addition to a cooking kit, water-carrying vessels are extremely important for camping. One economical way to get them is to save plastic milk cartons and other plastic bottles that can be cleaned and used as amphorae. Also, there are inexpensive 2½-gallon collapsible plastic water jugs being marketed that are lightweight and do not seem to present inordinate leakage problems. And as water is used, they can be collapsed to make more room in the boat.

Strictly speaking a canteen is not needed if you have one or more water jugs. But it is handy. By dipping a canteen in the water and wetting its cloth or canvas cover, you can take advantage of evaporation to keep drinking water reasonably cool. And, of course, the canteen is a great companion when hiking any distance from the boat.

201

*The Skatchet is an interesting tool for paddlers.*

Finally, in order to facilitate your cooking, use a shelf from an old refrigerator as your grate. It is strong, easy to clean, and can be tied to your craft to make a table from which to serve quick lunches when you do not feel like "setting up" ashore.

As far as tools are concerned, a saw, hatchet, and trenching tool or hand digger are necessities under almost all conditions. The saw and hatchet may be vital even if not used for cutting firewood: they may be the best implements for cutting through snags in the river itself. Many times paddlers, even those who make the best plans, find that the river they have chosen is blocked by debris and fallen limbs. Few maps can prepare one for blockage of this type. Because of their value, your saw and hatchet should be of top quality; do not skimp when buying these. Deal with a reputable hardware store or with a well-known outfitter, and buy items in the middle, or toward the top, of the price range. Be sure these tools are of adequate size and that they can be honed to razor sharpness. There are many lightweight compromises; avoid them. Look for a sturdy steel bow saw and a steel hatchet with a wooden handle.

In the final category on the checklist—Miscellaneous—the only item listed that is totally essential is a first-aid kit. Good first-aid kits can be purchased for $6 to $15. Other than this

*It is lightweight but can be used for a thousand jobs. (Photo Follins Corp.)*

crucial item, you need not take along any of the other miscellaneous items, and those you do take may be items you already have at home and need not invest in. A camera and binoculars are welcome, but not necessary. A compass can be useful, but in downriver canoeing or kayaking it, too, is not required; if you think yourself lost it is usually possible just to keep on going downriver and eventually come to your destination.

Twine, extra matches, a wash basin, garbage bags, and a sewing kit will have a thousand uses around camp. They can be packed together and cost you little or nothing since they are common household items. A log book and pencil cost about 30¢ in a dime store, and while not actually necessary, they allow you to keep records of the trips you take that will bring back many an enjoyable memory upon rereading during the winter months. Many other items on the list can be found around the house, and others admit to inexpensive substitutes. Items such as boating equipment and accessories, tents and sleeping gear are described elsewhere in this book.

## HOW TO PACK

Once you realize how much of the basic gear you already have, the checklist appears less formidable and you can dispose of the second two questions we asked originally: "How can I fit all this gear into a canoe or kayak?" and "How can I keep track of it on an extended camping trip?"

Actually, the answers to both of these questions are not mutually exclusive, and depend on each other. If you pack correctly, you will find that you can pack all the equipment on the checklist in one canoe or kayak, and even double up on such items as personal gear where two paddlers are concerned. Proper packing lets you assemble your gear in a fairly logical way so that it fits together compactly and neatly. The equipment listed need not total more than 150 pounds, and even less if you are fortunate enough to possess lightweight gear. It can all be stowed in two packs—one for food and cooking gear, and the other for clothes and personal goods. Tools should remain lashed to the top of the bundle so you can reach them readily, and your sleeping bag, mattress, and tent can remain separate unless you plan to mount them, along with your pack, on a rigid frame.

There is a logic involved in packing, and to some degree that logic is your own. For example, there is no reason not to pack a single-burner, lightweight stove in the tool kit or even along with personal gear, but it is probably wiser to stow it in the food bag along with the food it will cook. That way, when it comes time to make dinner, everything necessary for that function is concentrated in one place. Similarly, your first-aid kit is best placed in an outside compartment of a pack that is easily accessible. After all, you may need it at any time; and when you do, you will probably need it in a hurry.

Packing seems easiest if you initially group equipment into three piles, which should be established for the gear that will be carried in your personal pack, a food pack, and loose in the boat or lashed where it can be reached easily. Each paddler should have a personal pack, but there should be only one food pack for the group.

Into your personal pack goes everything designated in the list as "personal gear." For short trips, a single change of clothes is sufficient, as indicated on the checklist. For journeys of three or more days, it is wise to take an extra change of clothes (but do not take more than you need). Remember, the clothes you start out with constitute one change if they are clean.

If you are paddling in summer weather, it is best to wear your swimming suit as much as possible. This permits you to climb out and track your boat whenever necessary and prevents you from using up a change of clothes if you happen to fall into the water or are forced to remove an obstruction from the boat's path. And a swimming suit is comfortable. Let your swimming trunks be your shorts, and you will have to pack only one other pair of pants—long trousers for evening and town wear. But follow this advice only as far as sunburn lets you. If you have sensitive skin that burns easily, it is better to carry an extra pair of trousers and use them most of the time. Also wear the hat that is listed, so that it need not usurp space in your pack. Prefer brimmed hats with chin straps so they cannot get blown off your head.

When the weather is moderate, a lightweight nylon jacket is an ideal wrap. It folds up small enough to require virtually no space in the pack, weighs but a few ounces, and keeps you warm in the evening or when the sky clouds over. If you are canoeing in the northern autumn or if the weather is cool, few things beat a pull-over sweatshirt—the kind with a hand-warmer pocket on the belly and a hood that can be drawn tight by a drawstring. Most sweatshirts of this type are made of cotton, and are exceptionally warm in dry weather—as long as they do not get damp or wet. Even in the damp, chilly days of spring, however, they are wholly adequate when used under a poncho. Keep your jacket and poncho, along with your toilet paper and toilet kit, readily at hand—you may have to grab them in a hurry.

Every canoeist should carry two pairs of shoes—a good, comfortable pair of hiking high-tops and a pair of inexpensive tennis shoes that can get wet. The hiking shoes should be stashed in the personal pack or tied to the outside of it. Every effort should be made to keep them dry, since they will be used for sojourns away from the water and for comfortable walking around the campsite. The other pair of shoes are your "water-walkers," which should be kept near you on the floor of the canoe. When you must get out to track the boat through snags, or to walk it over sand bars where the water is shallow, put these shoes on, *sans* socks, to protect your feet from unseen dangers such as sharp branches, glass, or leeches on the river bottom.

Your personal pack should include toilet gear in one small kit. Other items that can fit into this pack are a small floating money box (optional), your flashlight, small tools such as an oil stone, a file, and a pair of pliers, and a small box of fishing tackle packed with lures, stringer, hooks, sinkers, etc. (If fishing is the real goal of your paddling, you will want a full tackle box that must be packed separately in the boat.) All the items that the checklist specifies as miscellaneous should also fit into your personal pack with the exception of

205

the wash basin (optional), which is kept separate in the boat, and the garbage bags, which should be put in the food pack.

The second important pack is for food. Be sure it is complete. It should have all the food, cooking, and clean-up supplies for the expedition. Besides the three items of semi-perishable food already mentioned (hard salami or sausage, cheese, and bread), four plastic containers of the Tupperware variety or, preferably, polyethylene bags that can hold powdered drink, powdered milk (good for use with portion packs of cereal), flour, and lard should be kept in this pack. The last two items are expendable if you pack foods that eliminate the need for them and do not intend to fry fish.

A food pack of moderate size will hold more than your food if you pay attention to packing it carefully. You should also be able to include in it a single-burner stove, extra fuel (in an outside pocket), tongs, a large spoon, fileting knife, and most other gear needed for cooking. Even your cooking kit may fit in. The food bag is also a good place to cache a supply of trash bags—handy both for carrying refuse and for covering gear to protect it against rain and splash.

Thus far most of the gear on the checklist has already been accounted for and consigned to two packs. That leaves only the gear that will be packed by itself in the boat or attached to the outside of the packs. Of this, tent, mattress, and sleeping bag take up the most space; but it should be possible to pack for two persons without even denting the carrying space of a 17-foot canoe or kayak. If your personal pack is of the large variety and is suspended on a pack frame, your sleeping bag, air mattress and tent can probably be attached or included within. Much of the remaining gear can be packed into the personal or food packs. What does not fit into either of these must be arranged logically in the bottom of the boat. Fishing rods, grate, wash basin, folding bucket, extra paddles, water jugs, boat-repair kit, tools, sponge, and spray cover or extra poncho all should be packed where they are easy to reach. When all is said and done, what looks like a vast list of needed belongings reduces itself to two bags and a bundle of utility items.

## TIPS FOR CUTTING WEIGHT AND SAVING SPACE

One way to minimize weight is to pack things that have more than one function. A good example of this is soap. Many campers pack either shaving soap or aerosol shaving lather in their toilet kit, a dishwashing liquid in their food bag, and another bar of soap for their personal hygiene. Instead, consider storing in your food pack a small plastic bottle of potent liquid soap that functions for all three uses. Such an all-purpose liquid soap is a remarkable product from Bestline called Liquid Concentrate (LC). Bestline products are marketed through door-to-door solicitation. You cannot buy the soap in a store, but it is worth an effort to find a distributor of this product and include some in your camping gear.

Liquid Concentrate can be used in small amounts for personal hygiene, and does an excellent job. Because it comes in a bottle, there is no problem with putting a wet, sloppy bar of soap back in your toilet kit. A tiny bit of LC also does an outstanding no-rinse job on dishes, cutting through grease in a way other products only talk about in commercials. When it comes to shaving, Liquid Concentrate has a wetting agent that softens whiskers as well or better than shaving cream, and its glycerine-like coating permits the razor to glide easily while preventing cuts. When you are finished shaving, you have the bonus of a razor that has lost the accumulation of dull scum commonly left by shaving soaps; the razor shines like a mirror.

If you want to milk every weight-saving possibility from this product, you can even use it to replace your toothpaste. I do not want to make this a commercial for Bestline, but I have tried competitive products and have not found one as functional as Liquid Concentrate.

Another suggestion for saving space and weight involves fishing gear: leave most of it home. You should be able to determine in advance of the trip conditions you will encounter. Sort out the most likely lures and tackle from your large tackle box, keeping it simple. Put a few trusted items in a small plastic kit, and pack the kit in your personal pack.

If you want to travel light, most of the items listed under *Miscellaneous* in the checklist can be left at home. A washpan is pure convenience; the kettle from your cooking kit will replace it for washing everything except a frying pan. Work around the frying pan by pouring washwater into it and scrubbing. After taking several trips, you may find that binoculars are used only occasionally if at all. You will probably not miss having them along, especially when paddling small, tree-smothered streams.

It is never a good idea to pitch camp in the dark. By all means plan to disembark in the afternoon and make camp before sundown. If you do this, you should be able to get by with a flashlight, leaving the gas or propane lantern home. And elimination of the lantern means that you need only enough fuel for your stove. For trips of not more than a few days, the fuel in a single gas cylinder should be enough.

While you must carry enough water to meet emergencies, it is not wise to lug more than you need. Not only is the extra weight difficult to paddle, but the water is likely to go stale anyway. If you paddle in an area where there are sources of clean water en route, take advantage of them. Assuming you can get water daily, you should need to carry no more than 2½ gallons of water for two paddlers per day, plus a quart of drinking water in the canteens.

To summarize—packing for canoe or kayak camping has its own logic, and you are that logic's source. Only if you think about gear, what you need and what can be left behind, can you minimize the amount needed to do the job. By all means strive to cut weight and bulk wherever possible, but do not be afraid to tolerate a few extra pounds here and there in order to make the trip enjoyable. It is best to start out overpacked. As time goes on, you will improve your packing technique by eliminating things that you find through experience are not used. The important thing is to get started. Once you take a trip in your canoe or kayak and spend a couple of nights under the stars, you will want to go back for more. There will be plenty of time to learn the science of packing the right gear for the specific job that gear has to do.

It is a curious fact that the experience of a paddler has often determines the pace he will set.

For example, take the person who works at a sedentary job all week and decides he needs some exercise to keep in shape. He decides to become a canoeist, plunks down the money on a boat and some camping gear. Perhaps he takes a day of his vacation and adds it to a weekend to give himself three days of paddling time. Next he looks at a map and spots a river he may have read about as being a haven for paddlers. He begins to calculate how many miles he can cover.

"Let's see, now. The current travels at about four miles an hour. I can figure on being on the water for about eight hours a day—that means I can cover about 32 miles. Since I have to be off the water by noon of the third day in order to make it home in time for work the following morning, I cannot quite triple the 32 miles. But then I should be able to add some miles each day, since I will be paddling in addition to riding the current. Thus, I can figure on about a 75-mile trip."

If the river is not navigable and no charts are available that show it marked in miles, the new paddler may apply his 75 miles to the map on the basis of about three miles of river to one of road. This is the way most inexperienced paddlers plan their trips. What are the results?

The paddler may well average 25 miles a day if the weather remains sunny, if the river really is three miles long for each mile or road, if the current actually does maintain a consistent four-mile-per-hour pace, if there is no wind to obstruct progress, if he can bear a full eight hours paddling in the hot sun, if there are no serious snags or unforeseen portages, and if everything else remains copacetic.

But these are a lot of "if's." Seldom does any paddle-camping trip proceed according to such preconceived plans. Storms may drive you ashore and even pin you down for a day or so. The river may undergo convolutions that are not shown on the road map, stretching its length. The concept of current is not as simple as it seems, for you seldom proceed directly down the center of a river where the current runs at a single speed. Rather, you will more likely weave from side to side as the fancy strikes, paddling among obstructions, eddies, and even back currents. You will find paddling easier at some times than at others, and often you will be content to float, simply using your paddle as a rudder.

On a good day you may spend eight or even more hours on the water. But it does take time to disassemble camp and pack the boat in the morning, not to mention making and eating breakfast, shaving, and cleaning up. Moreover, you do want to eat a leisurely and enjoyable lunch, even if it is kept simple, and, perhaps, lie down to rest or even take a short nap. It is utterly senseless to put yourself into a situation in which you must pull off the water late in the evening, pitch your camp in the dark, to say nothing of cooking in the dark. It is far better to get off the water in advance of your normal dinner hour so that you can make camp and prepare dinner in daylight.

Other drawbacks of planning too tightly and committing yourself to unrealistic distances include the elimination of stops for sightseeing and exploration as well as the incursion on your fishing time. And, of course, overriding concerns of safety must be faced when you push yourself too far physically, or when you compel yourself to paddle so rapidly that you cannot concentrate on critical situations or paddle with deliberation.

Despite all these drawbacks, almost every neophyte paddler starts by being overambitious. It is only after he has gotten a few exhilarating, but difficult, trips under his belt that he considers slowing down and planning so that he can gain relaxation from his trips rather than the thrill of mastering an almost impossible challenge.

And those who paddle slowly show clearly that they have been at it awhile. The trick of comfortable paddling, not to mention safe paddling, is to pace yourself properly. To do this you must make a realistic assessment of your own strength and endurance, and then plan the trip so that it will not tax this capacity.

For example, do not plan to paddle distances anywhere close to the sum of current-miles per hour plus the efforts (in miles per hour) of your paddling. Unless you are canoeing a river you know to be extremely fast-flowing, with no obstructions, do not plan to go more than ten to fifteen miles per

*Setting your pace demands that time be left for occasional leg-stretching and outside activities. Here, campers pause for lunch and repacking on Georgia's Alapaha River. (Photo Georgia Department of Community Development)*

day. Remember that the first few times out each year you need to rest often, letting the current carry you while you withdraw your paddle from the water. As the season progresses and your conditioning improves, you will assume a natural and comfortable rhythm and will be able to paddle hour after hour.

Do not plan your trip so you absolutely *must* make even a comparatively short distance on a given day. Sometimes headwinds not only retard your progress, but add psychologically depressing difficulties to paddling. There is the temptation to stay on the water late into the evening in an attempt to make up lost time. Do not succumb. Make camp at the predetermined time. If you have planned some flexibility into your trip, the chances are you can make up the distance the following day.

If you will travel for more than two days, try to plan an

entire extra day into the trip—that is, cut the intended mileage by the equivalent of a day's travel. If the trip comes off without a hitch, you can spend the extra day in sedentary camping, fishing, and exploring. But if you encounter rain and stormy conditions, you can stay put for a day. This decreases the necessity for making a downriver run in a storm.

Be sure to plan plenty of time into your itinerary for "fun" activities. Stop to swim when you get a chance. There is nothing as refreshing as washing the sweat from your body with a dip in cool water flowing over sandy bottoms. Fishing is always a welcome diversion. If traveling with a partner or with your family, take some games along—a portable chessboard or checker set are ideal. Camping must be play as well as work, especially if children are along.

In sum, the best advice that beginning canoeists and kayakists can receive about setting a pace is to slow down. Learn to enjoy the beauties of the natural world around you. Give in to the natural environment; do not try to conquer it. Remember, you are out to see things, to feel the breeze and hear the fish feeding in the backwaters at dusk. True, you also are pursuing the good feeling that accompanies muscles that are flexed and taxed, but this can be destroyed by overexertion.

If you set a slow-to-medium pace, there will be time for the unexpected portage, the unforeseen snag, the sudden shower. There will be time to erect a shelter and cook meals in a rational, logical, enjoyable way. Such aspects of the trip should never become unwanted interruptions in a mad dash from one point to another. Observe the ways of nature, the clouds that indicate the weather, the animals that inhabit the riverbanks, the wild flowers that form multicolored mats on the forest floor, the historical shrines that dot the landscape; the shops, the parks, and even the main streets of places you might otherwise miss.

Planning extra time into your trip, tempering your pace, is often the real key to enjoyment. If you cannot accept this advice for the first few trips, then paddle your heart out. You may enjoy it, but the greatest pleasure awaits the day when you tire and decide to take time to look just a little more deeply into the countryside through which you paddle.

# 19

## Planning Your Menu and Cooking

I have always found that time of year when the winter weather starts to break ideal for making menus, although they can be developed right up to the starting time of any paddle trip. Planning meals is an enjoyable pastime, and it can be done artistically if one gets an early start.

Planning menus today is no problem because of the vast array of dehydrated foods available. Not only are most of them light, but they are nutritious, tasty, and satisfying. Most really stick to the ribs. Today's food for backpackers, canoeists, and other back-country enthusiasts has come a long way from the suet and jerky of yesteryear.

Before the advent of dehydrates, restrictions on the menu were formidable obstacles to camping as a recreational activity. The hearty adventurers who broke trails to open the United States often set forth into the wilderness carrying little more than a supply of jerky, some parched corn, and a plug of sourdough. Variations in diet were left for those days when hunting or fishing were successful. As canned goods became available, the blandness of the camper's diet disappeared, and well-balanced, nutritious meals could be packed into the woods. But canned goods have two serious drawbacks on a camping trip: they are heavy and the tins must be carried empty until a place is found in which to deposit them. Thinking back to your youth, you probably remember the typical menus of Scout campouts: the omnipresent canned beans, Spam or similar canned meat, canned spaghetti, canned stew, canned hash, and so forth. These foods are still available and are most likely to be the ones you fall back on during the first few outings with your canoe or kayak.

But there are three significant advantages to using freeze-dried and dehydrated foods instead of canned goods. First, they are extremely light and compact. Your food bag weighs a fraction of what it would if filled with canned goods. Second, entire dinners are prepared and freeze-dried by the manufacturer. You can enjoy such one-pot delicacies as Turkey

213

Tetrazzini, Beef Alamonde, Mexican Omelette, and other dishes that would require numerous cans of ingredients and long preparation in the field. Third, and a very real advantage to conscientious outdoorsmen, is the fact that the containers from most freeze-dried or dehydrated foods can be burned. Those containers that are made of foil, and so cannot be burned, can be packed out in a very small parcel. In short, the disposal problems associated with tin cans and bottles are eliminated.

Campers use several methods to prepare the new lightweight foods. One of the best is the system required for Trail Chef foods, in which you simply pry apart the top of the plastic bag that holds the food and fill it to an indicated level with water from your supply. Then the bag is resealed with light finger pressure and placed in a pot of boiling water for a stipulated period of time. Since the bag is sealed completely, untreated river water can be used for boiling, saving precious drinking water. When the bag is removed from the boiling water and opened, the food is ready to eat.

Another easy method of preparation is employed by Tea Kettle Brand. In this case, each course comes in an aluminum pan in which it is directly prepared. The advantage of this method is that you need not dirty either a pan to cook the dinner or a plate on which to eat it. The disadvantage is that the aluminum pans must be cleaned and toted out of the wilderness. To their credit, they can be compactly crushed more easily than can tin cans and they are lighter. A third preparation method is offered by Mountain House, whose food comes in a plastic bag in which it is hydrated. The food then is poured into a pan and cooked almost as you would any other food.

The first few times you use freeze-dried products you are likely to appreciate their taste, but may find the texture unfamiliar. It is not always possible to hydrate this kind of food completely. A good example is freeze-dried hamburger. The patties must be immersed in room-temperature water for five minutes before they are fried in a skillet. The finished product has all the taste of fresh hamburger, but the texture sometimes comes suspiciously close to shoe leather. For one reason or another, complete hydration has not taken place.

Three factors determine your preferences for food—taste, texture, and appearance. Interesting experiments can be performed to show that your likes and dislikes are functions of these basic characteristics. For instance, conceive of adulterating fresh milk with a bright purple dye. While the taste and the texture of the milk would remain the same, the product as a whole would probably not be appetizing. By the same token, the taste and color of hamburger can be maintained but if the meat has the texture of a conveyor belt, you most likely cannot be compelled to eat it. At this point in time, most freeze-dried and vacuum-processed foods have come close to matching home-cooked counterparts in all three categories —taste, texture, and appearance. But some still have shortcomings. Many freeze-dried dinner dishes are casseroles that use spices and bits of highly flavored vegetables (such as peppers and onions) to mask their failings in texture. Spices and other flavoring techniques can offset deficiencies in the flavor of reconstituted vegetables and meat. Some campers have to grow accustomed to these foods, but it is worth the effort.

Before giving an unconditional recommendation to freeze-dried foods, one comment must be made: these foods are easy to portage and carry in your boat. And if water is available at every stopping point, they can save a lot of effort and aggravation. But water is precisely where the rub comes in. The reason these foods are light is that the water has been taken out. And you have to put it back. This means you must carry fresh water in the boat if you plan to stay where no water source is available. (You can rely on purification tablets and boiling to sanitize river water, but for health and taste reasons, employ these methods only in emergencies.) When the conditions of a trip impose the burden of carrying too much water, the light weight of the food ceases to be the advantage it appeared. Nevertheless, when all the advantages of freeze-dried and dehydrated food are combined, there is no question that these foods should be the preference of serious paddle campers. To exemplify the variety of these foods, consider the following excerpts from menus offered by Canadian Waters, a large canoe outfitter headquartered in Ely, Minnesota. These foods are available not only through Canadian Waters, but through thousands of sporting goods stores, outfitters, and camping-supply houses, so you should be able to match the delicious menus concocted by the pros.

Hash brown potatoes, mixed fruit, pancakes and syrup, oatmeal with brown sugar and raisins, bacon and eggs, French toast, eggs and Bacos, soups, macaroni, vegetables, fruit cocktail, chicken stew and rice, apple sauce, beef stroganoff, apple slices, spaghetti and meat balls, pudding, potatoes O'Brien, peaches, beef stew and rice, chili con carne, chili mac, chicken rice, and many more combinations are available for dinner and breakfast.

How can you beat this kind of selection?

Figure on three meals a day, although you may want to skip breakfast on the first day out and dinner and possibly lunch on the final day of the trip. Dehydrated foods lend themselves best to breakfast and dinner, when you are more likely to take the time to set up a stove or build a fire to boil the necessary water. Be sure to write down exactly what you plan to have for each meal, and keep the list handy on the trip so you do not overeat and consequently run out of food.

Once you plan breakfast and dinner, only lunch is left to plan for. What appears on the Canadian Waters menu for lunch? Simple but nourishing the satisfying items such as summer sausage and cheese sandwiches, cookies, powdered beverages, grilled cheese, soups, peanut butter and jelly sandwiches —and that is about it. On a paddle trip, lunch is usually eaten on the run, for each day's mileage is approximately planned and that precludes spending a lot of time boiling water to make lunch.

My own standard fare for lunch on paddle trips is hard sausage, dark bread, and a powdered drink. The sausage can be accompanied by a slab of cheese—the only perishables you really need take along. And they are not perishable in the commonly accepted sense, for the sausage keeps for several days even after being cut. Cheese, too, keeps better than some other foodstuffs, lasting for days if kept wrapped tightly in polyethylene. Dark bread is nourishing, and its use along with the sausage and cheese is wholesome. If you really want to enhance the delicacies of cheese and sausage, buy a Bota— a goat-skin bag available for about $6 from many outfitters— and fill it with wine. Your lunches will be modest but enjoyable, and will permit you to get back on the water without delay.

Many outdoorsmen like to fish. Often this is the main purpose of a camping trip. Paddle camping is especially attractive to fishermen because it lets them cover wide areas and test virtually unlimited waters. But one precaution must be mentioned: do not *depend* on fish for meals.

Take along some flour, lard, salt (and if you like them, onions and peppers) so that you can prepare any fish you might catch. But fish are not a sure thing. Sometimes they are taken in great numbers, and other times you must expect to get "skunked." Moreover, there are difficulties on a paddle trip where fish are concerned. It is almost impossible to keep them for any time without refrigeration. It does little good to catch twenty bass in the evening, before dinner. Three or four make a satisfying meal, but the rest will probably spoil before morning. You must figure on eating only those fish caught a short time before each meal.

## CAMPFIRES AND ECOLOGY

An exhortation—respect the environment. When talking of food preparation, the use of fire must be considered. Fire can be rapacious if not controlled. Keep in mind that the rivers, lakes, and woods are some of the few remaining places unspoiled by technology. They are the last bastions in which wildlife can be observed in its natural state, where men can take part in the world as it would be if they were unable to destroy it. The last thing you want to do is paddle into a natural place and burn it down.

It has become the custom of many light campers—backpackers, paddlers, bicyclists, and motorcyclists—to rely on lightweight stoves and to avoid traditional campfires. These campers boast that when they leave a campsite no one coming after them knows they have been there. Such camping *is* something to be proud of, and if you are taking up paddling for the first time, it certainly should be your goal.

It is not necessary in all instances to refrain from making fires; in many remote areas there are healthy supplies of fallen branches and dead wood lying on the ground, and along the banks of large rivers there are often mammoth supplies of driftwood. In such cases there is no other experience quite equal to sitting around a bonfire in the dark. Before building a fire, look for a spot at least ten feet from your tent and gear. Be sure there are no overhanging branches that could come ablaze. Rake away sticks, leaves, and other timber around the fire pit that might be ignited by a live spark or hot coal. Do not build the fire on or near tree roots, for they can ignite and smoulder underground for long periods of time, bursting into a conflagration far from the site of your campfire. Furthermore, never light a fire on a windy day—a single windborne spark can turn a woods into a roaring inferno. Do not use more wood than is needed for a small fire. It is important to leave wood behind for those who follow. Never cut a living tree to fuel a fire or for any other purpose. Not only is this a blemish on the environment, but the tree will not burn well anyway. And always be sure to take appropriate safety measures with fire. Keep a bucket of water nearby so the fire can be doused if it starts to get out of hand. Be sure to soak the fire thoroughly before you turn in at night or when you must leave it even for the shortest time.

217

A good, safe way to make a fire when you are camping on turf is to use a trenching tool to cut the turf in a square and lift it up. Placing it aside, build the fire in the shallow hole made by the vacated turf. When you are preparing to leave the campsite, simply douse the fire, with water and replace the turf over the ashes, so the fire will not keep burning.

# 20

# Boat Handling, Safety, Ecology:
## Tips and Common Sense

There are three interrelated aspects to keeping yourself safe and in good health when canoeing or kayaking or enjoying camping along with these activities. They are boat handling, comportment in the campsite, and treatment of the land around you.

Essentially, keeping safe and healthy is a matter of attitude. There are ways of viewing situations that engender caution. While the right attitude does not assure you will not meet with an accident, it can certainly minimize the chances.

Most books on canoeing and camping do not stress a pro-ecology sensitivity as part of good safety practice, and most material published on backpacking and other outdoor activities separates these two elements by chapter. But there are many instances where the two elements of outdoorsmanship overlap. For example, assume you camp in a very dry area in autumn, and that fallen leaves are spreading a red and gold carpet across your campsite. The leaves make a fine, soft mattress under the floor of your tent and add immeasurably to your comfort. They provide a colorful setting that combines visual beauty with aromas and sounds that induce a peaceful calm. Enjoying their crackle underfoot, it is easy to forget that those leaves also present a mighty fire hazard.

In this situation, you *must* practice every safety maxim possible. If you grind a cigarette into the leaves, a careless spark may ignite a conflagration that will kill you. If the campfire burns past its perimeter, and gets out of hand, at the very least you may lose hundreds of dollars worth of equipment.

But there is more to this than your own equipment or health. You can destroy acres of natural land, incinerate trees that took decades to reach their stately height, cause countless animals to flee helplessly choking in smoke, with charred skin, their habitat ravaged. In short, you can inflict a senseless scar on the country you wanted to enjoy, a scar that may not heal for centuries. Thus, it is important that your attitude toward nature be conditioned so that you always work *with* nature's forces, never to their detriment. Your attitude will then provide an additional motive in keeping you safe.

The attitude I am talking about is one of humility. Forget the Biblical conception that man was meant to dominate the garden. That's nonsense. You are but one more entity in the natural scheme, and should you fail to respect your surroundings, you can become a lethal agent of destruction. In exceeding your place in nature you can destroy the very thing you seek to enjoy—*and you can hurt yourself in the process.*

The attitude is also one of passivity. If you are injured and allow the currents to carry you downriver, you have every chance of reaching the journey's goal. But should you attempt to paddle upcurrent when injured, you exhaust yourself and face the possibility of not returning at all.

Your attitude toward nature should also be one of common sense. Never act precipitously in the face of danger. Rather, calmly consider the situation, seeking the most logical and rational means of meeting it. It makes no sense, for instance, to risk life on a wild rapid when you can portage around it with no risk. It makes no sense to paddle past the limits of endurance when a night's sleep will enable you to continue the voyage with sufficient strength to overcome any obstacles.

With humility, acceptance of the ways of nature, and common sense, paddle adventure is one of the safest ways to spend your time. On the other hand, if you assume an arrogant, rapacious attitude, you will destroy the medium in which you seek enjoyment, and also expose yourself to grave injury. In the spirit of these three virtues—humility, passivity, and common sense—the following maxims are offered to make your paddle camping safe and enjoyable.

## TIPS FOR HANDLING YOUR CANOE OR KAYAK SAFELY

Treat your craft gently and handle it with the utmost care. Never drop it, drag it, or run into things deliberately. Your boat's good condition is essential to keeping you safe and getting you to the end of your trip.

Be careful when boarding your craft. A canoe is stable only when floating along its entire length. Do not step into it when its bow is in the water and its stern is on an elevated area of land—it may spin over as if it were on an axle, not to mention the dangerous strain you inflicted on the keel.

As a corollary to the previous tip, steady the craft

*Paddlers show the proper way to launch a canoe from the bank. At no time should the canoe scrape on the ground. Ease the bow into a floating position and then let the stern slide into the water after it. (Photo Sportspal)*

for your partner when boarding or when climbing out. Such courtesy can save both of you a dunking and keep your gear dry.

For the sake of stability, hold on to both gunwales when assuming the paddling position. Above all, do not stand up in craft either when switching places or at any other time.

When in a K-2 kayak, paddle in unison so that you and your partner do not clash paddles. It is necessary for the bowman to set the tempo, so the sternman can observe him visually and adjust his stroke accordingly. In a canoe, if the sternman outpaddles the bowman, the craft veers off course.

Just as a snake with heads at each end tears itself apart in a battle of wills, in a canoe there is no room for schizophrenia. There can be only one head, and that, paradoxically, is most often in the stern. The sternman is in charge because he has greater control over direction. The bowman should defer to his decisions. In a K-2, the bowman participates in directional guidance to a greater degree.

When you have gained experience as a canoeist and have worked with canoeing partners, you will find times when the roles of the bowman and the sternman overlap. For example, in rapids or tortuous streams, the bowman is responsible for steering his end of the craft, and must initiate the course.

If you wear glasses, purchase and use a strap to hold them on your head. Even if you do not need them all the time, be sure to tie them at the top of your pack and protect them so they cannot be lost.

Watch for obstructions in the water and try to spot them far enough ahead to avoid them. Be especially careful of dams in small streams and rivers; they appear as almost invisible hairlines across the water but often are accompanied by sounds that indicate rushing water. If you have doubts about anything that looks like it may be a dam, climb onto the bank and walk downriver to investigate it. Another common obstruction is barbed-wire fencing that crosses rivers. This occurs in farm country where fences are erected by farmers required to do so. Never cut these wires. Portage around them.

In areas where you must climb out of the kayak or canoe and pull it over sand bars, be extremely cautious. Approach the river walking one step at a time. There may be dangerous drop-offs and undercurrents in your path.

When challenging fast water in a canoe, be sure to kneel, rather than sit on the seats. The kneeling position lowers the center of gravity so the boat cannot tip as easily.

If you tackle water that taxes the limit of your paddling experience and capabilities, rig your canoe with thigh and foot braces for maximum balance. These accessories permit you to put more muscle into paddling, especially in emergencies.

When you travel whitewater with a club or group of canoes, let the most experienced paddler lead the way. He has the best chance of finding routes among the rocks and ob-

*When the going gets rough— portage. Never risk wanton damage to your craft. (Photo Core-Craft)*

structions. By following his lead, you minimize the chance of encountering danger or making unpleasant mistakes.

If you travel with another canoe or kayak or in a group, keep the craft ahead in sight so that you can help if it gets in trouble, but do not stick so close that you run into it if the paddler makes a mistake or meets an unexpected obstruction.

Also, if you travel in a group, keep the group together and be ready to lend a hand to your companions at all times.

Always carry an extra paddle. In fact, when tackling difficult waters, it is good to have a spare paddle for each paddler, lashed where it can be easily reached. It is not difficult to lose a paddle. In calm waters, the paddler who has another can propel the craft after a paddle that is floating away. In difficult water, the extra paddle may be necessary to surmount difficulty before retrieving the lost paddle.

Obey the law concerning flotation devices. For calm waters, swimmers need only a floating cushion. Non-swimmers should have a vest or horse-collar of PFD type. In fast water, all paddlers should wear life jackets.

Examine questionable courses from shore before attempting them. Always decide exactly what you are going to do before doing it. This reduces maneuvering to a matter of execution, for in tight spots there is little or no time for analysis and planning.

Keep your craft parallel to the current as much as possible. One of the fastest ways to take a spill is to be washed broadside into a cluster of branches or upon a rock.

When cross-current turns are necessary to avoid obstacles, always lean downstream. This tends to balance the craft if it hits an obstacle. Leaning upstream merely accentuates the pitching motion.

When you ship water, bail it immediately. If too much water enters the boat, it sloshes around, rushing to the lowest spot. This creates forces that accentuate tipping or pitching and interferes with control.

A good piece of equipment to carry is a portable bilge pump. No matter what type of bailing receptacle you have—tin can or a plastic bucket—there are nooks and crannies it cannot reach. A portable bilge pump looks like a tire pump, with a plunger that moves up and down in a tube. Not only does it remove water fast, but it can be placed in the lowest point of the boat—that point to which all water flows.

Make the water work for you, not against you.

*When challenging fast water, be sure to kneel, both to lower the center of gravity and to maximize the potential paddle power. (Photo Moore)*

Wherever possible, use the force of the current for propulsion. It is advantageous to cut a bend wide where the water flows the fastest, or, if conditions warrant, paddle the inner bank to slow down and assure safety. In all cases, remember that water flows fastest in the line of least resistance. This does not mean that it refuses to flow circuitous or tortuous routes.

When tackling large, standing waves in an open canoe, move the bowman to a position aft of the normal bow thwart position. This moves the fulcrum of weight distribution farther abaft, lightening the bow and permitting it to ride up on the waves. It cuts down on the amount of water shipped over the bow.

When entering an eddy (or place where the water flows in the opposite direction from the main current) bow first, the bowman should lean upstream to offset the reverse current. Effectively, this prevents the canoe from being washed out from under you.

In leaving an eddy, put the bow out first and lean downstream, again preventing the canoe from being driven one way by the current while you are leaning the other way.

If you spill in fast current, remember that the force of the water pushing the canoe is tremendous. Stay upstream of the canoe. Do not get caught between the canoe and an obstacle; the canoe could injure you.

If you plan fastwater or whitewater paddling, become a student of water-flow interpretation. Read conditions carefully and make close observations when you are on the water. Do not try Niagara Falls the first time out. Take your time learning, never overtax your capabilities, and if lessons in whitewatering are available in your area, sign up.

There is no blanket rule on what to do if you spill. Of course, if the river is narrow and water downstream is dangerous, there is no point to sticking with your capsized craft; swim to shore as hastily as possible. On the other hand, if you know that the water downstream is not dangerous, or if the river is wide, stick with the boat and attempt to push it to shore as soon as possible. Be sure to hang on to it at the upstream end. Books on canoe craft spend many pages depicting methods of bailing a canoe while swimming, and making canoe rescues by hauling the submerged craft across the gunwales of another, thereby ridding the capsized craft of water and righting it for the rescued passenger. It is good to know and practice these techniques. But the novice should realize that they are not easy to accomplish, and that he is likely to bungle them if he has not practiced.

A healthy dose of humility mentioned earlier is essential to safety. Always underestimate your strength, experience, and abilities. In this way, you will be able to handle any situations that arise.

When paddling where there are many fallen trees and piles of debris blocking the watercourse, it may be necessary to attack the obstacles with ax and saw. Reserve the ax for situations where your feet are on solid ground, or at least on the river bottom. Chopping from a boat puts you in the position of swinging a sharp, heavy instrument from a base that can pitch or shift at any instant. This can cause serious injury or damage the boat. Any time you must chop or saw through snags, study and analyze the situation carefully. Do not chop a key log, only to have the entire pile of debris cascade upon you, driven by the river.

*It* can *happen.*
*PFDs are really no*
*substitute for*
*swimming. (Photo*
*Quapaw)*

When passing through locks where you are required to hold on to a rope while ascending or descending, never snub the rope or wrap it around your wrist. When you are being lowered, this could spell disaster.

## TIPS ON CAMPING

When camping, treat every animal as your equal in the struggle for survival. Animals are not cute. The bite of even the smallest squirrel can result in tetanus, rabies, or, in a rare instance, bubonic plague.

Sling your food sack from the limb of a tree where it is safe from nighttime marauders. Never store food in your tent while you sleep. This is an invitation for raccoons, skunks, or even bears to attempt to enter the tent.

During thunderstorms, stay away from isolated trees and poles; they are effective lightning rods.

Wherever possible, use existing campsites. In the Superior National Forest and the Boundary Waters Canoe Area, thousands of paddlers pass over trails every year. If every party were to pick a virgin stand of forest every night to pitch its camp, the entire area would become beaten down, erosion

227

would run rampant, and the land would be spoiled. People making trips in these areas are asked to used developed campsites that are carefully controlled and tended—an excellent suggestion for every paddler, wherever he may travel.

Leave your campsite without a trace of human occupancy, if possible. Nothing is more disturbing to parties that follow than to find clutter.

Smokers: when there is material on the ground that could serve as fuel, try not to smoke as you walk around the campsite. If you're going to smoke, stop, sit down, and relax. Use a flat rock as your ashtray or dig down to mineral soil with your heel. Make sure you crush out your butt.

Be careful in snake country. Do not grope along stony ledges or step over fallen logs without checking where your hand or foot will fall.

Do not wander around a campsite without a light at night. Since you will have pitched your tent and campsite only hours earlier, its layout will be comparatively foreign. It is easy to injure a foot on a tent peg or trip on a guy rope.

Whenever possible, pull your boat onto the land alongside your campsite and turn it over. This way it does not require bailing in case of rain. It also stays put if the river should happen to rise.

Remember that some rivers rise and fall as much as several feet when it rains or when dams are opened and closed. Always camp on a spot well above the water level. This precaution can prevent you from being awakened in the middle of the night to find your tent and gear in the water—an extremely serious situation in which the boat can wash away. Even if it doesn't float away, you may still have to paddle to shore in the dark, abandoning most of your equipment.

Do not build tables and shelters or other semi-permanent structures at a campsite. Also, do not pound nails into trees or otherwise permanently deface the foliage. Do not wrap wires around a tree. If the wire should remain as the tree grows, it will eventually cut into the tree itself. The best washline can be rigged by simply encircling a large tree with a piece of twine.

## GIVE A HOOT, DON'T POLLUTE

Trenching around a tent is out. This practice used to be advocated by most outdoor manuals. Not any more. Today's camper scrupulously avoids any act that mars the land on which he camps. Of course, he may have to trench if forced to camp on low-lying ground where water flows from higher areas, but usually he can find a campsite on high ground, even on a knoll.

Never use a soap to wash yourself or dishes in a stream or lake. For sudsing, use a bucket away from the water, and empty the soapy water at least 50 feet from the open river.

Nature will dispose of excrement. In the top six or eight inches of soil, there is a system of biological disposers that decompose organic material. To take advantage of it, carry a small digging or trenching tool. Select a suitable screened spot at least 50 feet from any open water. Dig a hole about six inches in diameter and eight to ten inches deep. Do not dig deeper, for you will pass the system of biological disposers. After use, fill the hole with loose soil and then tramp the sod. In a few days, nature does the rest.

Pick up extra pieces of refuse and tote them out with you. If enough paddlers make this their habit, it will be possible to clean up the nation's canoe and kayak streams, returning them to their original state.

### GENERAL SAFETY AND FIRST AID
Always tell someone where you are going and when you expect to return.

If you are ever paddling alone and are involved in an emergency that prevents moving and seeking help, signal by whatever means are available. The universal call for help is three signals in rapid succession, repeated at regular intervals: three shots of a gun, three flashes of light, three blasts on a whistle, three puffs of smoke. It is a good idea to carry a police whistle in your pocket for this purpose.

In case of injury, stop paddling immediately. Treat the injury if you can; make the injured party comfortable. Send or signal for help. Use extreme care in moving injured people.

If a person in your party is injured, restore breathing first (if necessary), using mouth-to-mouth artificial respiration. Tip his head back with the neck raised and extend his jaw. Clear the air passages. Pinch the nostrils, and blow in until his chest rises, then release. Repeat this procedure 12 times per minute for adults, 20 for children. Continue mouth-to-mouth resuscitation until normal breathing resumes.

Should an injured person bleed severely, apply direct pressure over his wound with a clean cloth, the fingers, or, the heel of the hand. Bandage when the bleeding stops. Use a tourniquet only as a last resort and do not leave the tourniquet on too long.

229

If an injured person needs treatment for shock, make him lie down and raise his legs slightly above his body level. Keep him warm and loosen his collar and belt. If he is conscious, give him stimulants such as tea or coffee—but never alcohol. Do not give him food or drink, however, if internal injuries are suspected.

# PART FIVE

# PADDLE TRAILS
# IN THE UNITED STATES
# AND CANADA

W e have discussed the cost of paddling as a hobby, investigated the differences and similarities between canoes and kayaks, described a great number of the more popular paddlecraft on today's market, examined camping equipment, and offered a number of tips for paddle camping. But a major question remains: Where can you launch your boat?

It is practically impossible to scratch the surface in listing trips for paddlers, and even more so to give a full description of each location. But it is possible to suggest some places and list other sources of information with addresses to which one can write.

When examining the following listings and descriptions of lakes, rivers, and streams, the ample opportunities that exist almost at the stoop of your back door are likely to surprise you. Few sections of the country lack at least a few areas suitable for leisurely Sunday-afternoon cruises. Most offer much more. An attempt has been made here to present canoeing spots that appeal to all paddlers, from amateurs to experienced competitors.

Sometimes the information you receive about various paddle trails grades the difficulty of the trip using Roman numerals. Rivers are commonly classified in six categories of difficulty. The Department of the Interior, Bureau of Land Management, describes the grades of difficulty in its publication *Alaska Canoe Trails:*

I. "Easy—sand banks, bends without difficulty, occasional small rapids and waves regular and low. Correct course easy to find but care is needed with minor obstacles like pebble banks, fallen trees, etc., especially in narrow rivers. River speed less than hard backpaddling speed. Spray cover unnecessary.

Gradient 0 to 5 feet. [I.e., 0 to 5 feet drop per mile. Gradient is expressed in feet of river drop per mile—five-feet drop per mile is generally slow water; 50 feet per mile is extremely fast water.]

II. "Medium—fairly frequent but unobstructed rapids, usually with regular waves, easy eddies, and easy bends. Course generally easy to recognize, river speed occasionally exceeding hard backpaddling speed. Spray cover useful. Gradient 5 to 15 feet.

III. "Difficult—maneuvering in rapids necessary. Small falls, large regular waves covering boat, numerous rapids. Main current may swing under bushes, branches, or overhangs. Course not always easily recognizable. Current speed usually less than fast forward-paddling speed. Spray cover recommended. Gradient 16 to 25 feet.

IV. "Very difficult—long extended stretches of rapids, high irregular waves with boulders directly in current. Difficult broken water, eddies, and abrupt bends. Course often difficult to recognize and inspection from the bank frequently necessary. Swift current. Spray cover necessary. Rough water experience indispensable. Gradient greater than 25 feet.

V. "Exceedingly Difficult—seldom attempted even by the very experienced.

VI. "Limit of navigability—cannot be attempted without risk of life."

# Paddle Trails in the United States

## [LISTED ALPHABETICALLY BY STATE]

Alabama provides excellent canoeing and fishing. Of the numerous trails, two suggested include tackling the Sipsey and Tallapoosa rivers. Following is an excerpt from an article entitled "Float Fishing on the Sipsey River" by Gerald Hooper, District Fishery Biologist, that appeared in *Alabama Conservation:*

"The Sipsey River lends itself well to float-fishing trips. . . . Canoes . . . are excellent craft for floating the stream and fishing. No major obstacles are present, although short portages around shoal areas may be necessary, depending on the water level. The most desirable area to float-fish extends from the Sipsey River Picnic Area, which is approximately four miles west of Grayson, to Payne Creek. This is the lower 11 miles of stream before it enters the Lewis-Smith Reservoir.

"There are three trips that could be made in this 11-mile section of stream, depending on the amount of available time. Trip number one could begin at the Sipsey River Picnic Area and end at the Old Payne Creek Road. This trip is eight miles and would take approximately nine hours. Trip number two could begin at the Old Payne Creek Road and end at the New Payne Creek Road. This trip is less than one mile and would take approximately one hour. Trip number three could begin at the Old Payne Creek Road and end at Payne Creek. This trip is three miles and would take approximately four hours . . . Overnight camping is permitted anywhere along the stream where it borders the Bankhead National Forest."

The other float trip might be taken on the Tallapoosa River, which rises in Paulding County, Georgia, near Embry, and flows in a southwesterly direction for some 250 miles to its junction with the Coosa River, a few miles above Montgomery. Much of this river flows through near-wilderness conditions. It is well to do some advance planning before tackling the various sections, but the river provides many good, short journeys

—especially for paddlers who want to try their luck at fishing bass. For more detailed information on these and other Alabama trips, contact the Administrative Division, Alabama Department of Conservation and Natural Resources, Montgomery, Alabama 36104.

## ALASKA

Alaska abounds in canoe trails of incredible beauty, almost all untouched and unspoiled by commercialization. "Seward's Icebox" is an unsurpassed Eden for wilderness paddling. For Alaskan residents these virgin water trails are right "out the back door," and paddlers who live in other parts of the United States often save their dollars for years, hoping to visit Alaska for canoeing or kayaking vacations.

A number of sources offer information about paddle trails in Alaska. One of the best is the Travel Information Officer, State of Alaska, Department of Economic Development, Division of Tourism, Pouch E, Juneau 99801. By writing the Travel Information Officer, you can get an invaluable pamphlet entitled *Alaska Canoe Trails*—a guide to the highway-accessible water routes of Alaska. The pamphlet identifies twelve canoe trails: Fortymile River—Yukon River to Eagle; Yukon River (Eagle to Circle), Birch Creek, Chatanika River and Chena River; Delta River, Upper Tangle Lakes to Dickey Lake and Gulkana River; Kenai River, Swanson River and Swan Lake; and Fish Creek. Featured in the pamphlet are index maps for the canoe trails. The descriptions of each trail contain difficulty and gradient ratings, supplemental map information, fish species available on the river, and specific trail details. You are also told how to figure travel time.

## ARIZONA

Even though many people from other parts of the United States think Arizona an arid state consisting of vast deserts with little or no water, there are some very attractive paddle adventures in the land of the sun. Some of the finest are found in the Coconino National Forest, where a number of lakes are suitable for paddlecraft. There is also a river in the forest—the Verde—that can be run in early spring when the waters run off the mountains. Canoeists usually put in at Cottonwood landing and take out at Camp Verde or continue on to Bartlett Reservoir in the Tonto National Forest. For information on the Verde River, write to the United States Forest Service, District Ranger, Camp Verde, Arizona 86322.

Arizona is also the home of the Grand Canyon National

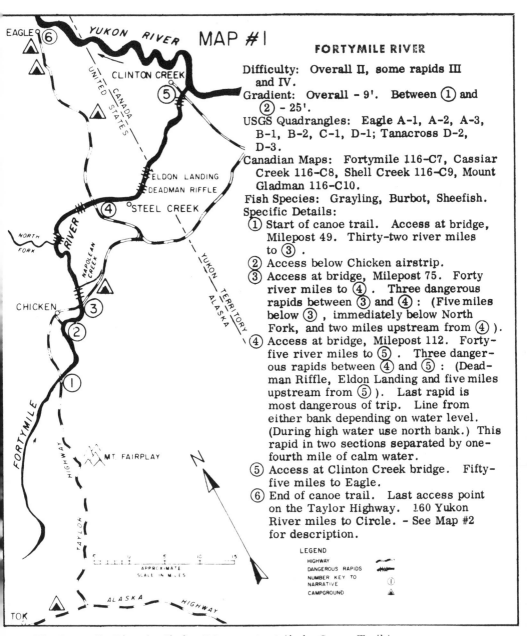

**MAP #1**

**FORTYMILE RIVER**

**Difficulty:** Overall II, some rapids III and IV.

**Gradient:** Overall - 9'. Between ① and ② - 25'.

**USGS Quadrangles:** Eagle A-1, A-2, A-3, B-1, B-2, C-1, D-1; Tanacross D-2, D-3.

**Canadian Maps:** Fortymile 116-C7, Cassiar Creek 116-C8, Shell Creek 116-C9, Mount Gladman 116-C10.

**Fish Species:** Grayling, Burbot, Sheefish.

**Specific Details:**

① Start of canoe trail. Access at bridge, Milepost 49. Thirty-two river miles to ③.

② Access below Chicken airstrip.

③ Access at bridge, Milepost 75. Forty river miles to ④. Three dangerous rapids between ③ and ④: (Five miles below ③, immediately below North Fork, and two miles upstream from ④).

④ Access at bridge, Milepost 112. Forty-five river miles to ⑤. Three dangerous rapids between ④ and ⑤: (Deadman Riffle, Eldon Landing and five miles upstream from ⑤). Last rapid is most dangerous of trip. Line from either bank depending on water level. (During high water use north bank.) This rapid in two sections separated by one-fourth mile of calm water.

⑤ Access at Clinton Creek bridge. Fifty-five miles to Eagle.

⑥ End of canoe trail. Last access point on the Taylor Highway. 160 Yukon River miles to Circle. - See Map #2 for description.

**LEGEND**

HIGHWAY

DANGEROUS RAPIDS

NUMBER KEY TO NARRATIVE

CAMPGROUND

*The Fortymile River in Alaska. (Map courtesy Alaska Canoe Trails)*

Park, through which flows the exciting Colorado. This is no trip for amateurs and should be attempted only by experienced kayakists and then with the utmost caution. Guidelines have been developed to help those managing the park determine if applicants are qualified to run the river. Information is available from the United States Department of the Interior, National Park Service, Grand Canyon National Park, Grand Canyon, Arizona 86023.

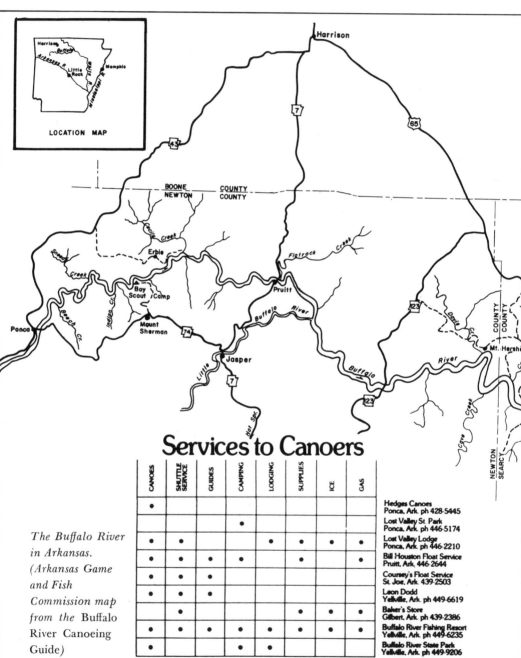

## Services to Canoers

| | CANOES | SHUTTLE SERVICE | GUIDES | CAMPING | LODGING | SUPPLIES | ICE | GAS | |
|---|---|---|---|---|---|---|---|---|---|
| | • | | | | | | | | Hedges Canoes<br>Ponca, Ark. ph 428-5445 |
| | | | | • | | | | | Lost Valley St. Park<br>Ponca, Ark. ph 446-5174 |
| | • | • | | | • | • | • | • | Lost Valley Lodge<br>Ponca, Ark. ph 446-2210 |
| | • | • | • | | | • | | • | Bill Houston Float Service<br>Pruitt, Ark. 446-2644 |
| | • | • | • | | | | | | Coursey's Float Service<br>St. Joe, Ark. 439-2503 |
| | • | • | • | | | | | | Leon Dodd<br>Yellville, Ark. ph 449-6619 |
| | | • | | | | • | • | • | Baker's Store<br>Gilbert, Ark. ph 439-2386 |
| | • | • | • | • | • | • | • | • | Buffalo River Fishing Resort<br>Yellville, Ark. ph 449-6235 |
| | • | | | • | • | | | | Buffalo River State Park<br>Yellville, Ark. ph 449-9206 |

*The Buffalo River in Arkansas. (Arkansas Game and Fish Commission map from the Buffalo River Canoeing Guide)*

236

**CHECK WATER CONDITIONS**  Except for extreme dry periods the lower half of the river can be floated most anytime. During some periods in late summer the stretch from Highway 123 to Highway 65 is too low for good floating. Normally after May 1, unless following local rains, the upper portion (Ponca to Pruitt) requires some dragging.

The Buffalo River of Northwest Arkansas is a fine free-flowing river that takes its origin in the Boston Mountains within the Ozark National Forest. There are numerous excellent pad-

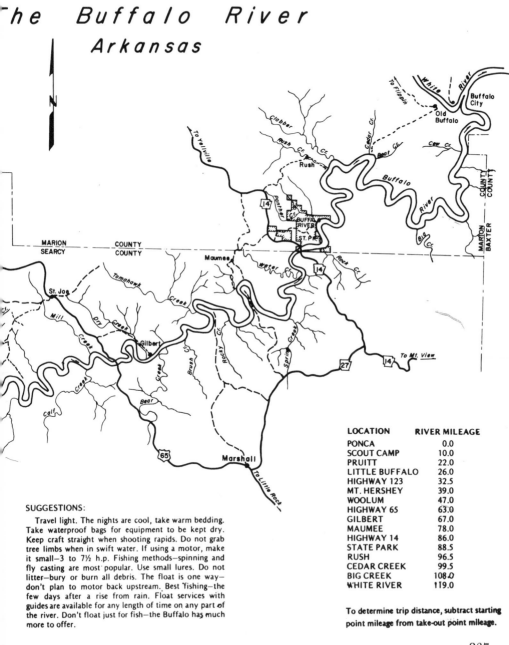

# The Buffalo River
## Arkansas

| LOCATION | RIVER MILEAGE |
|---|---|
| PONCA | 0.0 |
| SCOUT CAMP | 10.0 |
| PRUITT | 22.0 |
| LITTLE BUFFALO | 26.0 |
| HIGHWAY 123 | 32.5 |
| MT. HERSHEY | 39.0 |
| WOOLUM | 47.0 |
| HIGHWAY 65 | 63.0 |
| GILBERT | 67.0 |
| MAUMEE | 78.0 |
| HIGHWAY 14 | 86.0 |
| STATE PARK | 88.5 |
| RUSH | 96.5 |
| CEDAR CREEK | 99.5 |
| BIG CREEK | 108.0 |
| WHITE RIVER | 119.0 |

**SUGGESTIONS:**

Travel light. The nights are cool, take warm bedding. Take waterproof bags for equipment to be kept dry. Keep craft straight when shooting rapids. Do not grab tree limbs when in swift water. If using a motor, make it small—3 to 7½ h.p. Fishing methods—spinning and fly casting are most popular. Use small lures. Do not litter—bury or burn all debris. The float is one way—don't plan to motor back upstream. Best fishing—the few days after a rise from rain. Float services with guides are available for any length of time on any part of the river. Don't float just for fish—the Buffalo has much more to offer.

To determine trip distance, subtract starting point mileage from take-out point mileage.

237

Courtesy Arkansas Game & Fish Commission
Drawn By, Flaun Boyles    7-1-65

dle trips to be taken on the Buffalo and information is available to canoeists. For the key to top-notch canoeing in Arkansas write the Ozark Society, Box 2914, Little Rock, Arkansas 72203, for a copy of the *Buffalo River Canoeing Guide* by Harold and Margaret Hedges. Cost of this guide is $1.00.

The *Buffalo River Canoeing Guide* divides the river into twelve segments and gives mileage, water conditions, and descriptions of what you will encounter on each section. It mentions maps required for each trip and where to order them. And it lists services available to campers along the river—canoe rentals, shuttle service, guides, camping, lodging, and places for obtaining supplies. This fine publication enables you to plan a paddle adventure on the Buffalo in considerable detail, thereby getting the most enjoyment out of the time you spend on the river.

For those who like to travel with their canoe or kayak atop their cars and use it for fishing while staying at resorts or campgrounds, a packet of information is available from the Arkansas Department of Parks and Tourism, State Capitol, Little Rock, Arkansas 72201, that includes a tour guide of Arkansas and a camper's guide. These publications are indispensable in planning a vacation in Arkansas if you have never traveled to the state before. Best of all, they tell of places where the lakes are peaceful and the fish hungry.

## CALIFORNIA

The lakes of California beckon with excellent opportunities for travelers who pack canoes atop their cars. For extended paddling, however, the lakes may be too heavily populated with motorboats. For the canoeist or kayakist who wants adventure of a whitewater variety, there are numerous opportunities in the national forests, but most of these are suggested only for the experienced paddler who can negotiate difficult water. One such river is the Truckee, between Lake Tahoe and Truckee. This stretch of water is reserved mostly for kayakists and rafters. For maps of the Tahoe National Forest in which this route is found, contact the United States Department of Agriculture, Forest Service, Tahoe National Forest, Nevada City, California 95959.

More trips for the hardy, experienced paddle enthusiast can be found on the Trinity, Mad, and Eel rivers flowing through Six Rivers National Forest. These are difficult rivers, usually reserved for commercial float trips using rafts. For information on the region, contact the Visitor Information Clerk, Forest

Service, United States Department of Agriculture, Six Rivers National Forest, Eureka, California 95501.

Listed as having good canoeing potential are four reservoirs in the Whiskeytown-Shasta-Trinity National Recreation Area: Lake Clair Engle, Shasta Lake, Whiskeytown Reservoir, and Lewiston Reservoir. A river used for commercial float trips with rubber rafts is the Klamath, and this too should also be a good exercise for experienced kayakists. In the Groveland District of the Stanislaus National Forest is a usable portion of the Tuolome River, also popular for float trips. Maps of all these routes are available by contacting the United States Department of Agriculture, Forest Service, 630 Sansome Street, San Francisco, California 94111.

In the Sierra National Forest in California, the Merced and Kings rivers are attractive to whitewater enthusiasts, but are not suggested for average paddlers. On the other hand, the Mammoth Pool Reservoir, Hungtington Lake, Lake Thomas A. Edison, Florence Lake, Courtright Reservoir, and Wishon Reservoir are suitable for canoeing recreation, if not for paddle trips or camping.

The Inyo National Forest offers the Owens River to canoeists. This river is passable from Five Bridges to Big Pine, although heavy woods and grass are encountered in some portions. The Forest Service cautions that the Owens area has a high fire danger, making exact adherence to fire regulations and good camping practice mandatory. For a map of the Owens and its surrounding countryside contact Inyo National Forest, Attn: Maps, Office of Forest Supervisor, Bishop, California 93514. Needless to say, there are any number of other areas suitable for canoeing and kayaking in California.

## COLORADO

Colorado boasts top canoeing and kayaking opportunities in a land of incredibly varied, majestic landscapes. The White River National Park provides the following lakes for day canoeing and fishing: Avery, Trappers, Meadow, Heart, Deep, White Owl, Sweetwater, Beaver, Chapman, Homestake, Woods, Sylvan, and Blake lakes #1 and #2. Also suitable for paddling are Rifle Gap, Vega, Grizzly, and Ruedi reservoirs. Suggested river trips include the Colorado River, from Dotsero to Shoshoni Power Dam, which features three mild rapids before and after high water. During high-water spring runoff, only experts should tackle this stretch. Also three trips on the Colorado River from Newcastle to Silt, Silt to Rifle, and Rifle to

DeBeque are suggested for experts at high water. For maps and information on canoeing in the White River National Forest, contact the Office of Forest Supervisor, Post Office Building, P.O. Box 948, Glenwood Springs, Colorado 81601.

The Rocky Mountain region of Colorado also contains excellent paddling opportunities, mostly on lakes and rivers within one to three hours' driving time of the population centers. Some popular routes include the Arkansas, from Leadville to Buena Vista and on to Canon City; the South Platte, southwest of Denver; the San Miguel and Dolores rivers in the southwest part of the state; the Colorado in the central portion of the state; the Green River in Wyoming and northwest Colorado; and the Yampa in the northwestern part of the state.

For experienced kayakists looking for whitewater, the Cache La Poudre River in the Roosevelt National Forest offers challenge from May through June at some points. Information on where to put in is available from the United States Department of Agriculture, Forest Service, Arapaho-Roosevelt National Forest, Federal Building, 301 South Howes, Fort Collins, Colorado 80521. More worthwhile information on canoeing and kayaking in Colorado may be obtained from the Colorado Division of Parks and Outdoor Recreation, 6060 Broadway, Denver, Colorado 80216.

## CONNECTICUT

Connecticut offers extensive paddling for whitewater enthusiasts as well as those who like to cruise. For information, start by sending for a brochure entitled *Connecticut Canoeing Guide* from the Department of Environmental Protection, Public Information and Education, State Office Building, Hartford, Connecticut 06115. Along with basic advice on the sport of paddling, it lists and briefly describes lakes, ponds, and rivers that are worth considering.

*Lakes and Ponds.* In southeastern Connecticut: Beach Pond, Long Pond, Lake Gardner, Bashan Lake, Moodus Reservoir. In northeastern Connecticut: Bolton Lakes, Crystal Lake, Mashapaug Lake, Quaddick Reservoir. In southwestern Connecticut: Lake Lillinonah, Lake Waramaug, Lake Zoar, Quonnipaug Lake. In northwestern Connecticut: Highland Lake, East Twin Lakes, Wononscopomuc Lake, Colebrook Impoundment, Rainbow Reservoir, and West Hill Pond.

*Rivers.* The following rivers are listed: Housatonic, Connecticut, Farmington, and Thames.

More complete information is given for numerous rivers in Connecticut in the AMC *New England Canoeing Guide,* avail-

*Right: the Housatonic River. (Map courtesy of Riverrun Outfitters, P.O. Box 33, Falls Village, Conn. 06031)*

The Housatonic River offers some of the most pleasurable canoeing to be had in New England. Winding through the beautiful Berkshire Hills, its waters offer sport for the novice and expert canoeist as well.

The river above the Great Falls flows peacefully at all water levels with few hazards. From Sheffield, Mass., to Falls Village would be a fine lazy run with beautiful views that a whole family could enjoy. There is always substantial current but no rapids. The one danger spot is the old Canaan Dam, about 2½ miles south of the Mass. line. The dam is no longer used and there are breaks in the dam on the right and left. NO ONE should run these breaks as there are concrete reinforcing rods on the bottom that will destroy a canoe. Portage your canoe just to the right of the LEFT hand break, over the dam and across the small island. The portage is safe, easy and will save you or us a canoe.

The river resumes its lazy pace after the dam until you reach the next dam at Falls Village. This section of the river has an abundance of wildlife. Great Blue Herons have been seen along this stretch, and with the many other species of birds, this stretch should be a bird watchers paradise.

The portage at the Falls Village dam is on the left side just before the sluice gate. Carry down the railroad tracks about one hundred yards to a small bridge that crosses the

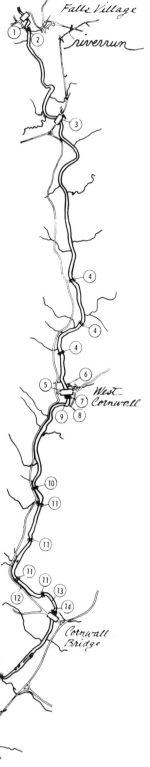

canal and put into the canal. Ride the canal to its end (the next bridge) then carry to the right down the dirt road to the river (1). BE CAREFUL when approaching the dam in high water as there is an eighty foot falls on the other side of the dam and the reservoir overflows the dam at high water. Approach carefully down the left side to the portage if these conditions exist.

The section of the river from Falls Village to Kent offers a more sporting run than the previous section. The profile of the river here is fast water broken at intervals with easy to difficult rapids. The majority of this water can still be handled by a novice with a couple of notable exceptions that I will deal with further on. This run begins with a nice little CLASS II rapid (2) to get the blood going. The inexperienced will probably want to stay close to the left hand side going through, however, for those with a little time at the paddle there is a nice slot between big boulders on the right. Calm water takes over for the next two or three miles, but the mountains close in on the river here hinting at faster water to come.

CLASS I & II rapids (4) begin coming about two miles south of the Rt. 7 bridge (3). These are easy rapids in high water and may be run full bore so to speak (if somewhat experienced). At low water go slow and pick your way through the rocks. When the red covered bridge (5) looms into view you will be approaching one of the finest rapids on the river. No matter how many times I run this one, I always seem to get a little lump in my throat.

This is a CLASS III rapid in low water, and a CLASS IV in high water (7). If you have little or no experience in canoes, portage around the left side. Take out before the

able from the Appalachian Mountain Club, 5 Joy Street, Boston, Massachusetts 02108. Cost of this hardbound manual is $6.00. The information is very complete and detailed, with excellent maps tucked into pockets in the cover. This publication is indispensable for those planning to paddle in Connecticut and its surrounding states.

## DELAWARE

Canoeing in Delaware is limited; most of the state rests on the Atlantic Coastal Plain. Delaware is relatively flat, and there is little water that can be considered "challenging." One river is considered delightful by paddlers, however—the Brandywine. A bulletin from the Division of Economic Development, 45 the Green, Dover, Delaware 19901, describes the Brandywine trip as follows:

"This is a lovely one-day trip by canoe. The creek flows through a very picturesque area. Symmetrical slopes, rising to 200 feet above the water, line the shores of the upper course. Although the upper river is more appealing from aesthetic standpoints, the whitewater enthusiast will enjoy views of the terracing slopes of the Brandywine battlefield, above the northeastern shore. In the lower reaches of the Brandywine, much of the industrial history of the United States and Delaware was written. . . . The Brandywine course begins at Lenape, State Route 52 (Pennsylvania) and ends directly above the Market Street Bridge in Wilmington at the tidewater mark."

Write to the Dover, Delaware, address for further information, including distances in miles, drop in feet, time in hours from one point to another, and degree of difficulty of each section (range from I to III). United States Geological Survey maps (7½ minute) of the Brandywine consist of Unionville, West Chester (Pennsylvania), and Wilmington North (Delaware).

In addition to the Brandywine, Delaware offers canoeists who prefer to cruise quiet waters some trails with beauty almost unsurpassed. Large tracts included in Bombay Hook National Wildlife Refuge and state-owned wildlife refuges can be explored by people interested in observing water fowl in their natural habitat. Because you must observe the regulations of the wildlife refuge, you should send for an information sheet and a map describing permitted activities. Write to the Refuge Manager, Prime Hook National Wildlife Refuge, Box 195, Milton, Delaware 19968.

*The Bombay Hook National Wildlife Refuge, right. (U.S. Department of the Interior, Fish and Wildlife Service map)*

One water system particularly interesting to paddlers is located in southern Delaware in the region known locally as the

# BOMBAY HOOK NATIONAL WILDLIFE REFUGE
## KENT COUNTY, DELAWARE

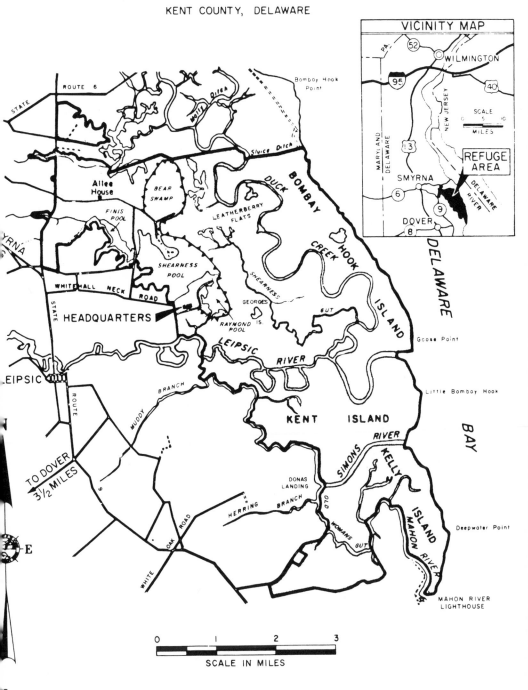

SCALE IN MILES

"Great Cypress Swamp." This area is reminiscent of the Mississippi Delta region and contains the northernmost stands of cypress in North America. According to G. Daniel Blagg, Travel Representative, Bureau of Travel Development of Delaware, "This is a strange, mystical environment where huge cypress spring from calm, eerie waters." Many of the old legends of southern Delaware emanate from this territory, and in fact Mason and Dixon, the two intrepid eighteenth-century surveyors, made their way through this very area in the 1760s.

## FLORIDA

The most popular spot for canoeing in Florida is Everglades National Park. Five paddle trails offer unsurpassed scenic adventure. The Bear Lake course begins about two miles from the main park road along Buttonwood Canal and ends at Cape Sable, a distance of 12 miles, or six hours' travel time. A 25-foot portage is necessary near the end of the trail, which passes through a dense mangrove-buttonwood environment and into open coastal prairie where thousands of wading birds and ducks feed during the winter months. There is a primitive campsite at the end of the trail, and camping also is permitted on the beach.

The Hell's Bay trail originates approximately halfway between Nine Mile Pond and West Lake along the Main Park Road. The route to the first campsite is marked with white stakes and is about 2½ miles from the starting point, or about three hours' travel. The second campground is in Hell's Bay and is 2½ miles from the first site. Here is your chance to travel through passageways of overgrown red mangrove and a brackish water environment. It is necessary to file a float plan with the ranger on duty before you paddle this trail.

Another paddle trail in the Everglades National Park is West Lake. This trail begins at the West Lake Interpretive Shelter. A long exposed crossing of West Lake is necessary, and it is advisable to use caution on windy days. The trail winds through the coastal lake country and is bordered by red and black mangrove trees as well as buttonwoods. A small campsite, containing picnic tables and cooking grills, is located at Alligator Creek. The length of this trail, which is marked with numbered white flags on wood poles, is eight miles, or an estimated seven hours' travel time.

Noble Hammock head is located between the Hell's Bay Trail head and Nine Mile Pond along the Main Park Road. This trail meanders through more open country than the Hell's Bay Trail and through small alligator ponds located in a mixture of buttonwood, red mangrove, and sawgrass. Travel time is about three hours.

Finally, the Everglades National Park offers the Wilderness Waterway, commencing at the Everglades City Ranger Station or the marina at Flamingo. The trail is a well-marked one-hundred-mile inside route that winds through creeks, rivers, and open bays in the mangrove wilderness of the park. Canoeists and kayak enthusiasts are required to check in and out with a park ranger at either end. Several days are needed to complete the trip. A booklet entitled *A Guide to the Wilderness Waterway* provides a wealth of information and is obtained by writing to the Everglades Natural History Association, P.O. Box 279, Homestead, Florida 33030. For more information on paddling in the Everglades, and for a map of the general area and water routes, contact the United States Department of the Interior, National Park Service, Everglades National Park, P.O. Box 279, Homestead, Florida 33030.

## GEORGIA

Georgia is one of those states that host a number of paddling opportunities for those persistent enough to pry loose information about the various rivers and streams. For some reason, it is difficult to get source material about Georgia's waters. James Maken, in his book *Maken's Guide to U.S. Canoe Trails,* lists the following trips.

*Alapaha River.* Willocoochee to Statenville 83 mi., remote country, clearest Ga. river, high sand banks, small rapids w/wave, minor obstacles, rises and is swift after rain, 4 campsites; Dif. Class I, easy; Trips—Willocoochee to Ga. U.S. 168 brdg., 20 mi.; on to U.S. 129 brdg, 18 mi.; on to U.S. 84 brdg., 18 mi.; on to Ga. 187 brdg.—Mayday, 12 mi.; on to Statenville, 15 mi.

*Chatooga River.* Northeast Georgia, borders South Carolina; Northern border of Georgia to Tugalo Lake, 30 miles; 4 access points—Burrell's Ford, Georgia Rt. 28, Earl's Ford and U.S. Rt. 76; a white water river for experienced only; Burrell's Ford to Georgia Rt. 28 and on to Earl's Ford, Dif. II-III; Earl's Ford to U.S. Rt. 76, Dif. IV, difficult, powerful waves, long rapids; Below Rt. 76, Dif. VI, extraordinarily difficult, very dangerous, experts only; good all year, good trout fishing.

*Chattahoochee River.* Habersham, White, Hall Cos.; Upper Chattahoochee—above Lake Lanier; Hidden Valley Campsite off Georgia Rt. 105 to Lake Lanier; Hidden Valley Campsite to Chattahoochee Paradise Park, 3½ to 4 hrs., several class II rapids with class III rapids at Smith Island, Buck Shoals and the Horseshoe, experienced canoeists only; Ch. Par. Park to Bellton Brdg. Recreation Facility, 10 mi., 4 hrs., 3 or 4 class II rapids and several class I; Below Bellton Brdg., back waters of lake, ok beginners; last take out point—Clark's Brdg. Rec. Facility; trout fishing in upper river, white and black bass in lower river; access points—Georgia 75, Georgia 255, Georgia 254/115, Duncan Brdg. Rd. (S. 1759), Bellton Brdg. Rd. and Georgia 52.

*Chestatee River.* Lumpkin Co.; Waters Creek off Ga. 19 to 5976, Dif. Class II, thru Good Spring Run IV, below 5976 is a 50′ water fall—this stretch experts only, old interesting gold and copper mines.

*Coosawattee River.* Gilmer Co., St. Hwy. 5 to St. Line, some good Class IV rapids, no other info.

*Etowah River.* Lumpkin, Dawson Cos.; easy Class II river, some challenging rapids and shoals, access from U.S. Rt. 19 near Dahlonega, Ga. at 2 pts. and from Ga. Rt. 53 and Ga. Rt. 136, DANGER—10′ falls, Ga. 136 to Tobacco Pouch Creek River, 3 hrs., good most year; Hwy. 52 to L. Altoona, 4.5 mi., fair fishing, canoeable.

*Satilla River.* Approx. 260 mi., beautiful river; Trips—area above Waycross 94 mi., low in dry season, raging in rainy season, good canoeing section, many small passages, obstructions in river, 30 access pts.; Waycross to Hoboken (Hwy. 121), 20 mi., seasonal water flow, many obstructions, 3 dangerous sections, high bluffs; Hoboken to Nahunta 29 mi., deeper than upstream, clear stream bed; Nahunta to Atkinson 23 mi., few obstructions, deep; Atkinson to Burnt Fort 41 mi., motorboat traffic, wide and clear channel; Burnt Fort to Atlantic Ocean 52 mi., very wide and deep, salt marsh border, tide influence, motorboat traffic; Best portion above Waycross to Woodbine; Bass, Crappie, Red Bellies, Bream.

*Toccoa River.* Fannin Co.; Canoeable from Cooper Creek to McCaysville thru Blue Ridge Lake, lightly traveled, Dif.—Gen. Class II, some Class III rapids, beautiful, forest, good trout fishing; Deep Hole Res. area to Blue Ridge L., 12 mi.

*Paddle trails in the Okefenokee Swamp, southern Georgia. (Map from the Slash Pine Area Planning and Development Commission, Waycross)*

*Withlacoochee River.* Ga. 94 brdg. to Suwannee River St. Park, Fla., 56 mi.; swampland, sandy beaches, many rapids, high waves, bends, minor obstacles, ptg. Aug.-Sept. over sand bars and rapids, high and swift Mar.-May; Dif.—Class III, fairly easy; Trips—Ga. 94 brdg. to U.S. 84 brdg., 8 mi.; U.S. 84 to Rocky Ford Rd. brdg., 12 mi.; Rocky Ford to Fla. 145 brdg., 4 mi.; 145 to Fla. 6 brdg., 20 mi.; Fla. 6 to finish 12 mi.

For further information about Georgia's paddle trails you can write to the Coastal Plains Tourism Council, Box 1223,

## OKEFENOKEE NATIONAL WILDLIFE REFUGE

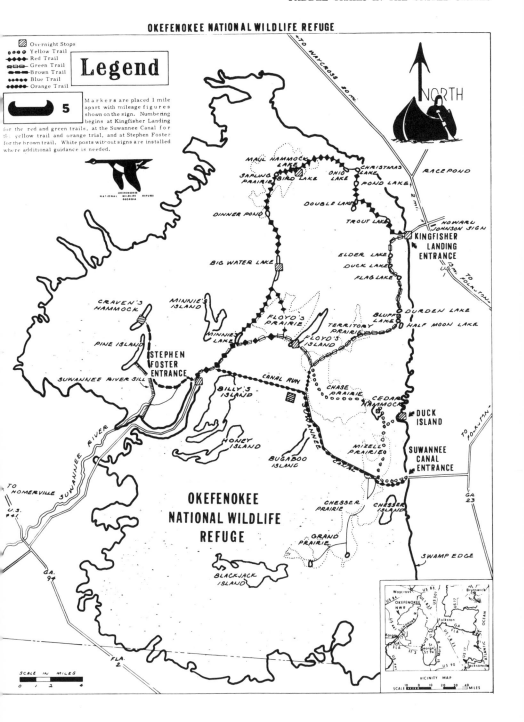

### Legend

- ▨ Overnight Stops
- ●●●●○ Yellow Trail
- ◆◆◆◆ Red Trail
- ▭▭▭ Green Trail
- ■■■ Brown Trail
- ◆◆◆◆ Blue Trail
- ●●●○ Orange Trail

Markers are placed 1 mile apart with mileage figures shown on the sign. Numbering begins at Kingfisher Landing for the red and green trails, at the Suwannee Canal for the yellow trail and orange trial, and at Stephen Foster for the brown trail. White posts without signs are installed where additional guidance is needed.

NATIONAL WILDLIFE REFUGE
OKEFENOKEE GEORGIA

NORTH

OKEFENOKEE
NATIONAL WILDLIFE
REFUGE

VICINITY MAP

SCALE IN MILES
0 1 2 4

247

Valdosta, Georgia, for their book *Canoe Guide to the Alapaha River Trail;* the Slash Pine Area Planning and Development Commission, P.O. Box 1276, Waycross, Georgia 31501, for their brochure *Canoe Guide to the Scenic Satilla River.* Other brochures are available from the Recreation Staff Officer, United States Department of Agriculture, United States Forest Service, P.O. Box 1437, Gainesville, Georgia 30501; the Georgia Department of State Parks, 7 Hunter Street S.W., Atlanta, Georgia 30334; and the Georgia Canoeing Association, Box 7023, Atlanta, Georgia 30309.

## IDAHO

Idaho is among the better paddle-adventure areas, although for the most part you must go it alone. There are, according to the State Department of Commerce and Development, no known canoeing organizations, canoe-trip outfitters, or listings of waters. About two-thirds of Idaho is public land, so there are ample opportunities for float voyages and camping, but a good round of local inquiry regarding conditions of the waters at any given point is in order.

Most of Idaho's potential paddling waters flow from north to southeast across the state. A partial listing of such waters includes the Moyie River, from the Canadian border to Meadow Creek Campground (Kootenai River Drainage). Two trips are suggested on the Pend Oreille River Drainage. The first is on the Priest River, a tributary to the Pend Oreille. The trip begins at Priest Lake Outlet and continues to the confluence with Pend Oreille. This is suggested as a two-day float trip to be taken in May. The second is on the Priest River Thoroughfare, a waterway between Priest Lake and upper Priest Lake, a trip of four miles.

Four other suggested voyages pertain to the Spokane River Drainage: the Spokane River from Post Falls to Spokane, Washington; the North Fork of the Coeur d'Alene River from the mouth of Teepee Creek to the confluence with the South Fork of the Coeur d'Alene; the St. Joe River from Red Ives Ranger Station to Coeur d'Alene Lake; and the St. Maries River from Clarkia to Mashburn, near Santa (suggested as an early-season float trip during April, May, and early June).

Six trips are suggested by the Department of Commerce and Development in the Clearwater River Drainage: the North Fork of the Clearwater, from Bungalow Ranger Station to Canyon Ranger Station (portages required); the Lochsa River from Split Creek to Lowell; the Selway River from Selway Falls to Lowell; the Middle Fork of the Clearwater from Lowell to Kooskia; the Clearwater River from Kooskia to Lewiston; and the South Fork of the Clearwater from Harpster to Kooskia.

The Salmon River Drainage reportedly offers no fewer than eight potential voyages: the Salmon River, from the confluence of Alturas Lake Creek to the steel bridge above Red Fish Lake Creek; the Salmon River from upper Stanley to the rapids above the old Sunbeam Dam; the Salmon River from Sunbeam Dam to North Fork, Idaho; the Salmon River from North Fork to the confluence with the Middle Fork; the Salmon from Vinegar Creek to Whitebird (take this one in the summer and early fall only, and then with some portages past rapids); Beaver Creek from Stanley Lake Creek to its mouth; Elk Creek from the twin bridges to the confluence with Bear Valley Creek; and Bear Valley from the mouth of Elk Creek to Fir Creek Campground.

Through an agricultural valley flows the Weiser River, which provides a good float trip from the Galloway Dam to the river's mouth.

The Payette River Drainage offers six paddle trips on the North Fork of the Payette—from Big Payette Lake outlet to Cascade Reservoir and from the bridge immediately south of Cascade to Cabarton Bridge; the Payette from Horseshoe Bend mill pond to Montour and from Black Canyon Dam to its mouth (on this segment of the trip there are irrigation diversions to portage); the South Fork of the Payette from Alder Creek Bridge to the mouth of the Middle Fork of the Payette, and the Middle Fork of the Payette from Hardscrabble Campground to the mouth of the river.

In the Boise River Drainage, suggested paddle trips include the North Fork of the Boise to Arrowrock Dam; the South Fork of the Boise from Baumgartner Campground to Anderson Ranch Reservoir; the South Fork of the Boise from Anderson Dam to Danskin Guard Station; the North Fork of the Boise from Swanholm Bridge to Barber Flat Bridge; and the Boise River itself from Barber Bridge to its mouth, with portages around irrigation diversions.

The Snake River Drainage also offers adventure in four trips on Henry's Fork; from Big Springs to Pond's Lodge, from Island Park Dam to the Highway #191 crossing, from Lower Mesa Falls to Ashton Reservoir, and from the Ashton Power Dam to the confluence with the South Fork of the Snake. Also listed by the Department of Commerce and Development is a trip from Henry's Lake Outlet to Henry's Fork, one down the Buffalo River, from its headwaters to U.S. 191-20, and another on Willow Creek from the Lincoln Road access to Valley Floor.

Other trips in the Snake Drainage include the Teton River from Spring Hollow to Teton Dam, and from Teton Dam to Teton City (St. Anthony Highway); the South Fork of the Snake from Palisades Dam to Heise; the Blackfoot River from Slug Creek Bridge to Lower Narrows, and from Diamond Creek Bridge to Trail Guard Station, as well as from the "narrows" to the mouth; the Portneuf River from the bridge above Pebble to the Highway 30N bridge above Lava Hot Springs (several short portages are required); the Snake from the mouth of the South Fork to Idaho Falls to American Falls Reservoir (with irrigation portages); from American Falls Dam in Milner Reservoir, and from C. J. Strike Dam to Swan Falls Reservoir; the Bruneau River from the upper Bruneau Valley crossing to the C. J. Strike Reservoir (suggested for an early float); and Salmon Falls Creek, from the Highway 93 crossing south of Jackpot, Nevada, to Salmon Falls Reservoir.

Two trips are listed in the Wood River Drainage—from Ketchum to Magic Reservoir and from Magic Dam to Richfield Canal Diversion—both of which are on the Wood River.

On the Big Lost River, try paddling from Mackay Dam to the Swauger Irrigation Diversion, from the Burnett Diversion to the Blaine Diversion near Leslie, and from there to the More Diversion.

On the East Fork of the Owyhee paddling is possible from the natural-gas pipeline crossing to Crutchers Crossing. And finally, on the Dear River, you will want to investigate trips from The Narrows to the Utah border and from the Wyoming line to the Rainbow Canal Diversion. On the former, it is suggested you check with the Oneida Dam about power-peaking operations to determine water flow.

## ILLINOIS

Although most Illinois water is not very clear, there are rivers and streams in all parts of the state that lend themselves to paddling. Whatever Illinois city you live in or whatever part of the state you plan to visit, you will find scenic and enjoyable voyages lasting from part of a day to several days. If you plan to paddle in Illinois, send for a booklet entitled *Illinois Canoeing Guide,* published by the Illinois Department of Conservation. This is a sterling little publication compiled in an effort to help canoeists; it is based on reports submitted to the department by canoeists who have made the trips themselves. You are told where to put in and take out, what to ex-

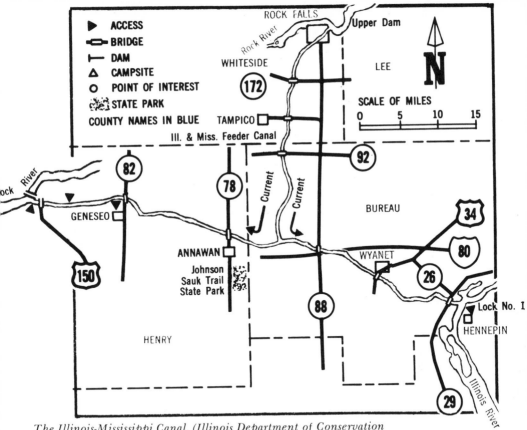

*The Illinois-Mississippi Canal. (Illinois Department of Conservation map from the* Illinois Canoeing Guide*)*

pect along the river banks, what the general conditions of the water are, where there are portages and obstructions. The guide also furnishes trip-report sheets on which you can record your trip to the Department of Conservation, so additional information can constantly be added to each new edition.

Those rivers covered in the guide include the Big Muddy, Cache, Des Plaines, Embarras, Fox, Green, Illinois, Kankakee, Iroquois, Kaskaskia, Shoal Creek, Mackinaw, Pecatonica, Rock, and Saline rivers; Salt Creek; the Salt Fork and the Middle Fork of the South Vermillion River; Sangamon, Spoon, Vermillion, and the Little Wabash rivers; Illinois-Michigan Canal, Illinois-Mississippi Canal.

Not included, but certainly worth mentioning, is an Illinois float trip from Galena, Illinois down the Galena and Mississippi rivers. The Galena is a gentle little river, without much challenge, but relaxing and quite scenic. When you reach the confluence with the Mississippi, higher water and wide stretches are encountered. You can pick your take-out point on the Mississippi—Belvue, Savanna, Clinton, Davenport, or anywhere in between.

Once you reach the Mississippi it helps to have navigational charts. Such charts for the middle and upper Mississippi from Cairo, Illinois, to Minneapolis, Minnesota, are prepared by, and are available from, the United States Army Engineer Division, North Central Corps of Engineers, Chicago, Illinois, and from the Milwaukee Map Service, 4519 W. North Avenue, Milwaukee, Wisconsin, at a cost of $6.00. These charts break the river down mile by mile, identify the channel, and indicate where there are islands, bridges, towns, dams, cable crossings, and everything else that affects navigation on the Mississippi. One of the most important things the charts do is indicate on which side of dams locks are located. Because the river is wide in most places, you will want to line yourself up on the passable side, well above the dams, in order to coast down to the locks.

It is worth saying something about passing through locks, for this can be a frightening experience the first time you do it. First, approach the lock from the upriver side and bring the craft alongside the yellow- and black-striped wall that protrudes from the door of the lock. Grab onto a cleat and hold the boat against the wall while waiting for the lockmaster to open the doors to let you in. When the doors are fully open (not while they are in the process of opening), paddle into the lock's interior and grab on to a rope dangling from the wall. You must hold the craft away from the wall with your free hand, since the waves and eddies are strong and could damage the canoe's finish by grating it against the wall. As water is released on the downriver side, you will feel yourself dropping, and can mark your progress downward by watching the watermarks on the walls. You must let the rope you are holding slip through your hand so the boat can go down with the water. NEVER, NEVER TIE OR SNUB THAT ROPE TO THE BOAT. It could cause a capsize; it could even cost you your life.

When you reach the point where the water level in the lock is the same as that on the downriver side, the lockmaster will open the downriver door and allow you to pass through. Be careful when leaving the lock not to run afoul of inconsiderate motorboaters who speed off, leaving washes that can push you hard against the wall.

Essentially, this is all there is to "locking through" and it is one of the thrills of paddling the Mississippi. Others include observing the towns along the river, and having the chance to visit a host of these fascinating places. Good campsites can be found along the river banks as well as on islands and sand bars in the river. In most places, an abundance of driftwood makes it enjoyable to cook over a wood fire. Scenery along the river includes everything from cornfields to bluffs. But remember paddling the wide stretches, especially when there is a moderate wind, may be taxing. Don't rush. Relax and enjoy your trip.

## INDIANA

The Indiana Department of Natural Resources lists numerous waterways as suitable for paddling. Among them are the Tippecanoe and the Eel rivers, the lengthy Wabash, the East Fork of the White River, and the Blue, Muscatuck, and Whitewater rivers. A packet entitled *Canoe Trails* is available that contains maps of fourteen of the most popular stretches in Indiana for canoeing, with information on access points, portages, supply stations, etc. To order this information send 30¢ per packet to the Department of Natural Resources, Map Sales, Room No. 604, 100 North Senate Avenue, Indianapolis, Indiana 46204.

## IOWA

Iowa is rich in history and proud of its natural beauty. And the canoeing is fine. The Iowa Conservation Commission publishes a brochure entitled *Iowa Canoe Trips*—a very complete and informative publication. Fourteen voyages are detailed: the west branch of the Des Moines River from the Mississippi to a point in central Palo Alto County near Emmetsburg and the east branch of the Des Moines to a point in Kossuth County near Algona; the Iowa River from the Mississippi to a point in Iowa County northwest of Marengo; the Cedar River, from the Iowa River to Cedar Falls in Black Hawk country; the Raccoon River from the Des Moines River to the west line of Polk County; the Wapsipinicon River from the Mississippi to a point just north of Central City in Linn County; the Skunk River from the Mississippi to the northeast corner of Jefferson County; the Turkey River from the Mississippi to a point near Clermont in Fayette County; the Nishnabotna River from the Missouri-Iowa border to a point near Riverton; the Upper Iowa River from its mouth to a point approximately nine river-miles upstream; the Little Maquoketa River —a very short portion of the stream from its mouth to a point upstream; the Mississippi River along the entire eastern border of Iowa; the Missouri River along the western Iowa border; and the Big Sioux River along the Iowa border.

*Iowa Canoe Trips* describes likely water conditions, the nature of adjacent lands, access points, distances, facilities, and

253

# .....THE WAPSIPINICON RIVER
## INDEPENDENCE TO STONE CITY

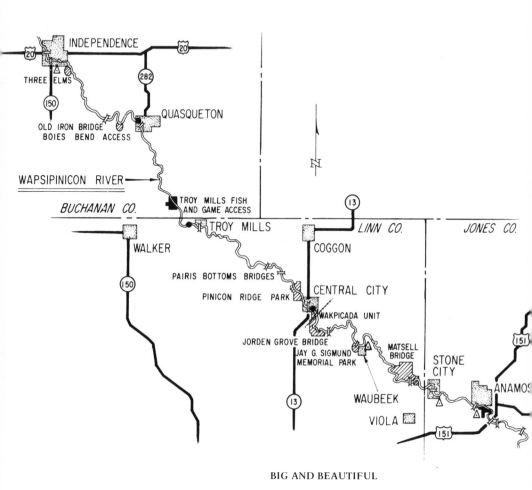

**BIG AND BEAUTIFUL**

*The Wapsipinicon River, from Independence to Stone City. (Iowa Conservation Commission map from Iowa Canoe Trips)*

The Wapsi is the largest stream in Northeast Iowa. Its headwaters are just over the Minnesota line and it flows southeasterly to the Mississippi roughly paralleling the Cedar River. The valley is narrow, the central and lower portions being more rugged and heavily timbered than the upper reaches. It is an excellent fishing stream, and is rich in historic landmarks and romantic Indian legends. Moreover, its scenery is superb, particularly in the vicinity of Stone City and Anamosa.

An interesting stretch of the Wapsi for a two or three-day canoe trip is that from Independence in Buchanan County to Stone City in Jones County. This is about 50 river miles. In unusually low water the trip requires about 24 hours of traveling time, and the estimated times given are for such conditions. In more normal water levels much faster progress can be anticipated.

254

even the history of the area through which you pass. It features excellent maps showing obstructions. To get this publication write to the Iowa Conservation Commission, 300–4th Street, Des Moines, Iowa 50319.

## KANSAS

Although Kansas is one of the flattest states in the nation, canoeists and kayakists will, nevertheless, find ample opportunity to paddle. Among the most likely spots are the Verdigris, Arkansas, Cottonwood, Kansas, Spring, Neosho, Fall, Marais Des Cygnes and Caney rivers; Lyons, Mill, Spring, and Shoal creeks. Most of these runs are best in the spring and early summer when winter runoff is greatest. All (except Caney River) are within the limits of most paddlers with some experience.

For more information write to the Tourist Division, State of Kansas, Department of Economic Development, State Office Building, Topeka, Kansas 66612. Also, a brochure *Where to Fish in Kansas* is available from the Forestry Commission, Box 1028, Pratt, Kansas 67124. Other information can be obtained from Ozark Wilderness Waterways, P.O. Box 8165, Kansas City, Kansas.

## KENTUCKY

Literature published by the Kentucky Department of Public Information lists no fewer than sixty-eight canoe trips in the Blue Grass state, ranging from 259 miles to two miles long. All trails are suggested for the average canoeist and feature Class I and II paddling conditions. Rivers said to provide excellent paddling opportunities include the Barren, Cumberland, Green, Kentucky, Laurel, Licking, and Pond; as well as Otter Creek, Rough River Lake, Salt and Rockcastle rivers, and many others. The literature is available from the Department of Public Information, State of Kentucky, Capitol Annex, Frankfurt, Kentucky 40601. When planning to canoe in Kentucky, it is suggested that you also write to Travel, Frankfort, Kentucky 40601, for a free highway map that helps locate the rivers mentioned above.

If you want to paddle in the Daniel Boone National Forest, the highway map is not sufficiently detailed to help you find the small roads that lead to the access points. To obtain this information, write to the Daniel Boone National Forest, 27 Carol Road, Winchester, Kentucky 40391.

All forest-ranger stations are indexed on the highway map (except Peabody, which is in I-5 near Big Creek). You are urged to contact the forest ranger of the district in which you wish to travel for instructions on how to get where you want to go and also on changes in water conditions. Remember, high water can alter a stream's character radically, especially when there have been rains in the mountain regions.

LOUISIANA

You should have no trouble finding good waters for paddling in Louisiana—even a road map graphically reveals the extent of water that flows in all parts of the state. Four places you should consider are the Mississippi River along Louisiana's entire eastern border with Alabama; Whiskey Chitto Creek

*Canoe trips in Louisiana. (Lafayette Natural History Museum map from* Canoeing Louisiana*)*

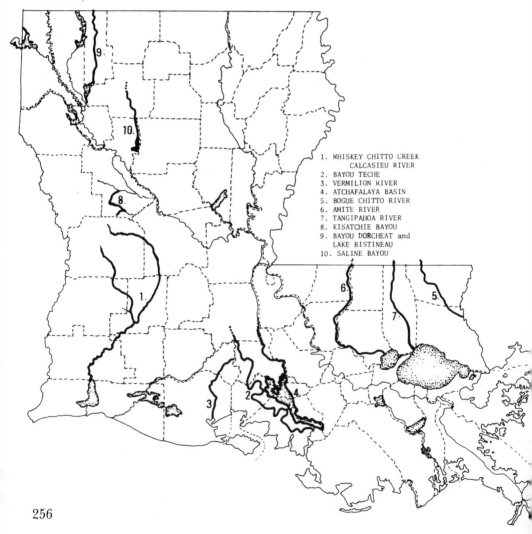

1. WHISKEY CHITTO CREEK
   CALCASIEU RIVER
2. BAYOU TECHE
3. VERMILION RIVER
4. ATCHAFALAYA BASIN
5. BOGUE CHITTO RIVER
6. AMITE RIVER
7. TANGIPAHOA RIVER
8. KISATCHIE BAYOU
9. BAYOU DORCHEAT and
   LAKE BISTINEAU
10. SALINE BAYOU

and Calcasieu River from Sugar to Lake Charles; the Tchefunte River from Highway 16 to Fairview Riverside Park; and the Bogue Chitto River from Warnerton to the Pearl River, which flows along the eastern border of the state.

An excellent booklet is available entitled *Canoeing in Louisiana,* published by the Lafayette Natural History Museum. It costs $3.00 and can be purchased from the Lafayette Natural History Museum and Planetarium, 637 Girard Park Drive, Lafayette, Louisiana 70501. This booklet describes a number of canoe routes: in southwestern Louisiana, the Whiskey Chitto Creek to Calcasieu River, Bayou Teche, Vermillion River, and Atchafalaya Basin; in southeastern Louisiana, the Bogue Chitto River, the Amite River, and the Tangipahoa River; the Kisatchie Bayou in central Louisiana; and the Bayou Dorcheat and Lake Bisinneau as well as the Saline Bayou in northern Louisiana. In addition to giving specific routes, maps, and general tips on canoeing, the booklet spins invaluable historical tales about the areas through which the waters flow.

## MAINE

Maine offers fabulous canoeing waters, among the best in the East. There are small ponds and large lakes, peaceful meandering brooks and tortuous whitewater courses. There is something here for paddlers of all stripes. To prepare yourself for canoeing or kayaking in Maine, purchase a copy of the Appalachian Mountain Club's *New England Canoeing Guide,* which costs $6 and is available from the Appalachian Mountain Club, 5 Joy Street, Boston, Massachusetts 02108. Although this book is fairly complete in its information, the State Department of Commerce and Industry urges you to check locally before starting on your trip. Those sources to contact include Forest Service Divisional or District Rangers, Fish and Game wardens, and Divisional supervisors. Also arm yourself with appropriate maps. United State Geological Survey topographic maps should be purchased.

A fine list of paddle trips is published by the Department of Commerce and Industry, State House, Augusta, Maine 04330. Among the flatwater trips listed for those who want leisurely, relaxing canoe camping are the Saco River from Swan's Falls to Hiram, a distance of 33 miles; a 45-mile voyage on the Rangeley Lakes; the Kennebec River from the Forks to Bath, a distance of 125 miles; Cobbossee Stream and Lake; Belgrade Lakes circle trip; several floats on the Chain of Ponds; voyages on Moosehead and Attean lakes, the Penobscot River, the

Mattawamkeag River, the Aroostock River, the Fish River Lakes, the Allagash Wilderness Waterway; Sebago and Long lakes, Damariscotta River and Lake, Bagaduce River; Chiputnecook Lakes, and the Grand Lakes Chain. For more detailed descriptions of these trips send to the Department of Commerce and Industry for its brochure entitled *Escape to Me.*

Maine is by no means all flatwater; there is excellent opportunity here for whitewater enthusiasts as well. The stretches for possible whitewater paddling are many, and it is impossible to mention all of them, rating their respective difficulties and stipulating their lengths. For a pamphlet listing more than 50 such trips, along with brief descriptions and recommendations as to their difficulty, contact the Department of Economic Development, Statehouse, Augusta, Maine 04330 for its brochure entitled *Wild Me.*

## MARYLAND

Maryland, one of the most scenic of eastern states, offers several fine paddling trips on Antietam, Big Pipe, Catoctin, and Bennett creeks, as well as on the Monocacy and Potomac rivers. For further information about paddle routes in Maryland write to the Department of Forests and Parks, State Office Building, Annapolis, Maryland 21404, or to the Tourist Department, Department of Economic Development, State Office Building, Annapolis, Maryland 21401. And don't forget about *Blue Ridge Voyages,* by Roger Corbett, Jr. and Louis J. Matacia, Jr., available from Blue Ridge Voyagers, 1515 N. Adams Street, Arlington, Virginia 22201. (See the section on Virginia for specifics regarding these volumes.)

## MASSACHUSETTS

For a state that has an abundance of paddling opportunities, it is surprising that Massachusetts does not offer a brochure on the subject. Trippers to Massachusetts should purchase a copy of the AMC *New England Canoeing Guide* for $6.00 from the Appalachian Mountain Club, 5 Joy Street, Boston, Massachusetts 02108. This publication tells all one needs to know in order to take paddle voyages throughout the state. In addition to detailed watercourse descriptions, the guide lists useful togographic maps one may want to buy and contains maps of its own.

The AMC guide contains information about the following trips on the Connecticut River watershed: Farmington River; Sandy Brook; Westfield River; Westfield River North Branch;

Westfield River Middle Branch; Westfield River West Branch; Westfield Little River; Chicopee, Swift, Ware, and Quaboag rivers; The Ox Bow; Manhan, Deerfield, Green, South, North, Falls, Millers, Tully, and Otter rivers.

The Quinebaug River, French River, and Mill Brook are covered in a discussion of trips in the Thames Watershed.

In the Merrimac Watershed, trips are described on the Powwow, Little, Spicket, Shawsheen, Concord, Assabet, Dudbury, Nashua, Nissitissit, Squannacook rivers; Middlesex Canal; and Beaver, Stony, and Salmon brooks to name only a few.

# MICHIGAN

The incredible paddling of the northern regions of Michigan is surpassed by very few places in the United States. The nights are cool and the tall pines provide a solitude settling to the soul. Michigan is popular for canoeing and kayaking not only among its residents, but every year tourists travel from all over the country to enjoy the exhilarating experience of its cool, clear lakes and rivers. There are legendary whitewater rivers, such as the Black and Presque Isle in the Upper Peninsula, and others, such as the Sturgeon in the northern sections of lower Michigan (i.e. below the peninsula), but these are for experts. There are countless trips that appeal to beginners and flatwater floating and camping enthusiasts too.

Fortunately there is an excellent canoeing guide to Michigan. You can request a free copy by writing to the State of Michigan, Tourist Council, Suite 102, 300 South Capitol Avenue, Lansing, Michigan 48926. Called the *Michigan Guide to Easy Canoeing*, this invaluable 34-page brochure concentrates on trips that any canoeist or kayakist will enjoy for the sheer fun of paddling—easy trips that do not require inordinate expertise.

The guide tells you where to procure still further information and lists no fewer than 54 potential voyages, complete with maps and descriptions of each. Rivers for which trips are charted include the Ontonagon, Otter, Sturgeon, Net, Paint, Fence, Brule, Carp, Escanaba, Ford, Au Train, Indian, Fox, Manistique, Tahquamenon, Waiska, Thunder Bay, South Branch of the Thunder Bay, Lower Platte, Betsie, Clam, Big Manistee, Pere Marquette, Big South Branch of the Pere Marquette, White, Muskegon, Au Sable, Rifle, Chippewa, Pine, Tittabawassee, Cass, Shiawassee, Flint, Maple, Looking Glass, Red Cedar, Grand, Flat, Thornapple, Kalamazoo, Paw Paw, St. Joseph, Black, Belle, Clinton, Huron, and Raisin.

If you live in Michigan, some of the top paddling in the

259

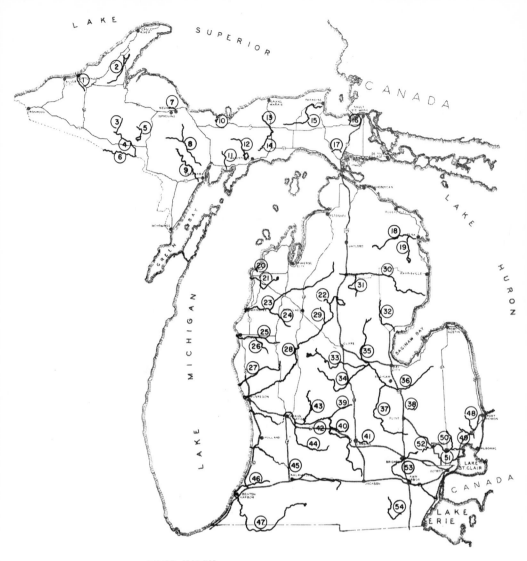

## RIVER INDEX

*Rivers in Michigan.*
*(Michigan*
*Department of*
*Natural Resources*
*map from their*
Michigan Guide to
Easy Canoeing)

260

country passes your back door; if you are an out-of-stater, you will find it difficult to plan a better paddle trip than one in Michigan for your next vacation. If you are a newcomer to paddling and do not yet know whether you will thoroughly enjoy canoeing as a hobby, there are many outfitters in Michigan who rent all the needed equipment except for personal gear. The Michigan Department of Natural Resources recommends you contact its field office nearest the river of your choice for information about such outfitters, and lists the telephone numbers of its various offices throughout the state in the guide.

## MINNESOTA

A land of cool, crisp evenings, towering pines piercing the sky like Egyptian obelisks, lakes set among them like embedded jewels, sunsets that inflame the soul—that is northern Minnesota, and unless you progress farther north into Canada, there is no more incredibly magnificent place in the world for the paddler. Mornings can be filled with the crackle and smoky aroma of bacon sizzling on the campfire, the splashing of fish in the lakes, and the rustling of pine needles overhead. Evenings are serene except for the twitters of furtive night creatures that inhabit the woods. Northern Minnesota has been rhapsodized countless times, and the brochures extolling tourist resorts seldom do it justice. Because there are so many potential paddle voyages there, I have selected a few to whet your appetite. Be sure to write to the addresses given for more facts and more possible trips. It will be worthwhile.

Let's start with two trips in the Chippewa National Forest. First there is the Turtle River beginning at Lake Julia, 12 miles north of Bemidji, and flowing through Turtle and Three Island Lakes into Turtle River Lake. Leaving Turtle River Lake the river enters the Chippewa National Forest. From there it flows through Rice Lake, then Kitchi Lake, and finally into Cass Lake on the Mississippi River, seven miles north of the village of Cass Lake.

The second trip is the Inguadona tour, which follows the lower part of the Boy River drainage that starts at Ten Mile Lake south of Walker and flows south and east, then north through Woman Lake to the entrance of the Chippewa National Forest at Inguadona. From this point the river flows through Boy Lake and on to enter Boy Bay of Leech Lake. Leech Lake, in turn, drains into the Mississippi through the Leech Lake River. The portion of river included in this tour is well suited for canoe travel. There are no portages, yet there

261

is a stretch of fast-flowing water that can be considered rapids. For pamphlets covering both trips write to the United States Department of Agriculture, Forest Service, Cass Lake, Minnesota 56633.

Excellent paddling is possible in all parts of Minnesota. Among the rivers suggested by the Department of Economic Development, Department of Natural Resources, and Division of Parks and Recreation are the Big Fork, Cannon, Cloquet, Crow, Crow Wing, Des Moines, Kettle, Little Fork, Minnesota, Mississippi, Red Lake, Root, Rum, Snake, St. Croix, and St. Louis. The "big-time" canoeing is done in the Superior National Forest, particularly in the Boundary Waters Canoe Area (see below for a discussion of this superb area). If ever you are so fortunate as to get away for a week or two, this area deserves your prime attention. For the moment, however, let us bypass the Boundary Waters Canoe Area (BWCA) and turn to trips within the Superior National Forest outside the BWCA itself.

A list of 14 float trips within the Superior National Forest is available from the Department of Agriculture, Forest Service, Superior National Forest, Forest Supervisor, Box 338, Duluth, Minnesota 55801. The list provides much useful information about these rivers: location, length of trip, points of access, portage locations, campsites, fishing areas, water character, and natural features. The following routes are covered: Timber-Frear Lakes; Crescent Lake-Rice Lake; Poplar River; Island River; South Kawishiwi River, Birch Lake, White Iron Lake; Stony River; Hegman Lakes; Fenske Lake-Grassy Lake-Low Lake Circle; Bass Lake-High Lake-Dry Lake-Little Dry Lake; Nels-Sandpit-Range River route; Burntside-Dead River-Twin Lakes circle route; Lake One to Farm Lake; Vermillion River; and Sturgeon River.

Located on more than one million acres of land in the northern third of the Superior National Forest is the world-famous Boundary Waters Canoe Area. Here you can paddle over some 1200 miles of water that honeycomb an area stretching for about 200 miles along the Minnesota-Canadian border. According to the United States Forest Service, July and August are the best months for paddling this area as far as weather is concerned, although you may find the region crowded (more than 125,000 people visit the BWCA each year). The best fishing will be found in the spring from mid-May through June. September has fewer insects, generally favorable weather, and fewer people. If you can endure frosty weather, October is also a good month for paddling, and at that time of year you will be

*The Boundary Waters Canoe Area, right. (Map from Greystone Outfitters, Ely, Minn.)*

Roland Lake
Darky Lake
Cone L.
Hurn
Elk L.
Milt Lake
Little
Argo Lake
Big Newt Lake
Paulene L.
Joyce Lake
Mari L.
McIntyre Lake
McNiece L.

CANADA

L. O.
Bay
Friday Bay
Wednesday Bay
Thursday Bay
Saturday Bay
Bart Lake
Robinson Lake
Cecil Lake
Dart L.
Tuck L.
Nuh L.
Lost L.
Moose Bay
Kett Lake
Low Lake
Side
Point Lake
Nest Lake
Isabella Lake
Shade Lake
Dell L.
West
Yum Yum
Sur
Grey L.

Bunggee Lake
Pappose L.
Chippewa Lake
Niki L.
Sauna L.
Jackfish Rabbit Lake
Wagosh L.
Gypo Lake
Thunder Lake
eartrap Lake

North Bay
Burke Lake
Bayley Bay

Gull L.
Gun Lake
Moose Camp Lake
No-See-Um Lake
Lake 16
River
Kings Point
Merriam Bay
Manomin Lake
Found L.
New Found Lake
Such

Fairy Lake
Fourtown Lake
Horse Lake
U.S. Point
U.S. Point

Boot Lake
Holy Lake

MINNESOTA

Sandpit Lake
Murphy Lake
Wind Lake
Bass L.

Mudro Lake
Range Lake
Picket Lake
Grassy Lake

4 Mile Portage
Ella Hall Lake
Good Lake
Hula Lake
Moose
Flash L.

**FALL LAKE LANDING**
Newton L.
Rice Lake
Mud Lake
Wood Lake
Jasper L.

**TTING ARTERS**
Hobo L.
Cedar L.
Browns Lake
Fall
Stump Lake
Fernberg
Road
Madden Lake
Twin L.
Twin L.
Lookout

Little Long Lake
WINTON
88
Fall
Garden Lake
Kemptons
Stone
Triangle Lake

LY
21
Lookout
Farm Lake
Pickerel Lake
South Farm Lake
Eskwagama L.
North
Kawishi
Clear Lake
**GRAYSTONE OUTFITTERS**
1829 EAST SHERIDAN STREET
ELY, MINNESOTA 55731
218 / 365-3251

263

treated to flamboyant fall colors and glistening paper birch.

Major entry points to the Boundary Waters Canoe Area are near Crane Lake, Ely, Grand Marais, and Tofte. Access also is possible from Tower, Minnesota, and from the Arrowhead Trail north of Havland.

The BWCA is unique in that crucial efforts are being made to preserve its original state for the outdoor recreation of future generations. Small outboards are permitted to enter the area only in certain places, and they may travel only a few designated streams. The rest of the area is reserved for paddlers. The effort to preserve this natural wonder is all-encompassing— you are not allowed to pack in cans or bottles; you are virtually limited to modern, lightweight packing foods of the dehydrated or freeze-dried variety. This requirement alone keeps the area clean and helps to make it one of the best in the world for communicating with the unspoiled environment.

When it comes time to camp, you can select a campsite from nearly 2000 that are beautifully managed. Most are provided with very simple camping facilities consisting of one or more tent sites, a fireplace, and simple toilet facilities. Tent poles left by previous campers often are on hand.

How can you prepare yourself for paddle adventure in this unsurpassed area? First write to the United States Department of Agriculture, Forest Service, Superior National Forest, Box 338, Duluth, Minnesota 55801, for a packet of information that explains the BWCA, its purpose, historical development, campsites, fishing and hunting regulations, and so forth. General maps come with the packet. Once you decide to visit the BWCA, contact the United States Geological Survey for quadrangle maps. In addition to topographic maps, you will probably want to carry canoe-route maps. Both are available from W. A. Fisher Co., Virginia, Minnesota 55792.

Because the BWCA is such an excellent haven for canoeists and kayakists, it bristles with professional outfitters who would like to arrange your vacation and rent you the equipment to enjoy it. Each outfitter takes pride in the beautiful brochure that expounds the virtues of his service, and from reading these pamphlets you can sample the mouth-watering adventure that awaits. But there is even more to be learned from these public-relations pamphlets. Many of them contain material on safety and camping tips. They also elaborate on menus, telling you what you will eat for each meal every day of the trip. These menus are valuable for your own canoeing at any time, and can make you aware of the lightweight foods available. They are also a good way to learn food combinations that provide reasonably balanced diets.

It would be difficult to get the names of all the outfitters in the BWCA and to contact each one individually. Fortunately, you do not have to. There are several central addresses to which you can write: the Chamber of Commerce, Ely, Minnesota 55731; the Chamber of Commerce, Grand Marais, Minnesota 55604; the Chamber of Commerce, Tower, Minnesota 55790; Minnesota Arrowhead Association, Duluth, Minnesota 55802; and the Commercial Club, Crane Lake, Minnesota 55725. When you write for information about outfitters, these organizations will pass your letter on to various outfitters, and you are sure to receive many replies.

If you live far from the Boundary Waters Canoe Area, you are better off putting yourself in the hands of an outfitter than attempting to truck your craft and gear all the way to the northernmost reaches of Minnesota. Outfitters provide many services that reduce the amount of planning you have to do at home—and that make your trip proceed smoothly and efficiently. When you reach their posts, they will sit down with you and your party and pore over maps, helping to plan the exact route. The outfitters know the backwaters; they can map trips that feature fastwater, picturesque flatwater set among the pine-forested shores, the best fishing areas, and good camping places in case you want to stay in one place for a while. They also can advise you of trips appropriate for your paddling skills. If you have never canoed before, they can provide abbreviated courses on handling your boat—in short, all you need to begin.

Outfitters do other things too. They can send you an itinerary in advance, make your airline reservations, pick you up at the airport, and procure motel accommodations. Once you reach their posts, many offer tow service, pulling you by powerboat deep into the backwaters where your trip begins. Most have guides if you wish to hire them. Some outfitters even provide fly-in service by which you can reach the remotest areas of the BWCA, and be picked up on a given day at a predetermined spot.

In short, working through an outfitter, you can drive or fly to northern Minnesota carrying nothing more than personal gear. Your plans are made easily at the time of arrival and your canoe and all your camping gear are ready for you. Professional paddlers help pack the boat so that it is done correctly. When you consider that complete canoe outfitting costs only $12 to

$15 per day, and that children are charged less, you cannot take a much more inexpensive vacation. Nor, for that matter, a more enjoyable one.

## MISSISSIPPI

Float trips are popular in Mississippi, and fishing is usually the main purpose. One of the most popular float trips is a 50-mile junket on the Black and Beaver Dam creeks. Both are highly scenic and boast wide, white sand bars along their shores that give paddlers a chance to camp, relax, and swim.

The following description appears in a pamphlet, the *DeSoto National Forest:*

"The floating speed [of the Black and Beaver Dam creeks] is about one mile an hour unless you linger to fish the deep, quiet pools along the way. Most of the major obstructions have been cleared from the channel, and few portages are required. Floaters should watch for underwater snags and shallow water. Access points are at Brooklyn, Moody's Landing, Janice Recreation Area, Cypress Creek Recreation Area, Fairly Bridge, and Big Creek. Paved boat launching ramps have been constructed at Cypress Creek, Big Creek, and Fairly Bridge." For more information on this float-fishing trip, contact the United States Department of Agriculture, Forest Service, P.O. Box 1291, Jackson, Mississippi 39205.

## MISSOURI

One dollar brings you extensive information on excellent paddling in Missouri's Ozarks. Write to the Missouri Conservation Commission, Jefferson City, Missouri 65101, for their 114-page booklet entitled *Missouri Ozark Waterways* by Oz Hawksley. Dr. Hawksley, a professor of zoology at Central Missouri State, spent many years exploring the streams in the Ozarks and covered over 3500 miles by canoe in gathering data for this guide. General pointers on canoeing, equipment, safety, conservation, and paddlers' legal rights are included, as well as descriptions of more than 35 paddle trips. Each trip is rated for difficulty and gradients and the appropriate quadrangle maps are listed. Extensive details are provided on the watercourses themselves. This is one of the best canoeing guides available—well worth the dollar it costs.

*The Sac River, right. (Map from Missouri Ozark Waterways, Missouri Ozark Society)*

The rivers detailed include, in the Osage region: Sac, Pomme de Terre, Niangua, Moreau, Weaubleau Creek, Osage tributaries, Little Niangua, Grand Augleize Creek, Tavern Creek, and Maries River.

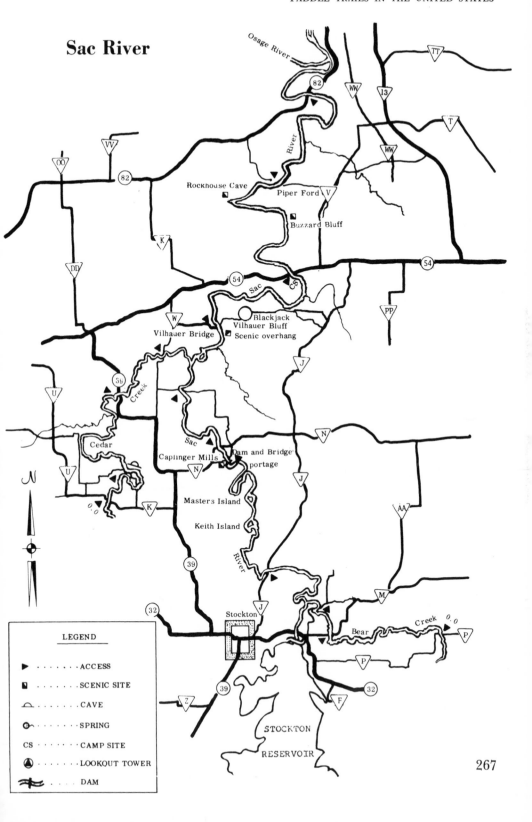

# Sac River

Osage River

82

WW

13

TT

T

VV

WW

OO

82

WW

Rockhouse Cave

Piper Ford V

Buzzard Bluff

K

54

DD

54

Sac

CS

PP

W

Blackjack
Vilhauer Bluff
Vilhauer Bridge    Scenic overhang

J

39

Creek

U

U

N

J

Cedar

Sac

Caplinger Mills

Dam and Bridge
portage

N

AA

0.0

K

Masters Island

Keith Island

River

39

M

32

Stockton

J

Bear        Creek    0.0

P

Z

39

P

32

F

STOCKTON

RESERVOIR

## LEGEND

▶ · · · · · · ACCESS

◪ · · · · · · SCENIC SITE

⌒ · · · · · CAVE

◓ · · · · · SPRING

CS · · · · · CAMP SITE

◬ · · · · · LOOKOUT TOWER

〰 · · · · DAM

267

In the central ozark region: Grasconade, Osage Fork, and Big Piney River.

In the Meramec Valley region: Meramec River, Curtois and Huzzah creeks, Bourbeuse River, and Big River.

In the southwestern region: Spring River, Center and Shoal creeks, Big Sugar-Elk River, and Indian Creek.

In the White River region: Roaring, James, and North Fork rivers; Flat, Bull, Swan, Beaver, and Bryant creeks.

In the Ozark National River region: the Current, Jacks Fork, Eleven Point, Black, and St. Francis rivers.

## MONTANA

Montana, "The Land of the Big Sky," displays a vast panorama of unspoiled forests, mountains, and rivers. The state is so large that any information presented on paddling opportunities within its generous boundaries must be very incomplete.

Fortunately, for those who wish to visit Montana there is information available on streams in all parts of Montana. One of the best publications is entitled *Montana's Popular Float Streams,* which is put out by the Montana Fish and Game Department as Information Bulletin 1970. You can procure a copy of it by contacting the United States Department of Agriculture, Forest Service, Missoula, Montana 59801.

This bulletin lists 23 potential float trips in all parts of the state and describes the types of paddling and obstacles to be met with in each. Rivers listed in southwest Montana include the Upper Missouri River Drainage, the Madison River, the upper Missouri River to Townsend, the Beaverhead River, the Big Hole River, and the Jefferson River. In south-central Montana is listed the Yellowstone River. Western Montana features the Clark Fork River, the Big Blackfoot River, and the Bitterroot River. For northwest Montana are listed the Kootenai River, the Main Flathead River above Flathead Lake, the middle fork of the Flathead above Bear Creek, the middle fork of the Flathead below Bear Creek, the north fork of the Flathead, and the south fork of the Flathead as well as the Swan River. Central Montana features the Marias River, the Dearborn River, the Sun and Smith rivers, the Missouri River below Townsend, and the Missouri River from Fort Benton to Fred Robinson Bridge.

All in all, this brochure merely scratches the surface of paddling in Montana. Never forget the remarkable fishing opportunities on the many fine lakes not designated as potential float trips. Here is a titanic land that any paddler will be proud to challenge.

Many outsiders think Nebraska consists of uninteresting, flat land. Few seem to realize the fine opportunities for canoeing and kayaking there. If you want a lead on nine enjoyable paddle trips in Nebraska, write to the Nebraska Game and Parks Commission, 2200 North 33rd Street, Lincoln, Nebraska 68503, for a profusely illustrated brochure entitled *Canoeing in Nebraska*. Trips are described on the Niobrara River, the Dismal River, the Elkhorn River, the Calamus and North Platte rivers, the Republican and Missouri rivers, the Big Blue River, and the Platte River. You are told where to put in and take out, mileages, and the type of paddling encountered at each stretch along the way.

New Hampshire prides itself on its variety of paddling waters and is among the states foremost in publicizing both flatwater and whitewater events. For an excellent accumulation of descriptive information on water trails, contact the Department of Resources and Economic Development, P.O. Box 856, Concord, New Hampshire 03301.

New Hampshire's mountains are among the highest in the northeastern portion of the United States, and initiate rugged rivers that reach considerable size as they approach their foothills. Many are boulder-strewn, whirlpooled, and have rapids. Among the more prominent rivers in the northern part of the state are the Bearcamp, Ossipee, Magalloway, Androscoggin, Connecticut, Upper Ammonoosuc, Saco, and at high water, the Pemigewasset, Israel, and Baker. Some of the more prominent in the south include the Blackwater, Contoocook, Lamprey, Suncook, and Warner.

Those interested in whitewater participation on mountain streams should contact the Appalachian Mountain Club, 5 Joy Street, Boston, Massachusetts, for its *New England Canoeing Guide* ($6.00). Also, the New Hampshire Office of Vacation Travel, P.O. Box 856, Concord, Massachusetts 03301, has fact sheets on whitewatering that are offered free upon request.

Fact sheets from the Department of Resources and Economic Development detail a number of trips including some on the Magalloway, Androscoggin, Connecticut, Upper Ammonoosuc, and Saco rivers, and other rivers that can be navigated when water is high. Summer canoe streams include the lower part of the Ammonoosuc, the Androscoggin downstream from Berlin, the Blackwater River, the Connecticut River downstream from Beechers Falls, Wilder Lake, Moore Reservoir, and Contoocook River.

Another useful pamphlet on paddling in New Hampshire is *Summer Canoeing and Kayaking in the White Mountains of New Hampshire*, put out by the White Mountains Region Association, Box K, Lancaster, New Hampshire 03584, which also lists the larger lakes and streams in the New Hampshire area that have public boat accesses, as well as listing local distributors.

## NEW JERSEY

A good starting point for planning canoeing or kayaking trips in New Jersey is to write the New Jersey Bureau of Parks, P.O. Box 1420, Trenton, New Jersey. This source can provide several maps, a list of canoe liveries, and descriptions of the more popular paddle areas in the state.

Among rivers suitable for paddling in New Jersey are the Paulins, the Musconetong, the Raritan River (both its north and south branches), the Passaic and Ramapo rivers, the Millstone River and Raritan Canal, the Metedeconk and Toms rivers, the Rancocas River, the Mullica, Batsto, Wading, and Oswego rivers, the Great Egg Harbor River and its Hospitality Branch, the Tuckahoe River, and the Maurice, Manumuskin, and Manantico rivers. Also, of course, there is the Delaware River, which forms the western border of New Jersey.

## NEW MEXICO

Through the vastness of New Mexico run such rivers as the Chama and Rio Grande. There are stretches of these rivers that can be listed in all grades, for every paddler from the rankest novice or casual joyrider to the most serious expert.

Fortunately for those living in New Mexico, as well as for paddlers across the nation who would like to try their hand at river running in the state, there is a remarkable little monthly publication called the *Rio Grande Gurgle* that offers maps of various streams, reports from paddlers who have attempted them, water levels, and countless other valuable tips. The *Gurgle* is available from Ms. Helen F. Redman, Editor, Route 1, Box 177, Santa Fe, New Mexico 87501. Cost of a subscription to this newsletter is $2.00 per year. It is a must if you contemplate visiting the Southwest with your canoe, kayak, or inflatable on your car.

## NEW YORK

Too often people entertain the mistaken idea that New York is a megalopolis, covering the eastern seaboard with cement. Nothing could be further from the truth. There are great stretches of farmland and wooded areas within the state, and there are terrific canoeing and kayaking opportunities. In fact, some delightful canoe trails exist within a couple of hours' drive of New York City itself. To find excellent paddling in New York, contact the New York State Department of Environmental Conservation, Albany, New York 12201. Ask for two informative publications: *Adirondack Canoe Routes* and *Canoe Trips.*

The first publication gives worthwhile details about canoeing in the Adirondacks. It describes the most popular paddle trip as being from Old Forge, at the foot of the Fulton chain of lakes, through various other lakes and the upper reaches of

*See next page for larger map and key.*

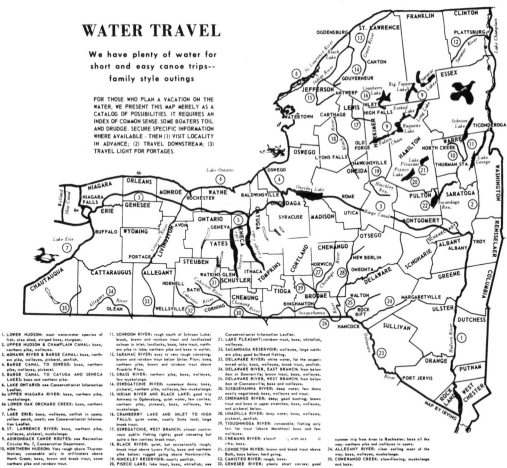

**WATER TRAVEL**

We have plenty of water for short and easy canoe trips-- family style outings

FOR THOSE WHO PLAN A VACATION ON THE WATER, WE PRESENT THIS MAP MERELY AS A CATALOG OF POSSIBILITIES. IT REQUIRES AN INDEX OF COMMON SENSE. SOME BOATERS TOIL AND DRUDGE. SECURE SPECIFIC INFORMATION WHERE AVAILABLE - THEN (1) VISIT LOCALITY IN ADVANCE; (2) TRAVEL DOWNSTREAM; (3) TRAVEL LIGHT FOR PORTAGES.

1. LOWER HUDSON: most warm-water species of fish; also shad, striped bass, sturgeon.
2. UPPER HUDSON & CHAMPLAIN CANAL: bass, northern pike, walleyes.
3. MOHAWK RIVER & BARGE CANAL: bass, northern pike, walleyes, pickerel, panfish.
4. BARGE CANAL TO OSWEGO: bass, northern pike, walleyes, pickerel.
5. BARGE CANAL TO CAYUGA AND SENECA LAKES: bass and northern pike.
6. LAKE ONTARIO see Conservationist Information Leaflet.
6a UPPER NIAGARA RIVER: bass, northern pike, muskalonge.
6b LOWER OAK ORCHARD CREEK: bass, northern pike.
7. LAKE ERIE: bass, walleyes, catfish in spots, yellow perch, smelt; see Conservationist Information Leaflet.
8. ST. LAWRENCE RIVER: bass, northern pike, walleyes, pickerel, muskalonge.
9. ADIRONDACK CANOE ROUTES: see Recreation Circular No. 7, Conservation Department.
10. NORTHERN HUDSON: Very rough above Thurman Station; canoeable only in stillwaters above North Creek; bass, brown and brook trout, some northern pike and rainbow trout.
11. SCHROON RIVER: rough south of Schroon Lake; brook, brown and rainbow trout and landlocked salmon in inlet; landlocks, bass, lake trout, northern pike in lake; northern pike and bass in outlet.
12. SARANAC RIVER: easy to very rough canoeing; brown and rainbow trout below Union Flow; bass, northern pike, brown and rainbow trout above Franklin Flow.
13. GRASS RIVER: northern pike, bass, walleyes, few muskalonge.
14. OSWEGATCHIE RIVER: numerous dams; bass, pickerel, northern pike, walleyes, few muskalonge.
15. INDIAN RIVER AND BLACK LAKE: good trip Antwerp to Ogdensburg, quiet water, few carries; northern pike, pickerel, bass, walleyes, few muskalonge.
16. CRANBERRY LAKE AND INLET TO HIGH FALLS: quiet water, mostly State land; large brook trout.
17. OSWEGATCHIE, WEST BRANCH: almost continuous public fishing rights; good canoeing but quite a few carries; brook trout.
18. BLACK RIVER: quiet, but occasionally rough; brook trout above Lyons Falls, bass and northern pike below; rugged going above Hawkinsville.
19. HINCKLEY RESERVOIR: mostly panfish.
20. PISECO LAKE: lake trout, bass, whitefish; see Conservationist Information Leaflet.
21. LAKE PLEASANT: rainbow trout, bass, whitefish, walleyes.
22. SACANDAGA RESERVOIR: walleyes, large northern pike; good bullhead fishing.
23. DELAWARE RIVER: white water, for the experienced only; bass, walleyes, brook trout, panfish.
24. DELAWARE RIVER, EAST BRANCH from below dam at Downsville; brown trout, bass, walleyes.
25. DELAWARE RIVER, WEST BRANCH: from below dam at Cannonsville; bass and walleyes.
26. SUSQUEHANNA RIVER: deep water; few dams easily negotiated; bass, walleyes and trout.
27. CHENANGO RIVER: deep; good boating; brown trout and bass in upper stretches; bass, walleyes and pickerel below.
28. UNADILLA RIVER: deep water; bass, walleyes, pickerel, panfish.
29. TIOUGHNIOGA RIVER: canoeable; fishing only fair for trout (above Marathon) bass and few walleyes.
30. CHEMUNG RIVER: slow-d_____, with acc\_\_\_\_\_l riffs; bass.
31. CONHOCTON RIVER: brown and brook trout above Bath, bass below; hard going.
32. CANISTEO RIVER: rough; bass.
33. GENESEE RIVER: plenty short carries; good summer trip from Avon to Rochester; bass all the way; northern pike and walleyes in spots.
34. ALLEGANY RIVER: clear sailing most of the way; bass, walleyes, muskalonge.
35. CONEWANGO CREEK: slow-flowing; muskalonge and bass.

MAP BY IRVING

271

*Paddle trails in New York. (N.Y. State Department of Environmental Conservation map from* Canoe Trails*)*

the Raquette River to either Tupper Lake, Saranac Inn or Paul Smith's landings or Saranac Lake.

More excellent paddling is described in *Canoe Trips*. Among the places suggested are Black Creek, Cayuga Lake, Upper Mohawk River, West Canada Creek, Kunjamuk River, Fall Stream, Unadilla River, Fish Creek, Delaware River, Ramapo River, the Susquehanna River, Chenango River, Hudson River, Champlain Canal-Lake George, Normanskill River, Allegheny River, Sacandaga River (the west branch), Oswegatchie Inlet, Indian River, and Nisequoque River. Each of these rivers is discussed for disembarkation and embarkation points, lengths of journey, time of year best suited for a journey, type of fishing, and so forth. Maps are presented. Do not sell New York short as a bastion of exhilarating paddle adventure.

FOR THOSE WHO PLAN A VACATION ON THE WATER, WE PRESENT THIS MAP MERELY AS A CATALOG OF POSSIBILITIES. IT REQUIRES AN INDEX OF COMMON SENSE. SOME BOATERS TOIL AND DRUDGE. SECURE SPECIFIC INFORMATION WHERE AVAILABLE - THEN (1) VISIT LOCALITY IN ADVANCE; (2) TRAVEL DOWNSTREAM; (3) TRAVEL LIGHT FOR PORTAGES.

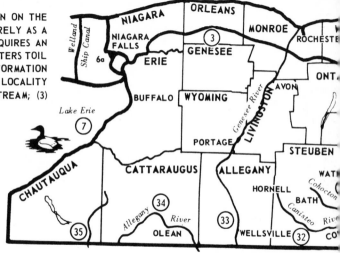

1. **LOWER HUDSON:** most warm-water species of fish; also shad, striped bass, sturgeon.
2. **UPPER HUDSON & CHAMPLAIN CANAL:** bass, northern pike, walleyes.
3. **MOHAWK RIVER & BARGE CANAL:** bass, northern pike, walleyes, pickerel, panfish.
4. **BARGE CANAL TO OSWEGO:** bass, northern pike, walleyes, pickerel.
5. **BARGE CANAL TO CAYUGA AND SENECA LAKES:** bass and northern pike.
6. **LAKE ONTARIO:** see Conservationist Information Leaflet.
6a **UPPER NIAGARA RIVER:** bass, northern pike, muskalonge.
6b **LOWER OAK ORCHARD CREEK:** bass, northern pike.
7. **LAKE ERIE:** bass, walleyes, catfish in spots; yellow perch, smelt; see Conservationist Information Leaflet.
8. **ST. LAWRENCE RIVER:** bass, northern pike, walleyes, pickerel, muskalonge.
9. **ADIRONDACK CANOE ROUTES:** see Recreation Circular No. 7, Conservation Department.
10. **NORTHERN HUDSON:** Very rough above Thurman Station; canoeable only in stillwaters above North Creek; bass, brown and brook trout, some northern pike and rainbow trout.

11. **SCHROON RIVER:** rough south of Schroon Lake; brook, brown and rainbow trout and landlocked salmon in inlet; landlocks, bass, lake trout, northern pike in lake; northern pike and bass in outlet.
12. **SARANAC RIVER:** easy to very rough canoeing; brown and rainbow trout below Union Flow; bass, northern pike, brown and rainbow trout above Franklin Flow.
13. **GRASS RIVER:** northern pike, bass, walleyes, few muskalonge.
14. **OSWEGATCHIE RIVER:** numerous dams; bass, pickerel, northern pike, walleyes, few muskalonge.
15. **INDIAN RIVER AND BLACK LAKE:** good trip Antwerp to Ogdensburg, quiet water, few carries; northern pike, pickerel, bass, walleyes, few muskalonge.
16. **CRANBERRY LAKE AND INLET TO HIGH FALLS:** quiet water, mostly State land; large brook trout.
17. **OSWEGATCHIE, WEST BRANCH:** almost continuous public fishing rights; good canoeing but quite a few carries; brook trout.
18. **BLACK RIVER:** quiet, but occasionally rough; brook trout above Lyons Falls, bass and northern pike below; rugged going above Hawkinsville.
19. **HINCKLEY RESERVOIR:** mostly panfish.
20. **PISECO LAKE:** lake trout, bass, whitefish; see

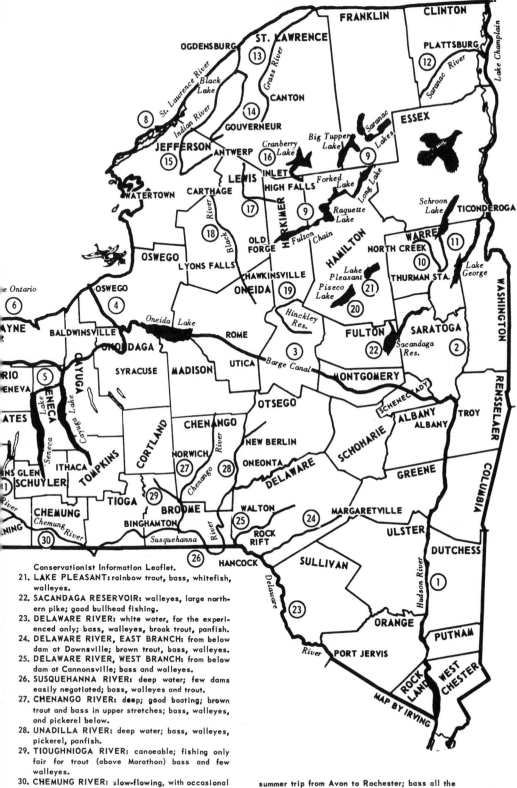

Conservationist Information Leaflet.

21. **LAKE PLEASANT:** rainbow trout, bass, whitefish, walleyes.

22. **SACANDAGA RESERVOIR:** walleyes, large northern pike; good bullhead fishing.

23. **DELAWARE RIVER:** white water, for the experienced only; bass, walleyes, brook trout, panfish.

24. **DELAWARE RIVER, EAST BRANCH:** from below dam at Downsville; brown trout, bass, walleyes.

25. **DELAWARE RIVER, WEST BRANCH:** from below dam at Cannonsville; bass and walleyes.

26. **SUSQUEHANNA RIVER:** deep water; few dams easily negotiated; bass, walleyes and trout.

27. **CHENANGO RIVER:** deep; good boating; brown trout and bass in upper stretches; bass, walleyes, and pickerel below.

28. **UNADILLA RIVER:** deep water; bass, walleyes, pickerel, panfish.

29. **TIOUGHNIOGA RIVER:** canoeable; fishing only fair for trout (above Marathon) bass and few walleyes.

30. **CHEMUNG RIVER:** slow-flowing, with occasional rifts; bass.

31. **COHOCTON RIVER:** brown and brook trout above Bath, bass below; hard going.

32. **CANISTEO RIVER:** rough; bass.

33. **GENESEE RIVER:** plenty short carries; good summer trip from Avon to Rochester; bass all the way; northern pike and walleyes in spots.

34. **ALLEGANY RIVER:** clear sailing most of the way; bass, walleyes, muskalonge.

35. **CONEWANGO CREEK:** slow-flowing; muskalonge and bass.

## NORTH CAROLINA

It is hard to beat the scenic opportunities for canoeing and kayaking afforded by the rivers of North Carolina. Unfortunately the state has not yet prepared a compilation of all, or even most, of its paddle trails. But nonetheless, they are many.

Some that show potential are the Nantahala River, from the Nantahala Powerhouse at Beechertown to Wesser; the Little Tennessee River; the French Broad River, from Rosman to the town of Pisgah Forest; the Tuckaseigee River from the junction of the east and west forks below Glenville Lake to Sylva; the Green River near Saluda; the New River above and below Route 16 east of Jefferson; and the Nolichucky River west of Bakersville. In the eastern part of the state there is Brice Creek ease of Pollacksville, and the White Oak River from Belgrade to Stella.

## NORTH DAKOTA

Do not think North Dakota is no more than a necessary place to pass through on a vacation trip west.

Among the many fine river trips in North Dakota is the Souris Canoe trail, beginning at Johnson Bridge and lasting for either 5½ or 13 miles, depending on how long you want to pursue it. To conclude the shorter trip, take your boat out at the Thompson Well site. The longer trip ends at Dam 1. These trips afford opportunities to observe the wonder of nature. A pamphlet by the North Dakota State Highway Department suggests watching for beaver lodges, wood ducks, hooded mergansers and other waterfowl, and white-tailed deer.

Other trips in North Dakota are:

*Northeastern part of the state:* the Pembine River from the Canadian line to Neche (spring, summer, and fall).

*Eastern North Dakota:* the Park River, from Park River (town) to Grafton (early spring).

The Cheyenne River (northern sector) from the Highway 20 bridge to Lake Ashtabula (spring, summer, and fall).

The Cheyenne River (southern sector) from Valley City to Kindred (spring, summer, and fall) and the James River, from Jamestown to the South Dakota state line.

*Southwestern North Dakota:* The Hearst River from State Highway 6, south of Mandan, as far west as water level allows (spring, summer, and fall).

The Cannonball River from near Shields to Cannonball (spring, summer, and fall).

The Knife River from Beulah to Stanton (late spring, early summer).

274

The Missouri River from the Garrison Dam Trailrace Area to Bismark (spring, summer, and fall).

The Little Missouri River, from the North Dakota state line to U.S. Highway 85 (late spring, early summer.)

The Little Missouri Bay, from U.S. Highway 85 bridge to the State Highway 22 bridge.

*North Central part of North Dakota:* The Mouse River from Minot to near Towner (spring, summer, or fall).

For three pages of typed information on the Little Missouri River float trip, contact the United States Department of Agriculture, Forest Service, Custer National Forest, P.O. Box 2556, Billings, Montana 59103. This guide details likely river conditions, tells the time the trip should take, makes suggestions for equipment to bring along, discusses weather, details the prospects for fishing, etc. It also tells where to write for maps, and what maps are needed.

OHIO

Not only does Ohio contain a surprising number of paddling opportunities within its borders, but it has some of the best-documented canoeing-kayaking trails in the nation. To mention a few: There is a 95-mile journey on the Little Miami River; a 140-mile trip on the Great Miami River; a 163-mile journey on the Mohican, Walhonding, and Muskingum rivers; a 56-mile journey on the Cuyahoga River; an 81-mile jaunt on the Maumee; and a 65-mile sojourn on the Sandusky River. You can get a free pamphlet detailing these trips and containing information on some other opportunities by writing the Ohio Department of Natural Resources, Publications Section, 1500 Dublin Road, Columbus, Ohio 43215.

If you have any intention of dipping your blades in Ohio waters, you will find indispensable a catalog entitled *1,000,000 Miles of Canoe and Hiking Routes* available from Ohio Canoe Adventures Incorporated, 5128 Colorado Avenue, P.O. Box 2092, Sheffield Lake, Ohio 44054, for $1.00.

*1,000,000 Miles of Canoe and Hiking Routes* claims that Ohio has over 43,000 miles of perennial streams, and that while not all are canoeable, at some time of year one-fourth, or over 10,000 miles, offer unlimited paddling possibilities. This guide represents years of research into the characteristics of Ohio's paddling waters. It lists hundreds of river programs, providing factual descriptions of water routes, that are the result of comprehensive study. The programs are written to depict recreational opportunities for paddlers and other outdoorsmen. Descriptions are complete, with mileages, access points, float times, water conditions, camping areas, points of interest, etc. Prices are given for the various programs. In addition, the brochure offers hundreds of canoe-trail maps, and books on canoeing.

Of course, Ohio Canoe Adventures Incorporated (OCAI) is in the business of selling information, and your catalog for $1.00 is simply their promotion piece for ordering more information. Nevertheless, the material available from this source is about the most complete and detailed available. OCAI devotes several months a year to seeking out new Ohio canoe trails and exploring them. Thus the collection of trip descriptions and maps grows all the time. Some of the rivers detailed in the guide at this time include the Sandusky, Portage, Mohican, Walhonding, Huron, Cuyahoga, Grand, Dokosing, Muskingum, Michigan Au Sable, and Wills and Killbuck creeks. Among the literature offered by OCAI are canoe-trail guides for states other than Ohio. Paddlers who intend to take to the water in Michigan, Pennsylvania, Wisconsin, Maine, Indiana, Iowa, Illinois, and Canada will also find material here. Everything considered, *1,000,000 Miles of Canoe and Hiking Routes* is a valuable investment. It introduces you to a vast cache of literature that can make your paddling more enjoyable and add variety to your itinerary.

## OKLAHOMA

An attractive paddle trip for those who want to cruise in Oklahoma is the Illinois River from Twin Falls, near the Arkansas border, to Carter's Landing—a distance of about 70 miles. The voyage can be made in shorter legs for day cruising.

A brochure entitled *Floating the Illinois* is available from the Oklahoma Tourism and Recreation Department, 500 Will Rogers Building, Oklahoma City, Oklahoma 73501. It describes the Illinois as flowing easily, with delightful scenery, yet with several stretches of mild rapids. Included is a chart listing locations where one can rent canoes, buy groceries, bait and tackle, ice, and get shuttle service, boat access, and other goods and services. There is also a detailed description of the course and an excellent map.

Those interested in canoeing Oklahoma may wish to contact two canoeing clubs in the state:

| | |
|---|---|
| OK Canoers | or Tulsa Canoe & Camping Club |
| Mr. B. L. Smith | Jean Estep |
| 3112 Chaucer Drive | 5810 East 30 Place |
| Village, Oklahoma 73120 | Tulsa, Oklahoma 74114 |

There is no dearth of canoeing or kayaking opportunities in Oregon, and the tall pines and majestic, unspoiled landscapes make it prime territory for those who like exploring. According to the United States Department of Agriculture, Region 6, headquartered in Portland, Oregon, paddling is a fairly new form of outdoor activity in the Northwest, so there is practically no written information about suitable lakes and rivers. However, the Department lists five opportunities in Oregon.

1. The Willamette River, from Eugene to Oregon City, is placid in summer and fall and more challenging in winter and spring.

2. The Deschutes River, from Wickiup Dam to Benham, is reportedly a fine float trip in spring and summer.

3. The Oregon Cascades are full of lakes of varying size and accessibility. Sparks, Waldo, and Cultus are said to be some of the best canoeing lakes, with a season from July 1 to September 30.

4. The John Day River is a challenging float trip in spring and early summer.

5. The Columbia is a big river, and has great potential for those capable of handling it.

Other popular drifting and paddling streams in Oregon include, in the southeastern part of the state, the Owyhee, a 100-mile trip of many hazards, which may be negotiated from May through mid-June; in central Oregon, the John Day, a 114-mile trip with some hazards—negotiable from March through mid-June; the Deschutes, a 100-mile paddle trip with many hazards that can be attempted year round. Seven streams suggested in northwest Oregon include the Willamette, McKenzie, North Santiam, Clackamas, Nestucca, Aslea, and Nehalem. All these present varying degrees of hazards. Check with local sources and procure the appropriate topographic maps before negotiating them. Two other rivers in Oregon that show promise are the Powder River and the Grande Ronde River, the latter for well-experienced paddlers only.

Paddling opportunities abound in the Deschutes National Forest. For information on the Deschutes River, contact the Deschutes National Forest, Office of Forest Supervisor, P.O. Box 751, Bend, Oregon 97701. The material from this source also lists the following for enjoyable, if brief, paddle trips: Summit Lake, Wickiup Reservoir, Charlton Lake, Crane Prairie Reservoir, and others.

## PENNSYLVANIA

Excellent information is available on canoeing and kayaking in Pennsylvania. One suggested area is the Allegheny National Forest. Although this Forest has no mapped canoe routes, you may canoe on portions of Tionesta Creek, Conewango Creek, Bokenstraw Creek, Allegheny River, and Clariton River. There are also impoundments at Chapman Dam and Beaver Meadows. Canoeing is possible on the Allegheny and Tionesta reservoirs, although caution is advisable to avoid the powerboats. For good, specific information about canoeing in this region, send for a booklet entitled *Canoeing in Kinzua Country,* by Bill Rusin. The booklet is available by writing Kinzua Dam Vacation Bureau, 305 Market Street, Warren, Pennsylvania. It costs $1.00.

For a bulging packet of information on paddling opportunities in Pennsylvania, contact the Commonwealth of Penn-

*Susquehanna River paddle trails key map, below. At right, details of Map 4, top, and Map 2, below. (Endless Mountains Association map, from* Susquehanna Water Trails)

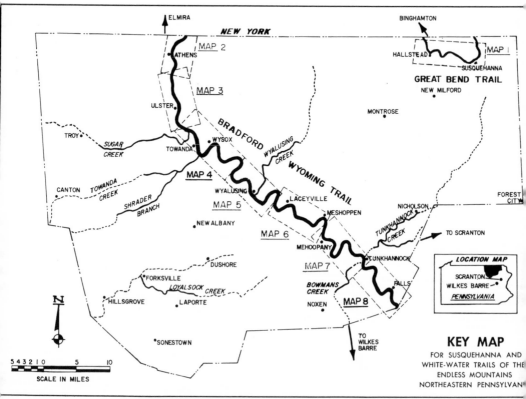

278

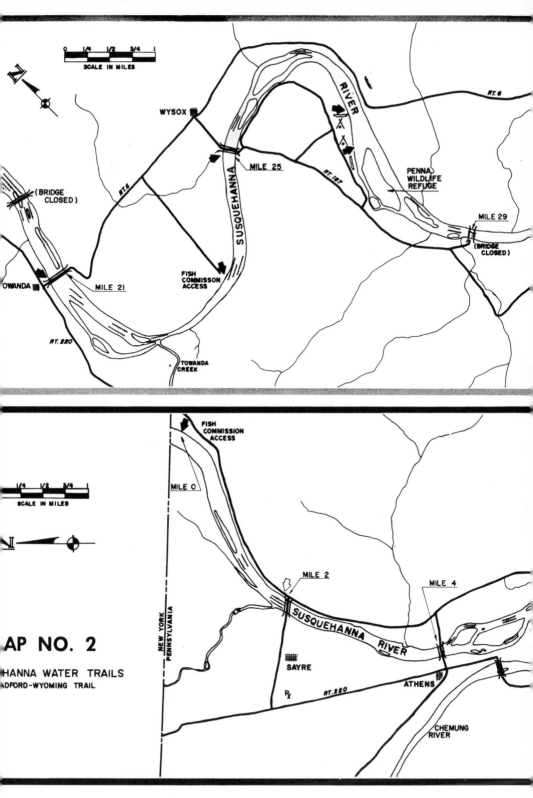

**SCALE IN MILES**

WYSOX

RT. 6

(BRIDGE CLOSED)

TOWANDA

MILE 21

RT. 220

TOWANDA CREEK

SUSQUEHANNA

MILE 25

RT. 187

PENNA WILDLIFE REFUGE

MILE 29

(BRIDGE CLOSED)

RIVER

RT. 6

FISH COMMISSON ACCESS

FISH COMMISSION ACCESS

MILE 0

MILE 2

MILE 4

NEW YORK
PENNSYLVANIA

**MAP NO. 2**

**SUSQUEHANNA WATER TRAILS**

**BRADFORD-WYOMING TRAIL**

SCALE IN MILES

SUSQUEHANNA RIVER

SAYRE

RT. 220

ATHENS

CHEMUNG RIVER

sylvania, Department of Commerce, Harrisburg, Pennsylvania 17120. Included are brochures and maps detailing conditions, facilities, and recreational opportunities on the Susquehanna water trails in the Endless Mountains of the northeastern portion of the state. Areas covered include the Great Bend Trail, a 19-mile watercourse extending from the Pennsylvania Fish Commission access above Lanesboro to the Kirkwood-Conklin Bridge off Route 7, at Kirkwood, New York. Also described is the Bradford-Wyoming Trail, 88 miles of water extending from the Pennsylvania Fish Commission access near the Pennsylvania-New York line above Sayre, Pennsylvania, to Falls, Pennsylvania. Also covered are eight whitewater trails, all of which are graded.

The packet from the Department of Commerce contains pamphlets from professional outfitters offering rafting and kayak trips and guided whitewater adventures. Some of these trips include the Youghiogheny Wilderness, Cheat Canyon, and Stony Creek. Commercial outfitting is also advertised for trips in Kittatinny country on the Delaware River.

One excellent river for paddling is the Brandywine, which also flows into Delaware. The following is quoted from the AAA's regional magazine, *The Lancaster Motorist:* "For eleven miles of nearly continuous waterway, the inveterate paddler may combine relaxation with a remarkable nature education. In all the miles there are only two places on the stretch from Lenape, Pennsylvania, to Rocklands, Delaware, where dams break into the watery highway. Seven different access points make it possible to try a number of small trips through the summer.

"One of the access points, two hours downstream from Lenape, is at the Brandywine River Museum, at Chadds Ford, where the Tri-County Conservatory also holds forth. The Conservancy has a very special interest in the Brandywine River, offering a number of conservation and preservation activities that are tied in with maintaining water quality and educating the general public in the importance of a balanced ecology."

A book entitled *Canoeing the Brandywine: A Naturalist's Guide,* by Charles Aquadro is available from the Tri-County Conservatory, Chadds Ford, Pennsylvania 19317.

## RHODE ISLAND

*The Pawcatuck River and Wood River,* a brief pamphlet available from the Rhode Island Development Council, Tourist Promotion Division, Hayes Street, Providence, Rhode Island

02908, contains a map of the rivers and a discussion of the fishing to be enjoyed on the Pawcatuck and Wood rivers. Included is the following discussion of the Pawcatuck:

"There are relatively few opportunities in Rhode Island for extensive canoeing. The best watercourse for this purpose is found in the Pawcatuck River watershed. Three long trips are possible. One can commence at One Hundred Acre Pond in West Kingston, and proceed through Thirty Acre Pond, into the Chepuxet River to Worden Pond, thence down the Pawcatuck to Westerly or Watch Hill. Another, somewhat shorter, could originate in the village of Usquepaug and proceed down the Queens River until it intercepts the Pawcatuck and the other long trip could commence in Exeter at Route 165 in the Arcadia Management Area and proceed down the Wood River to the Pawcatuck through Barberville, Wyoming, Hope Valley, Woodville and Alton with each location requiring a portage over dams."

In addition to the Pawcatuck, Chepuxet, and Wood rivers, the AMC *New England Canoeing Guide* details a trip on the Pettaquamscutt River. The Guide is available from the Appalachian Mountain Club, 5 Joy Street, Boston, Massachusetts 02108 for $6.00.

## SOUTH CAROLINA

South Carolina offers some of the best paddling adventures on the east coast—and some of the toughest, including parts of the infamous Chattooga River. Before attempting this incredible river make certain you obtain information about it from the United States Department of Agriculture, Forest Service Southern Region, Sumter National Forest, P.O. Box 1437, Gainesville, Georgia 30501; and from the Recreation Officer, United States Forest Service, United States Department of Agriculture, 1801 Main Street, Columbia, South Carolina 29202. Rivers that can also be run, in addition to the Chattooga, are the Broad, Catawba, Wataree, Santee, Congaree, Tugaloo and the Chauga (though the beginner should beware of the latter two).

## SOUTH DAKOTA

South Dakota lists its best places for boating as Pactola Lake, Sheridan Lake, Bismark Lake, Horsethief Lake, Cook Lake, Deerfield Dam, Roubaix Lake, and Angostura Reservoir. No motors are allowed on Roubaix, Horsethief, Cook, and Bismarck lakes, making them good for paddling. Check at boat launches for other rules and regulations posted by the Forest Service and the State of South Dakota.

## TENNESSEE

Among the rivers for floating in Tennessee are the Hatchie, Buffalo, Duck, Elk, Harpeth, Red, Roaring, Collins, and Sequatchie; the Big South Fork of the Cumberland River; the Obed, Powell, Clinch, Holston, and Conasaugo rivers; the Ocoee, Hiwassee, Little Tennessee, and Little rivers; and the Little Pigeon, French Broad, and Nolichucky rivers. For a colorful brochure entitled *Canoeing in Tennessee* contact the Department of Conservation, 2611 West End Avenue, Nashville, Tennessee 37203. Also available from this source are maps of some of these waterpaths.

## TEXAS

At the time this material was prepared, Texas lacked a comprehensive publication covering its waters for paddlers. However, a booklet was in the making. Two publications that present worthwhile information for canoeing and kayaking in Texas are entitled *Texas Rivers and Rapids* and *Texas Rivers and Rapids, Volume II.* These are obtainable from *Texas Rivers and Rapids,* P. O. Box 673, Humble, Texas 77338.

Texas has numerous paddle adventures for those who prefer easy enjoyment in beautiful scenery and who do not care to challenge fast water. There is the Angelina River, from its headwaters to its confluence with the Neches River above Sam Rayburn Reservoir (100 miles) and below the reservoir (another 20 miles). Another opportunity is found on Big Cypress Creek between Lake o' the Pines and Caddo Lake, a distance of 45 miles. A 60-mile trip is possible on the Big Sandy Village Creek from the Alabama-Coushatta Indian Reservation to the Neches River. Other rivers that may be paddled include the Brazos, Colorado, Little, Red, Sabina, and Trinity, as well as the Pine Island Bayou.

Whitewater rivers in Texas include the Concho, Erio, Guadalupe, Lampasas, Llano, Medina, Nueces, Pecos, Perdernales, Rio Grande, San Gabriel, San Marcos, and San Saba rivers. For further descriptions of the embarkation and take-out points for these rivers, contact the Texas Parks and Wildlife Department, John H. Reagan Building, Austin, Texas 78701.

## UTAH

Utah is a land of giant rock outcroppings and rugged mountains that boast a fantastic paleontological and geological heritage. Many rivers pound with rapids and rocks. They are rugged and far beyond the prowess of most paddlers, no matter how expert. Many of them are reserved for commercial float trips, using big neoprene and rubber rafts. For the most part, rigid craft such as canoes and kayaks would be pounded to pieces in the churning whitewater.

Nonetheless, there are also placid rivers and lakes in Utah. For pleasurable canoeing and good fishing, consider three lakes in the Dixie National Park, all with accompanying campgrounds: Navajo Lake, Pine Lake, and Posy Lake. For a trip with more adventure, examine the Green River in the Flaming Gorge National Recreation Area. Here twelve miles of the Green (below the Flaming Gorge Dam) provide popular float and fishing experiences among the best in the West. The scenery is outstanding and rapids are moderate to easy. Another rugged float trip is on the Salmon River. For initial information on these trips, contact The United States Department of Agriculture, Forest Service, Federal Office Building, 324 25th Street, Ogden, Utah 84401.

## VERMONT

An excellent brochure from the state of Vermont, Department of Forests and Parks, Montpelier, Vermont 05602, describes the attractions and hazards of paddling the Connecticut River. Entitled *Canoeing the Connecticut River,* the brochure details water conditions and many other facts about the Connecticut along the approximately 235 miles over which it forms a boundary between New Hampshire and Vermont. The length of the watercourse is divided into sections and is mapped. Space also is devoted to sights you may see while paddling the Connecticut.

## VIRGINIA

The Commonwealth of Virginia has not published a definitive listing of the paddle opportunities within its boundaries, but fortunately would-be explorers of Virginia can procure several privately written books that can prepare them for adventure second to none.

One such book is entitled *Canoeing Whitewater: A Guidebook to the Rivers of Virginia, Eastern West Virginia, and the Great Smoky Mountain Area.* The book, by Randy Carter, may be purchased from Mr. Carter, 158 Winchester Street, Warrenton, Virginia 22186, at a cost of $4.75.

Virginia paddling also fills four volumes of *Blue Ridge Voyages* by Roger Corbett and Louis Matacia. Volume I costs $3.00

283

and presents 10 one- and two-day trips within 150 miles of Washington, D. C. It indicates take-outs, put-ins, hazards, campsites, and local history, with photographs and scale maps of each trip. Rappahannock River, Antietam Creek, Thornton River, Potomac River, Shenandoah River, and Cedar Creek are discussed.

Volume II, which consists of 84 pages, presents ten more trips within approximately the same radius from the nation's capital. Illustrations, descriptions of side hikes, cave trips, historical sites, and other information is assembled. Of particular interest are Smoke Hole Canyon, Caudy's Castle, Potomac Gorge, Burnside Bridge, Catoctin Creek, Cacapon River, Monocacy River, Antietam Creek, Potomac River, Cedar Creek, and South Branch, Potomac River. This volume is $3.00.

Volume III also costs $3.00. It presents an illustrated guide to ten whitewater canoe trips in Virginia and West Virginia. Detailed maps and photographic coverage of beginning to intermediate trips on the Hughes River, Lost River, Shenandoah River, Passage Creek, Sleepy Creek, Goose Creek, Rappahannock River, South Anna River, and North Anna River are found within these pages.

The last volume, Volume IV, also $3.00, is an illustrated log of the Shenandoah River and its south fork. It offers a mile-by-mile description of the river starting above Waynesboro on the South River and continuing 200 miles downstream to Harpers Ferry. The log is illustrated with photographs and maps of the entire river. Access points, rapids, dams, and danger points are described in text and located on maps. Points of interest along the river, such as old mills, early Indian fish dams, battle sites, and locations of industrial centers add a historical flavor. Chapters on the Shenandoah headwaters, the canoeable tributary streams, and selected short trips round out the guide. All four volumes may be purchased from Louis J. Matacia, 2700 Gallows Road, Vienna, Virginia 22180.

If you are interested in paddling the Shenandoah, you may want to take advantage of the services of an outfitter who can provide you with excursions including "wild food" options, or with partial outfitting. If this is the case, contact the Shenandoah River Outfitters, Route 3, Luray, Virginia 22835.

Other suitable streams in eastern Virginia include the Mattaponi River, the Pamunkey River, Mount Landing, Big and Little Totuskey, and Farnum Creeks. There is Nomini Creek north of Warsaw, and Occupacia Creek. Or you may want to try the James River, Grays Creek, Wards Creek, and Floridieu

Hundred Creek. Among these waters you should find exhilarating paddling with outstanding fishing, swimming, and exploration.

WASHINGTON

Among paddling opportunities in Washington are the Elwha and Hoh rivers. In the Gifford Pinchot National Forest canoeing is gaining popularity at Spirit Lake at the base of Mount St. Helens. Also, Walupt Lake at the edge of the Goat Rocks Wilderness is popular for fishing, and should be a good place to stop if you are carrying a canoe or kayak atop your car.

In the Okanogan National Forest, the Twisp, Methow, and Okanogan rivers are reported floatable at certain times of the year. (Every July Fourth, the Rat River Race is held on Methow River between Winthrop and Twisp. There are separate divisions for kayaks, canoes, rafts, and other craft.)

The Wenatchee National Forest offers paddling opportunities on Keechelus, Kachess, Cle Elum, and Wenatchee Lakes. Fifty-mile long Lake Chelan has outstanding scenery and numerous boat-in campsites but is susceptible to strong winds and 3- to 5-foot waves. Finally, Ross Lake, a reservoir, leads to wild country and has several boat-in campsites.

For information on the waters in Washington, contact the Washington Kayak Club, Route 2, Box 6377, Issaguah, Washington 98027.

WEST VIRGINIA

West Virginia has not compiled material on paddling opportunities in the state, but fortunately the private sector has taken on the task. If you are interested in the excellent streams of this state, prepare yourself by purchasing the very comprehensive book, *Whitewater West Virginia,* published by Dr. Robert Burrell, 1412 Western Avenue, Morgantown, West Virginia 26505. This is a well-integrated book detailing the characteristics of rivers and streams and containing maps for all navigable streams (for canoes at least) in the state.

WISCONSIN

Like its sister state Minnesota, Wisconsin boasts some of the finest canoeing and kayaking streams in the nation. A sample of its enjoyable paddle adventures may be found in the Chequamegon National Forest, which has 411 lakes over 10 acres in size. There are 32 miles of rivers and streams. Within the Chequamegon National Forest the Bad, Chippewa, Yellow, Flambeau, and Namakagon rivers flow essentially as

285

they did when they were the major routes of travel for Indians, explorers, missionaries, voyageurs, traders, and loggers. The Flambeau, Chippewa, and Namakagon are considered fine canoeing waters. The Jump and Yellow rivers, located northwest of the town of Medford, are also good canoeing streams. The upper reaches of all these rivers are often shallow in the late summer and early fall. You should, therefore, expect to portage around some stretches. Specific information on a canoeing stream or lake within the Chequemegon National Forest can be obtained by contacting the District Ranger's office nearest your point of interest. The five District Ranger offices are located in Park Falls, Glidden, Medford, Hayward, and Washburn.

Numerous excellent publications are available on the canoeing possibilities in Wisconsin. Among them are the following:

*Canoe Trails of Northeastern Wisconsin.* This is a guide to the Brule, Deerskin, Embarrass, Manitowish, Menominee, Oconto, Pelican, Peshtigo, Pike, Pine, Popple, Prairie, Red, Spirit, Tomahawk, Wisconsin, and Wolf rivers. It is published by *Wisconsin Trails Magazine* and costs $4.75. Write to *Wisconsin Trails,* P.O. Box 5650, Madison, Wisconsin 53705.

*Canoe Trails of North-Central Wisconsin.* This is another fine book by *Wisconsin Trails.* It presents a guide to the Chippewa, Flambeau, Couderay, Jump, Turtle, Manitowish, Yellow, and Thornapple rivers, and Deertail and Main Creeks. It costs $4.00 and is available from the address listed above.

*Wisconsin's North-Central Canoe Trails.* This publication is offered by North-Central Canoe Trails Incorporated of Ladysmith, Wisconsin 54848. It covers ten major streams in the north-central portion of the state and is printed on water-resistant paper. The price is $2.50.

But paddling is by no means reserved for the northern portions of Wisconsin. Even if you live in Milwaukee or out of state, say in Chicago, there are excellent and reachable streams in the southern part of the state. There is a booklet entitled *Wisconsin Water Trails* published by the Wisconsin Department of Natural Resources, Division of Conservation, Information and Tourism Section, Madison, Wisconsin, 53701, which details canoe trips in all parts of the Badger State. Listed among the possibilities are: Manitowish, Turtle, and Flambeau river water trails; Big Elk, Bear, and Trout River water trails; Horsehead to Lac du Flambeau water trail; Three Lakes to Eagle River water trail, Wisconsin River water trails; Tomahawk, Lemonweir, the east fork of the Chippewa, Chippewa, St. Croix, and Namakagon water trails;

*The Peshtigo Water Trail, right. (Map from Wisconsin Water Trails, Wisconsin Department of Natural Resources, Division of Conservation)*

286

## Peshtigo River Water Trail

### Trip No. 44

**Highway C to Green Bay**—For the canoeist who desires a stream with ever-changing northwoods scenery, long stretches of tall pines and hardwoods, good fishing and many a breathtaking dash through white waters, this river trip has definite appeal. The country traversed is very picturesque and quite wild, and the trip includes a few dams, flowages, and steaming rapids.

Although some trips start at Cavour, the usual put-in place is County Trunk Highway C or the upper end of Caldron Falls Reservoir. Water levels along the Peshtigo fluctuate considerably, and it is a good idea to check conditions before a trip. There are a number of portages indicated on the map, and except for experts, a portage is also advisable around the rough water about three miles below Johnson Falls. Use the right bank.

The Upper Peshtigo is considered one of the toughest and most adventurous of all white-water river trips. The lower portion is more peaceful. The trip can be extended downstream through Peshtigo all the way to the waters of Green Bay.

Restrictions by the Wisconsin Public Service Corporation on the use of the Caldron and High Falls Flowages include no fires or overnight camping except at Twin Bridge County Park on High Falls. There are numerous well-kept landings on these flowages.

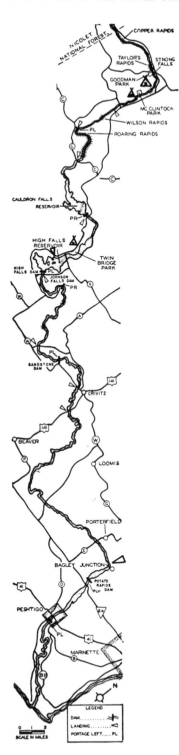

287

Totogatic, Yellow, Clam, and Bois Brule river water trails; Menominee, Bad, Marengo, Wolf, Fox, and Little Fox water trails; Waupaca River water trail; Pelican, Peshtigo, Rock, Yahara, Kickapoo, and Black rivers. In short, there is something for everyone, no matter what part of Wisconsin you want to paddle or how good you are. If your plans will take you to Wisconsin, write for this booklet.

## WYOMING

Wyoming is big country with abundant natural beauty and solitude for paddlers. Some of the lakes and rivers suggested by the Wyoming Travel Commission include, in Yellowstone National Park, Yellowstone Lake, Lewis Lake, Shoshone Lake; in Grand Teton National Park, Jackson Lake, Jenny Lake, Spring Lake, Phelps Lake, the Snake River; in Badger National Forest, Fremont Lake, New Fork Lake, Half Moon Lake, Boulder Lake, Green River Lake, Willow Lake, Middle Piney Lake, the Green River, and Palisades Lake. Also there are Meadowlark Lake, Sibley Lake, and West Tens Sleep Lake in the Big Horn National Forest.

Cook Lake is suggested in the Black Hills National Forest. In the Shoshone National Forest there are Louis Lake, Fiddlers Lake, Brooks Lake, Beartooth Lake, Island Lake, Long Lake, and the north fork of the Shoshone River. Teton National Forest offers the Snake River, Buffalo River, Gros Ventre River, Lower Slide Lake, and Hoback River.

In Medicine Bow National Forest there are Lake Marie, Sand Lake, Silver Lake, Lake Owen, Rob Roy Reservoir, Hog Park Reservoir, and North Platte River.

Wyoming parks conducive to paddling include Alcova and Big Sandy parks, Boysen State Park, Buffalo Bill State Park, Glendo State Park, Guernsey State Park, Keyhole State Park, Seminoe State Park, and Curt Gowdy State Park.

Other places to canoe include the Fontenelle Reservoir and Viva Naughton in southwest Wyoming; Lake Hattie, Saratoga Lake, and Springer Reservoir in southeast Wyoming; Lake DeSmet in northeast Wyoming; and the Big Horn River and Ocean Lake in northwest Wyoming.

Paddle Trails in Canada

Canada, land of voyageurs and fur traders, boasts terrific canoeing and kayaking in almost all sectors. And Canada promotes this sport as a tourist attraction, so that a wealth of material is available on canoe trails. So many lakes are joined together that it is possible to take "loop" trips, trips in which you end up back at the point of embarkation.

Because of the proliferation of brochures and maps that flow from sources of tourist information in Canada, several books would have to be written just to list the various canoeing possibilities by name, let alone provide maps and descriptions. It is possible, for the purpose of this guide, only to extend some pointers on where to write for information, and in some instances hints on where attractive routes lie.

## ALBERTA

Together with British Columbia, Alberta offers some of the most awesome and majestic scenery in North America. Its forests and waterways are vast, and one can easily get the urge to stay longer than originally intended. Here, paddlers can see nature in all her resplendent beauty. The Saskatchewan River provides close to 225 miles of paddling pleasure; the Athabasca almost 350 miles! Needless to say, hundreds of shorter—and longer—trips are to be found. As an initial source of material write to the Canadian Government Travel Bureau, Ottawa, Ontario, for its book *Canoe Trips in Canada;* and the Government Travel Bureau, 331 Highways Building, Edmonton, Alberta.

## BRITISH COLUMBIA

A packet of brochures from the Department of Travel Industry, Government of British Columbia, Victoria, British Columbia, Canada, gets you started on planning a memorable vacation in the resplendent Northwest wilderness. Write, asking for a list of canoe clubs in the province. Study a map and then write to the canoe club located nearest the general area in which you wish to plan a trip. Also worth writing for is Key 14 (available from the Province of British Columbia, Department of Lands, Forests, and Water Resources, Vancouver, British Columbia) to the topographic maps published in the National Topographic Series pertaining to British Columbia. Using Key 14 in conjunction with a highway map, you can order the necessary topographic maps to plan your trip. Finally, a book entitled *Canoe Trip Guide to British Columbia,* which costs $2.75, can be purchased from Canoe British Columbia, 1606 West Broadway, Vancouver 8, British Columbia.

## LABRADOR AND NEWFOUNDLAND

The forests of Newfoundland and Labrador remain shrouded with the same enchantment as when Norsemen sailed the fogbound banks of the province over 1000 years ago. This is an excellent, remote place for a vacation. But before you go, be aware of the following regulations: under the Forest Travel Act, all forestland within the province is declared a Forest Travel Restricted Area, generally between mid-May and mid-September each year. Non-residents are not permitted to travel in the restricted areas without a guide, and when two or more non-residents travel together, the number of guides shall not be less than one guide for each two non-residents. This can be waived in extenuating circumstances, such as for laboratory or exploratory expeditions, but in this case you must receive a permit issued by the Minister of Agriculture and Forests, Confederation Building, St. John's, Newfoundland.

For topographic maps of the province, contact the Crown Lands and Survey Division, Department of Agriculture and Forests, Confederation Building, St. John's, Newfoundland. The following descriptions of canoe and kayak routes in Newfoundland are published by the Tourist Development Office, St. John's.

*Northwest Gander River.* "Starting at Glenwood logging settlement, accessible by highway or railway . . . supplies can be purchased; Glenwood to mouth of Northwest Gander River . . . 14 miles through Gander Lake . . . first 16 miles of river easy canoeing . . . short portages on upper river where rough water occurs . . . all wilderness country . . . moose and caribou frequent all season . . . total canoeing distance, including return trip, approximately 100 miles."

*Lower Gander.* "Starting at Glenwood, river flows to sea through a series of lakes . . . two rapids in first three miles . . . remainder of river smooth . . . very beautiful scenery . . . salmon and trout fishing available . . . Glenwood to Gander

Bay settlement at the mouth of the river is a distance of 30 miles . . . excellent for seven-to-ten-day trip, including return . . . this trip can be combined for a 14-to-20 day trip with the Northwest Gander."

*Upper Exploits.* "Starting at Buchans Junction, rail and highway junction . . . forty miles to head of Red Indian Lake . . . thence by river into Lloyds Lake and King George IV Lake . . . 14-day trip, including return . . . portages necessary around rapids on Lloyds River and King George IV River . . . excellent scenery, moose and caribou frequent . . . complete wilderness country . . . speckled trout and ouananiche fishing available . . . total distance approximately 150 miles."

*Lower Exploits.* "Beginning at Bishops Falls or Main Dam, Millertown . . . two-day trip . . . floating pulpwood makes it necessary to enquire if drives intended . . . portage necessary around falls and power dam at Grand Falls . . . holding booms at Grand Falls and Bishops Falls to be avoided . . . excellent scenery for short trip."

*Upper Humber River.* "Starting at Deer Lake, thence ten miles of easy river to Harrison Steady . . . rougher water from Harrison Steady, about six miles to Little Falls . . . Little Falls to Big Falls (Provincial Park Area) 3½ miles easy traveling . . . Big Falls to Alder Pond 13 miles easy traveling . . . Alder Pond to Adies Lake, 25 miles easy water . . . moose photography possible . . . log drives at intervals during June and early July . . . salmon and trout fishing."

*Gambo Lake Area.* "Short canoe and camping trip—15 to 20 miles additional river canoeing available at head of lake for one- or two-day duration . . . scenic area . . . salmon and trout fishing . . . moose photography possible."

*Terra Nova to Long Pond.* "A cross-country trip for hardy canoeists . . . can begin at Terra Nova settlement or North West River, Lake Kepenkeck . . . about 40 miles by logging road further up river . . . route from Terra Nova to Mollyquajeck Falls—Lake St. John to Lake Kepenkeck . . . rough and many short portages are required . . . Lake Kepenkeck to Rainey Lake is a 3-mile portage over rough trail . . . Rainey Lake to Lake Kaegudeck, Kaegudeck to Jubilee, Jubilee to Hungry Grove Pond . . . portage from Hungry Grove Pond to Long Harbour River is about 6 miles . . . Long Harbour to settlements at mouth of bay is 15 miles. This trip requires 15 to 20 days, all through wilderness country . . . moose and caribou frequent this area . . . speckled-trout fishing in all lakes and ponds."

*Grand Lake to Sandy Lake—Birchy Waterways.* "Approximately a 40-mile trip beginning from the power house at Deer Lake through the northern portion of Grand Lake, then on to Sandy and Birchy lakes . . . some pulpwood is present in Birchy Lake but presents no obstacle . . . this route may be subdivided into shorter lengths because of its proximity to the trans-Canada Highway. The entire route offers steady water through scenic countryside."

## MANITOBA

For assistance in planning a trip to Manitoba, contact the Department of Mines and Natural Resources, 1007 Century Street, R3H OW4, Winnipeg 1, Manitoba, Canada. Ask for *Information Bulletin 4,* which provides a key to Canadian nautical charts for Rainy Lake, Lake of the Woods, Lake Winnipeg, Lake Winnipegosis, and Lac La Ronge. The canoe trips in these regions are too many even to enumerate.

Two excellent chart-maps are published by the Manitoba Department of Tourism and Recreation, Parks Branch; they cover the Sassiginnigak canoe country and the Riviére Aux Rats canoe routes. Also from this source come guide maps and descriptions of the Kautunigan and Whitemouth River canoe trips.

## NEW BRUNSWICK

For a booklet detailing canoe or kayaking travel opportunities in New Brunswick, contact the Department of Tourism, Research and Planning Branch, P.O. Box 1030, Fredericton, New Brunswick. This booklet can assist your selection of rivers. Then write the Department of Tourism for further details on the river of your choice. Described in the booklet, entitled *Canoe Tripping in New Brunswick* are the following rivers: St. John River (upper, lower, and middle); St. Francis River; Tobique River; Eel River; Keswick River; Portobello Creek; Oromocto River; Salmon River; Canaan (Wahademoak) River; Nerepis River; Kennebecasis River; St. Croix Headwaters and River; Little Digdeguash (North Brook); Main Southwest Miramichi River; Cains River; Restigouche River; Kedgwick River; Upsalquitch and Northwest Upsalquitch River; Nepisquit River; Pokemouche River; Tracadie River; Kouchibouguac River; and Richibucto River.

## NOVA SCOTIA

Suggested paddle trails in Nova Scotia include the Shannon River Bridge (Squirreltown Station), via Alma Lake, Ponhook

Lake, and Medway—60 miles of trout and salmon fishing; and Shannon River Bridge via Alma Lake, Ponhook Lake, Lake Rossignol and Liverpool River to Liverpool, a distance of 82 miles. The trip can be continued and increased to 107 miles by starting at Shannon River Bridge and taking the Medway River, Lake Rossignol, Kejimkujik Lake, Liverpool River, Alma Lake, and returning to Shannon River Bridge.

Another suggested trip is Halifax to Truro through Dartmouth locks, Banook Lake, Micmac Lake, two locks at Port Wallace, and Porta Bella locks. Then to Lake Williams and Lake Thomas, Wellington River, Shubenacadie Lake to Maitland, and following the eastern shore of Cobequid Bay and Salmon River to Truro. Total distance is 74 miles. Hubbard Cove to Windsor, via Dauphinee Mill Lake, West Haver Lake, Ponhook lakes, St. Croix River to Windsor—40 miles of excellent fishing for trout is another fine trip.

Finally suggested is a trip from St. Peter to Strathlorne, via Bras d'Or Lakes, to Baddeck through St. Patrick's Channel, to Lake Ainslie to Strathlorne. This trip provides 105 miles of good fishing for trout and salmon.

Perhaps the best source of information on canoeing the waters of Nova Scotia is the Trail Shop Cooperative, 6260 Quinpool Road, Halifax, Nova Scotia. In addition to providing general information, this source has available a book entitled *Canoe Routes* of Nova Scotia for $2.50. You can also order the book (including 50¢ for handling) from Nova Scotia Camping Association, Box 1622, Halifax, Nova Scotia.

## ONTARIO

If you want to plan a paddle vacation in Ontario, start by writing the Engineering Branch, Map Office, Ministry of Natural Resources, Parliament Buildings, Queen's Park, Toronto, Ontario, for its publication entitled *Northern Ontario Canoe Routes*. The cost of the latest edition of the guide is 50¢; it provides general information and lists further sources on 125 separate routes.

By writing the Ministry of Natural Resources at 101 Holiday Inn Drive, Respeler, Ontario, you can receive numerous small pamphlets describing various canoe routes, among which are the following: Saugeen River, Rankin River, Grand River, Beaver River, Kishkebus, Mississippi, Mattawa Provincial Park, Moon River, Pickerel River, Wolf and Pickerel River Canoe Route, Quetico Provincial Park, North Georgian Bay Recreational Preserve, the Black Lake Canoe Route, and the south branch of the Miskoka River canoe route.

## QUEBEC

Quebec is the province most famous for its early trappers, who helped introduce the canoe to the newly arriving French and English. And there is no dearth of adventure on Quebec waterways. Some of the rivers suitable for paddling are the Kipawa, Rupert, Sasaginaga, Metabetchouan, and Riviére du Chef. Lakes also provide ample opportunities: Lac Des Loups, Lac Jean-Pére, Lac Antostagen, Poulter Lake, Lake Mistassini, Lake St. John, Lac Le Meule, Lake Peribonca, and Lake Manouan will give you at least a start. For much more extensive information write to the Department of Tourism, Fish, and Game, Parliament Building, Quebec City, Quebec for its book *Canoe Routes in La Verendrye Park* and its map of the Metabetchouan River Canoe Trip, a 60 mile trip through the Laurentide provincial park.

## SASKATCHEWAN

A list of canoe routes, giving starting and finishing points, numbers of portages, length of trips in days and miles, and features to note along the way is presented in *Canoe Saskatchewan,* a pamphlet that can be procured from the Conservation Information Service, Department of Natural Resources, Administration Building, Regina, Saskatchewan. Pertinent local information may be obtained at Department of Natural Resources regional offices and Conservation Officers' Headquarters. *Canoe Saskatchewan* lists the following trips:

Lac Ile-la-Crosse to Otter Rapids, 240 miles, 10 to 15 days; Otter Lake to La Ronge, 75 miles, 5 days; Otter Lake to La Ronge, 90 miles and 6 days; Otter Lake to La Ronge, 64 miles, 5 days; Otter Lake to Pelican Narrows, 100 miles, 5 to 7 days; La Ronge to Otter Lake, 57 miles, 4½ days; La Ronge to Hanson Lake Road (Highway 106, mile 146), 175 miles, 8 to 10 days; La Ronge to Jan Lake Road, 148 miles, 6 to 8 days; La Ronge to Hanson Lake Road (Highway 106, mile 190), 151 miles, 7 to 10 days; Wadin Bay to Wadin Bay, 126 miles, 8 to 10 days; La Ronge to La Ronge, 106 miles, 6 days; La Ronge to La Ronge, 120 miles, 8 to 10 days; Hanson Lake Road (Highway 106, mile 146), to Hanson Lake Road (Highway 106, mile 190), 94 miles, 5 to 6 days; Hanson Lake Road (Highway 106, mile 190), to Denare Beach, 53 miles, 3 days.

Other trips include: Cumberland House to Pas, Manitoba, 83 miles, 2 to 3 days; Nemeiben Lake to Otter Lake, 63 miles, 6 days; Nemeiben Lake to Otter Lake, 100 miles, 7 to 9 days; Saskatoon to Nipawin, 220 miles, 5 days; Lynx Lake to Kuskawac Lake, 13 miles, 1 to 2 days; Pelican Narrows to Hanson Lake Road (Highway 106, mile 190), 74 miles, 6 to 7 days; Pierce Lake to Lac des Iles, 22 miles, 1 to 2 days; Waterhen River to Beaver River, 70 miles, 1 to 2 days; Squaw Rapids to Cumberland House, 70 miles, 2 or 3 days; Black Lake to Selwin Lake, 105 miles, 7 to 11 days; and finally, Brabant Lake to Missinipe, 77 miles, 5 or 6 days.

# CHECKLIST FOR PACKING CAMPING GEAR

## PERSONAL GEAR

*Clothes*
—sweatshirt or jacket
—swimming trunks
—long trousers
—belt
—T shirt
—underwear
—2 pr. socks
—extra shoes
—pajamas
—hat
—bandannas
—poncho

*Toilet Gear*
—towel
—washcloth
—toothbrush
—toothpaste
—razor
—shaving cream
—after shave
—soap
—toilet paper
—sunburn lotion
—insect repellent

## SHELTER AND SLEEP

*Shelter*
—tent
—tarpaulin
—extra rope
—extra tent pegs
*Sleeping gear*
—sleeping bag
—mattress

*This checklist can
be torn out
and used or duplicated.*

## BOATING EQUIPMENT
—boat
—extra paddles
—life preservers
—repair kit
—spray cover or
—extra poncho(s)
—sponge
—kneeling pads
—padded yoke

## COOKING GEAR

*Gear to cook with*
—cook kit
—knives, forks, spoons
—tongs
—can and bottle opener
—canteen
—plastic or flexible
  water jugs
—stove and fuel
—matches
—candles
—grate
—large spoon or ladle
—fileting knife
—paper plates
*Gear to clean with*
—liquid dishwashing soap
—scouring pads
—dish cloth
—dish towel
—paper towels
—tinfoil

## TOOLS
—flashlight or lantern
—hatchet
—campsaw
—trenching tool
—bilge pump
—folding bucket
—oil stone
—file
—saw
—pliers

## FISHING GEAR
—rod
—reel
—line
—sinkers, bobbers
—stringer
—lures
—hooks and leaders

## FOOD
—water
—cheese
—sausage
—dark bread
—wine
—flour
—powdered milk
—powdered fruit drink
—margarine or lard
—salt and pepper
—cereal
—coffee
—dried foods
  as on planned menu

## MISCELLANEOUS
—jackknife
—Boy Scout field book
—log book and pencil
—camera
—binoculars
—radio
—first-aid kit
—twine
—extra rope
—compass
—wash basin
—extra matches
—sewing kit
—stop-ravel
—litter bag and
  garbage bags
—money box
—.................
—.................
—.................

# CHECKLIST FOR PACKING CAMPING GEAR

## PERSONAL GEAR
*Clothes*
—sweatshirt or jacket
—swimming trunks
—long trousers
—belt
—T shirt
—underwear
—2 pr. socks
—extra shoes
—pajamas
—hat
—bandannas
—poncho

*Toilet Gear*
—towel
—washcloth
—toothbrush
—toothpaste
—razor
—shaving cream
—after shave
—soap
—toilet paper
—sunburn lotion
—insect repellent

## SHELTER AND SLEEP
*Shelter*
—tent
—tarpaulin
—extra rope
—extra tent pegs
*Sleeping gear*
—sleeping bag
—mattress

*This checklist can
be torn out
and used or duplicated.*

## BOATING EQUIPMENT
—boat
—extra paddles
—life preservers
—repair kit
—spray cover or
—extra poncho(s)
—sponge
—kneeling pads
—padded yoke

## COOKING GEAR
*Gear to cook with*
—cook kit
—knives, forks, spoons
—tongs
—can and bottle opener
—canteen
—plastic or flexible
  water jugs
—stove and fuel
—matches
—candles
—grate
—large spoon or ladle
—fileting knife
—paper plates
*Gear to clean with*
—liquid dishwashing soap
—scouring pads
—dish cloth
—dish towel
—paper towels
—tinfoil

## TOOLS
—flashlight or lantern
—hatchet
—campsaw
—trenching tool
—bilge pump
—folding bucket
—oil stone
—file
—saw
—pliers

## FISHING GEAR
—rod
—reel
—line
—sinkers, bobbers
—stringer
—lures
—hooks and leaders

## FOOD
—water
—cheese
—sausage
—dark bread
—wine
—flour
—powdered milk
—powdered fruit drink
—margarine or lard
—salt and pepper
—cereal
—coffee
—dried foods
  as on planned menu

## MISCELLANEOUS
—jackknife
—Boy Scout field book
—log book and pencil
—camera
—binoculars
—radio
—first-aid kit
—twine
—extra rope
—compass
—wash basin
—extra matches
—sewing kit
—stop-ravel
—litter bag and
  garbage bags
—money box
—. . . . . . . . . . . . . . . .
—. . . . . . . . . . . . . . . .
—. . . . . . . . . . . . . . . .